The World Bank Annual Report 1998

The World Bank, Washington, D.C.

Photo credits	page vi, Michele Iannacci/World Bank
	page x, Jean-Louis Sarbib
	page 15, 54, 70, and 87, Richard Lord
	page 28, 36, 45, 62, 66, and 73, Curt Carnemark/World Bank
Design	Book and cover design: Joyce Petruzzelli, Graphic Design Unit, The World Bank Group
	Chart design: Spot Color
	Typography: Debra Malovany, Graphic Design Unit, The World Bank Group
Editorial	Lesley Anne Simmons, Office of the Publisher, The World Bank Group
Editorial assistance	Carolyn Knapp and John McCain, Office of the Publisher, The World Bank Group
Production	Stephanie Gerard, Office of the Publisher, The World Bank Group
World Wide Web design	Sherry Holmberg, Office of the Publisher, The World Bank Group

ISSN: 0252-2942
ISBN: 0-8213-4091-3

This Annual Report, which covers the period July 1, 1997, to June 30, 1998, has been prepared by the executive directors of both the International Bank for Reconstruction and Development (IBRD) and the International Development Association (IDA) in accordance with the respective by-laws of the two institutions. James D. Wolfensohn, president of the IBRD and IDA and chairman of the boards of executive directors, has submitted this

World Bank Executive Directors, April 1998 From left to right (front) Khalid M. Al-Saad; Khalid H. Alyahya; Juanita D. Amatong; Ali Bourhane; Kacim Brachemi; Andrei Bugrov; Juan Cariaga; Joaquim R. Carvalho; Enzo Del Bufalo; (back) Leonard Good; Luc Hubloue; Jannes Hutagalung; Young-Hoi Lee; Yong Li; Jean-Claude Milleron; Ilkka Niemi; Atsuo Nishihara; Gus O'Donnell; Franco Passacantando; Helmut Schaffer; Surendra Singh; Pieter Stek; (missing from photo: Matthias Meyer; Jan Piercy)

Report, together with accompanying administrative budgets and audited financial statements, to the board of governors.

Annual Reports for the International Finance Corporation (IFC), the Multilateral Investment Guarantee Agency (MIGA), and the International Centre for Settlement of Investment Disputes (ICSID) are published separately.

The World Bank, which consists of the International Bank for Reconstruction and Development (IBRD) and the International Development Association (IDA), has one overarching goal: helping its borrowers reduce poverty. It is a partner in strengthening economies and expanding markets to improve the quality of life for people everywhere, especially the poorest.

The IBRD and IDA make loans to borrower governments for projects and programs that promote economic and social progress by helping raise productivity so that people may live better lives. Along with these loans, the World Bank provides advice and technical assistance. The International Finance Corporation (IFC)—which works closely with private investors and invests in commercial enterprises in developing countries—and the Multilateral Investment Guarantee Agency (MIGA)—which encourages direct foreign investment in developing countries by offering insurance against noncommercial risk—share the same overall goals. The International Centre for Settlement of Investment Disputes (ICSID) shares the World Bank's objective of promoting increased flows of international investment by providing facilities for settling disputes between foreign investors and their host countries. Collectively,

these five institutions are known as the World Bank Group.

The IBRD, established in 1945, is now owned by the governments of 181 countries. To join the IBRD, countries must first be members of the International Monetary Fund (IMF). Upon joining the IBRD members subscribe to its capital stock. The amount of shares each member is allocated reflects its quota in the IMF, which in turn reflects the country's relative economic strength in the world economy. Members pay in a small portion of the value of their shares; the remainder is "callable capital" and would only be paid should the IBRD be unable to meet its obligations—a situation that has never arisen.

The IBRD lends only to credit worthy borrowers and only for projects that promise high real rates of economic return to the country. As a matter of policy, the IBRD does not reschedule payments, and it has suffered no losses on the loans it has made. While it does not aim to maximize profits, but rather to intermediate development funds at the lowest cost, the IBRD has earned a net income every year since 1948.

The IBRD borrows most of the money it lends through medium- and long-term borrowings in capital markets across the globe. It also borrows funds at market-based rates from central banks and other government institutions.

Conservative lending policies, strong financial backing from members, and prudent financial management give the IBRD strong standing in the markets. As well as borrowings, the IBRD is funded by the capital its members have paid in, its retained earnings, and repayments on its loans.

IDA was established in 1960 to provide assistance to poorer developing countries that cannot meet the IBRD's near-commercial terms. IDA provides credits to the poorest countries—mainly those with an annual per capita gross national product in 1997 of $925 or less. By this criterion, about seventy countries are eligible *(see appendix 6)*.

All members of the IBRD are eligible to join IDA, and 160 have done so. Unlike the IBRD, most of IDA's funds are contributed by its richer members, although some developing countries contribute to IDA as well. In addition, IDA receives transfers from the net earnings of the IBRD and repayments on its credits.

IDA credits are made only to governments. The repayment period is thirty-five to forty years. Credits carry no interest, but there is a small service charge, currently 0.75 percent. There is also a commitment charge, which is set annually, within a range of 0–0.5 percent of the undisbursed balance; the commitment charge is currently set at zero percent. Although IDA is legally and financially distinct from the IBRD, it shares the same staff, and the projects it supports have to meet the same criteria as do projects supported by the IBRD.

Under its Articles of Agreement, the World Bank cannot allow itself to be influenced by the political character of a member country: Only economic considerations are relevant. To ensure that its borrowers get the best value for the money they borrow, Bank assistance is *untied* and may be used to purchase goods and services from any member country.

The IFC, established in 1956, helps promote private sector growth in developing countries and helps mobilize domestic and foreign capital for this purpose. It has 174 members. Legally and financially the IFC and the World Bank are separate entities, and the IFC has its own operating and legal staff. It draws upon the World Bank for administrative and other services, however.

The IFC provides loans and makes equity investments in support of projects. Unlike most multilateral institutions, the IFC does not accept government guarantees for its financing. Like a private financial institution, the IFC seeks profitable returns and prices its finance and service, to the extent possible, in line with the market while taking into account the cost of its funds. The IFC shares full project risks with its private-sector partners. The IFC issues its own annual report.

ICSID was established in 1966 to help promote international investment. It does this by providing facilities for the settlement, by conciliation and arbitration, of disputes between foreign investors and their host countries. Provisions referring to arbitration under the auspices of ICSID

are a common feature of international investment contracts, investment laws, and bilateral and multilateral investment treaties. ICSID has 129 members. In addition to its dispute-settlement activities, ICSID undertakes research, advisory services and publishing in the fields of arbitration and investment law. Its publications include multivolume collections of "Investment Laws of the World" and "Investment Treaties" and the semi-annual "ICSID Review—Foreign Investment Law Journal." ICSID issues its own annual report, which may be obtained from the ICSID Secretariat.[1]

MIGA was established in 1988 to promote the flow of foreign direct investment in member countries. It does this by providing guarantees to private investors against major political risks and offering investment marketing services to host governments to help them attract foreign investment.

MIGA is an independent self-supporting agency of the World Bank Group. Like the IFC, it has its own capital base and country membership, but it shares the World Bank's development mandate to promote the economic growth of its developing member countries.

MIGA has 145 members. MIGA issues its own annual report, which may be obtained from its Office of Central Administration.[2]

---

1. International Centre for Settlement of Investment Disputes, Secretariat, 1818 H Street N.W., Washington, D.C. 20433, USA.

2. The Multilateral Investment Guarantee Agency, Office of Central Administration, 1818 H Street N.W., Washington, D.C. 20433 USA.

MESSAGE FROM THE CHAIRMAN OF THE BOARD OF EXECUTIVE DIRECTORS

Last year's *Annual Report* described a year of change and renewal. This year many of those changes have begun to bear fruit. Disbursements and quality are up; projects at risk are down; and our clients are reporting improvements across the institution—from more client responsiveness to more humility.

This year has seen further changes: the implementation of the Cost Effectiveness Review; further decentralization of decisionmaking powers to the field; a new budgeting and planning process for the first time linked to strategic objectives; and the introduction of a new human resources policy designed to end the traditional divisions between headquarters and local staff in the field and between regular and nonregular staff. Much remains to be done. But the progress of the last twelve months provides us with a solid foundation on which to build. None of this would have been possible without the whole-hearted support and guidance of our executive board.

For many of our clients the year has also brought profound change. We do not yet know what the long-term effects of the East Asian crisis will be, but the impact on the poor has already been savage. For all of us at the World Bank Group, the crisis has highlighted the fact that financial and social policy must go hand in hand. With the support of our shareholders we have set up the new Special Financial Operations Unit to look at financial and social issues in crisis countries on an urgent basis. We are also expanding our work on long-range financial sector reform and focusing much more attention on social assessments.

With its threat of returning millions to poverty, the crisis has also underlined the fact that, as I put it in my speech at the Annual Meetings in September 1997, the challenge of inclusion is the key development challenge of our time. Across the globe, too many people are missing out on the fruits of economic success. Our goal must be to reduce these disparities across and within countries; to bring more and more people into the economic main-

stream; to promote equitable access to the benefits of development, regardless of nationality, race, or gender.

To do this we must boost our work with our partners in government and in the other donor agencies, civil society, and the private sector. We must reach out much more proactively to disadvantaged groups—especially women and indigenous peoples—and we must take a more holistic view of development itself. It is my strong belief that we will not make development meaningful, sustainable, and inclusive until we put people at the center of the development process. This means a much greater focus on country ownership and participation, a better appreciation of local conditions, and more attention to the role of culture.

You will find these themes reflected in the pages of this Annual Report. Taken together, they show an institution which is repositioning itself to meet the demands of a new millennium—an institution committed to results, partnerships, and inclusive development. The 4.8 billion people who are our ultimate clients deserve nothing less.

JAMES D. WOLFENSOHN

INTERNATIONAL BANK FOR RECONSTRUCTION AND DEVELOPMENT

Operational results

IBRD commitments: $21,086.2 million

115 new operations in 43 countries

32.3 percent of investment lending directly targeted to the poor

IBRD disbursements to countries: $19,232 million

Three largest commitments to countries:

Republic of Korea ($5,000 million), China ($2,323 million), and Mexico ($1,767 million)

Financial results

Net income: $1,243 million

Outstanding borrowings at fiscal year end: $105,577 million

Average borrowing costs after swaps: 6.10 percent

Borrowers selected single-currency loan terms for $20,060 million (95 percent) of new loans

INTERNATIONAL DEVELOPMENT ASSOCIATION

IDA commitments:[a] $7,507.7million

67 new operations in 19 countries

IDA disbursements:[b] $5,630 million ($198 million from the Interim Trust Fund)

54 percent of IDA investment credits directly targeted to the poor

Three largest commitments to countries:

India (1,073.6 million), Ethiopia ($669.2 million), and Bangladesh ($646.4 million)

IBRD/IDA PROGRAMS

40 percent of investment lending directly targeted to the poor

Adjustment lending: $11,289.2 million (39 percent of total lending)

a. Excluding $75 million in development grants.
b. Excluding $74 million in development grants.

The World Bank's purpose is to help borrowers reduce poverty and improve living standards through sustainable growth and investment in people. In fiscal 1998, the Bank made strong headway in implementing the Strategic Compact,[1] aimed at increasing development impact and playing its part in the fight against poverty more effectively. The Board of Executive Directors reviewed two progress reports on the compact in fiscal 1998 that documented improvements in the quality, timeliness, and quantity of operational work, and in organization, processes, and ways of doing business *(see box 1)*.

The Bank's renewed capacity to deliver high-quality services through effective partnerships was tested in fiscal 1998 in its ability to respond to a new challenge—the East Asian financial crisis, which speeded up the pace of change across the institution—and in the strong turnaround in the performance of the Africa region, which had been the starting place of the Bank's renewal program.

Following the dramatic downturn in financial markets in several East Asian countries early in the fiscal year, the Bank moved quickly to adjust both lending programs and advisory services. The crisis risks undermining one of the most remarkable economic achievements of the twentieth century—and perhaps the single

most effective antipoverty performance in history. As an institution whose core mandate is poverty reduction, the Bank helped support the international effort to restore confidence and sustainable growth by focusing on both the financial and the human dimensions of the crisis—including unemployment, food shortages, and the effects on the poorest and most vulnerable groups.

The Bank pledged some $16 billion to support reform programs in the countries facing critical situations, of which $5.65 billion was disbursed. This included a $3,000 million loan to the Republic of Korea, the largest loan in the Bank's history, which was processed in record time.

The East Asian crisis underscored the prudence of the Bank's renewed financial sector emphasis under the Strategic Compact. As the East Asian financial crisis rapidly escalated, the Bank geared up to respond quickly and credibly. Additional resources were approved to reinforce the financial sector program, and the Special Financial Operations Unit was established to help respond to the crisis in all affected countries, not just in East Asia, by providing support to help its clients strengthen weak financial systems and reduce the impact of the crisis on poor and other vulnerable people. Staff capacity was built up through recruitment; collaboration and

coordination with external partners were enhanced, including with the new Financial Sector Advisory Service established with the help of a PHRD[2] grant, and with European donors through the Asia-Europe Meeting (ASEM) Trust Fund; and a Central Bank secondment program was established in several countries.

The international effort consisted of close partnerships—from other multilateral institutions, particularly the International Monetary Fund (IMF), and with nongovernmental organizations (NGOs). Working in close coordination with the IMF, for example, the Bank promptly organized a series of technical assistance missions to assist the governments of Indonesia, the Republic of Korea, and Thailand—including helping to identify and address problems in the financial and corporate sectors.

1. The Strategic Compact, endorsed by the Board of Executive Directors on March 31, 1997, set ambitious objectives for the Bank, including: strengthening the development effectiveness of lending and nonlending services; improving responsiveness to client needs; developing a broader range of products and services; reducing overhead and shifting resources to the front line; further decentralizing activities; rebuilding professional expertise and technical capacity; and sharing the best global knowledge on development with clients and partners.
2. The Policy and Human Resource Development (PHRD) Fund is a collaborative effort between the government of Japan and the World Bank to extend untied grants to meet technical assistance needs of Bank client countries.

BOX 1.   THE STRATEGIC COMPACT: PROGRESS AND CHALLENGES

One and a half years after member countries approved the Strategic Compact—the World Bank's ongoing effort to strengthen its development effectiveness through a comprehensive renewal program—progress is apparent in a number of key areas. There is clear evidence of improved quality and timeliness and an increase in demand for products and services. These results are underscored by emerging positive feedback from clients through, for example, client surveys. But a lot remains to be done. Internally, staff are still adjusting to matrix management and other new ways of working, and there is a need to strengthen trust and teamwork. Externally, it is imperative to sustain the emerging progress on quality, delivery, and results for clients. The compact is a work in progress. The challenge of implementation remains.

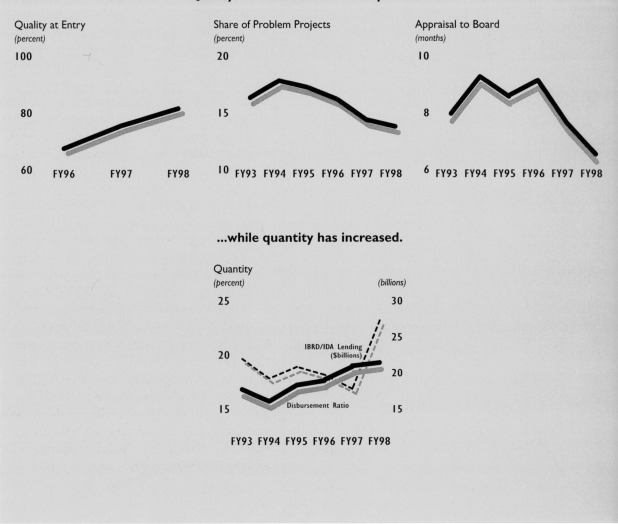

Quality and timeliness have improved...

Quality at Entry
(percent)

Share of Problem Projects
(percent)

Appraisal to Board
(months)

...while quantity has increased.

Quantity
(percent)   (billions)

IBRD/IDA Lending
($billions)

Disbursement Ratio

FY93 FY94 FY95 FY96 FY97 FY98

THE STRATEGIC COMPACT: Goals and Progress

Goal	Progress
Improve operational quality	• *Reduction in problem projects in portfolio* • *Higher quality of projects entering portfolio* • *Faster delivery of products*
Increase level of services	• *More timely delivery of country assistance strategies* • *Increased resources to advisory services* • *Lending in FY98 at record levels*
Enhance responsiveness	• *22 Country Directors located in field* • *Response to East Asian crisis* • *Response to El Niño effects in client countries*
Address broader development agenda	• HIPC: *Six countries at decision point* • *Mainstreaming social analysis/ anti-corruption programs* • *Additional $25 million per year to reinforce financial sector*
Introduce new products	• *Single-currency loans* • *Adaptable lending instruments (APLS and LILS)* • IDA *guarantees approved*
Strengthen partnerships	• *Collaboration with all partners in East Asia* • *Stronger relationship with EC/EBRD in Eastern Europe* • *Cooperation with private sector and civil society*
Build knowledge management	• *Knowledge systems in fifteen major sectors* • *Web sites/help desks for clients/partners* • *Distance education program*
Lower costs/increase Productivity	• *Cost effectiveness review under implementation* • *On track to return FY01 budget to FY97 level in real terms*
Revamp internal capacities	• *Human Resources policy reform approved* • *400 managers in Executive Development Program* • *Systems renewal driving efficiency teamwork/productivity*
Focus on Results	• *Scorecard measuring performance and results under development* • *Client surveys gauging Bank impact* • *Semi-annual reports to Board on progress*

While addressing new challenges to meet the needs of client countries facing crises in East Asia, the Bank and its African clients began to reap the rewards of stronger partnerships and closer client focus.

Continued growth, improved economic policies, and increased political openness in many parts of the region, together with a new generation of African leaders, created greater opportunity for development in the region. Lending commitments to Africa increased by almost two thirds to $2,873.8 million after fiscal 1997's downturn, reflecting significant policy improvements in some African countries and the completion of the Bank's renewal process, which had delayed the pace of commitments in fiscal 1997. At $2,506 million, disbursements also remained high.

The Bank's focus on working more closely with client partners was exemplified in Africa in fiscal 1998. The Bank's president participated in two key meetings in Kampala and Dakar with African leaders where he learned from them firsthand about their development priorities and how the Bank could best help meet them.

The special needs of Africa's heavily indebted countries progressed as Uganda became the first country to reach its completion point under the Heavily Indebted Poor Countries (HIPC) Debt Initiative in April 1998, when the Boards of Executive Directors of the IMF and IDA agreed that the necessary conditions had been fulfilled. The Bank's assistance was provided in the form of grants for education, purchase and cancellation of outstanding debt owed to IDA, and servicing debt owed to IDA over the next five years *(see also box 2-1)*. Decisions to provide assistance under the initiative were taken for three African countries (Burkina Faso, Côte d'Ivoire, and Mozambique) and two South American countries (Bolivia and Guyana). Eligibility for the initiative was reviewed for four more African countries—with Guinea-Bissau and Mali expected to receive HIPC debt relief, while the debt situations for Benin and Senegal were confirmed sustainable after the full application of existing debt relief mechanisms *(see table 1)*.

Both the World Bank and IMF remain committed to meeting their full shares of the cost of the initiative. The IBRD's Board of Governors approved the transfer of $250 million from IBRD surplus and net income to the HIPC Debt Initiative Trust Fund, the principle vehicle through which the Bank will deliver its debt relief. The IMF has provided SDR 250 million to its Enhanced Structural Assistance Facility (ESAF)-HIPC Trust to finance special ESAF operations under the initiative and approved an additional transfer of SDR 40 million. In addition, fifteen bilateral donors made contributions or pledges of about $275 million to the HIPC Trust Fund to assist other multilateral creditors (including the African Development Bank Group) in providing their respective shares of debt relief to qualifying HIPCS.

This year several East Asian and African nations, along with some Latin American countries, were among those confronted by another external event that caused them to turn to the Bank and its partners for urgent support: the severe weather conditions resulting from El Niño oscillation. Several governments anticipated damage and disaster and requested the Bank's help to prepare themselves. Partnership with the Inter-American Development Bank (IDB), the United States Agency for International Development (USAID), and the United States National Oceanic and Atmospheric Administration (NOAA), together with the Bank's streamlined

procedures, helped facilitate speedy responses to these requests for help. A seminar held in collaboration with the Bank's Environment Department, the Economic Development Institute (EDI), and the International START Secretariat[3] provided a forum for participants from governments, NGOs, the private sector, and others to plan for long-term activities to mitigate the impact of drought induced by El Niño.

Supporting reconstruction after conflict remained a major activity in several countries, including Angola, Bosnia and Herzegovina, Rwanda, and Tajikistan.

The Bank is committed to the development targets adopted by the international community for improving the lives and environment of people who live in its client countries *(see box 2)*. While more people in its client countries are healthier, better fed, and more educated than ever before,[4] progress is uneven among countries, and much more needs to be done. Increasing its development effectiveness lies at the heart of the Bank's renewal. Evaluations completed in fiscal 1998 showed steady improvements—Bank operations achieved better results, portfolio quality was improved, and evaluation processes were enhanced—but indicated that

3. START is a coalition that includes the Global Change System for Analysis, Research and Training of the Human Dimensions of Global Environmental Change Program; the International Geosphere Program; and the World Climate Change Research Program.

4. World Bank. 1998. *World Development Indicators 1998.* Washington, D.C.

TABLE 1. HIPC INITIATIVE: STATUS OF COUNTRY CASES

| | Decision point | Completion point | NPV debt/export target (in percent) | Assistance at completion point (US$ millions, present value at completion point) | | | of which: | | Percentage reduction in NPV of debt[1] | Estimated total nominal debt service relief (US$M) |
				Total	Bilateral	Multilateral	IMF	World Bank		
Completion point reached:										
Uganda	Apr-97	Apr-98	202	347	73	274	69	160	20	650
Decision point reached [2]										
Burkina Faso	Sep-97	Apr-00	205	115	21	94	9.6	44	14	200
Bolivia	Sep-97	Sep-98	225	448	157	291	29	54	13	600
Guyana	Dec-97	Dec-98	107[3]	253	91	161	35	27	25	500
Côte d'Ivoire	Mar-98	Mar-01	141[3]	345	163	182	23	91	6	800
Mozambique	Apr-98	mid-99	200	1,442	916	526	105	324	57	2,900
Total agreed debt relief	...	...	2,950	1,421	1,528	271	700	...	5,650	1
Preliminary HIPC document issued [4]										
Mali	2nd Q. 98	4th Q. 99	200[5]	196	63	133	20	65	14	350
Guinea-Bissau[6]	3rd Q. 98	mid-01	200[5]	300	148	153	8	73	73	500
Debt judged sustainable										
Benin	Jul-97	...	...	...	...	...	...	...	...	...
Senegal	Apr-98	...	...	...	...	...	...	...	...	...

SOURCES: IMF and Bank board decisions, completion point documents, final HIPC documents, preliminary HIPC documents, and staff calculations.

1. Percent of net present value (NPV) of debt at completion point, after full use of traditional debt relief mechanisms.

2. Assistance committed by Bank and IMF. Further countries that could reach the decision point within the coming year include Chad, Guinea, Mauritania, Togo, and, possibly, Ethiopia and Vietnam. Not all would be expected to require assistance under the HIPC Debt Initiative.

3. Eligible under fiscal/openness criteria; NPV of debt to exports target chosen to meet NPV of debt-to-revenue target of 280 percent.

4. Targets based on majority view in preliminary discussions at Bank and IMF boards; assistance based on preliminary HIPC documents and subject to change.

5. Reflects the view of most executive directors advocating a target at the low end of the 200–220 percent range, with many recommending a 200 percent target.

6. Country case will need to be re-assessed after civil disturbances end.

continued progress in meeting the development effectiveness goals set out in the Strategic Compact will depend on current efforts to sustain and strengthen the portfolio. *The Annual Report on Portfolio Performance* (ARPP) showed improvement in the overall portfolio performance as both actual and potential problem projects de-clined from 31 percent of the portfolio to 26 percent by commitment value and from 34 percent to 30 percent by number of projects.

The Bank's strategic underpinning for refocusing the development agenda to improve development effectiveness is the country assistance strategy (CAS), the centerpiece of

FIGURE 1
Operations Approved for Bank and IDA
Assistance by Region, Fiscal Year 1998
(US$ millions)

LAC **6,040**

MNA **969**

ECA **5,224**

SAS **3,864**

EAP **9,623**

AFRICA **2,874**

Bank-government interaction. A CAS evaluation report prepared in fiscal 1998 documented improvements in CASs, and identified three priorities for further advances: sharper strategic selectivity, more candid treatment of risks, and enhanced self-evaluation and monitoring of CAS implementation. Improvements were evident in two directions: increased client focus and strategic selectivity.

Mainstreaming the social dimensions of development is key to effective and sustainable development, and some 125 social assessments were completed or underway in fiscal 1998. Regional social development action plans were prepared, and resources for social development were provided under the Strategic Compact. An increasing number of CASs paid special attention to social development issues, and the involvement of key stakeholders in the preparation process of many also helped meet social objectives.

The goals and targets of the Rural Development Action Plan, approved in fiscal 1997, also are supported under the Strategic Compact. Initiatives in support of the plan included development of rural strategy papers for Guinea,

Madagascar, Mali, and Uganda; dissemination of a rural development and water strategy in Morocco and Yemen and development of a rural water strategy for Tunisia; and initiation of a regional rural development strategy for South Asia and of sector studies on agricultural marketing and land markets in Sri Lanka.

The important role that partnerships are playing in reinforcing the Bank's development activities and enhancing development effectiveness is illustrated throughout the pages of this *Annual Report*. The Partnership Group was established in fiscal 1998 to help build and facilitate further partnerships to make the Bank a more efficient player in development.

A central tenet of the evolving role of the World Bank is to build it into a world-class knowledge institution through a knowledge management system that extends across the World Bank and outside—to mobilize knowledge and learning for better results. Underpinning this effort in fiscal 1998 was an action plan for consolidating information management and technology systems to ensure that individual Bank units' efforts align with institutional priorities. Prototype knowledge management systems in education and health were established, and a common framework for the systems was set up in the Bank's regional offices.

While the regional offices' knowledge management efforts focused on developing country-level information and live databases, the thematic networks[5] began implementing a knowledge management program in fifteen sectors (such as education, finance, health, infrastructure, and poverty), with information being compiled around eighty "knowledge domains." Work began on establishing a community of practice for each topic, which includes help desks, advisory services, a directory of expertise, collections of statistics and information about the Bank's operations and activities, and collections of know-how emphasizing best practices

5. Networks comprise and link staff working in the same sectors throughout the Bank and provide a mechanism to help deliver the best possible products for clients. The four thematic networks are Human Development; Environmentally and Socially Sustainable Development; Finance, Private Sector, and Infrastructure; and Poverty Reduction and Economic Management.

and lessons learned. Provision is being made for external clients to access the system.

The Bank helps to facilitate learning and strengthen client country capacity through EDI's activities.[6] As greater emphasis has been placed on knowledge as a catalyst of reform, EDI's role has increased. In fiscal 1998 the efficiency of EDI's services was improved and its reach extended: some 23,250 direct participants, including national leaders, government officials, parliamentarians, journalists, private entrepreneurs, NGOs, and educators were reached through 402 EDI learning activities. Partnerships within the Bank were strengthened: with the Bank's thematic networks, for example, EDI launched and piloted core courses on development priorities—from banking, finance, and regulation to environment and sustainable development and from governance to human and social development. These courses help spread up-to-the-minute knowledge on key development challenges. To integrate client training programs into overall development efforts, EDI provided program support, on a selective basis, in the preparation of twelve CASs in fiscal 1998.

The Global Distance Education network, established in fiscal 1998, is using interactive television, videoconferencing, and the Internet to deliver training and policy services to more development partners than is possible through face-to-face learning. An interactive electronic classroom was set up in the Bank's Main Complex, and core courses are being converted to distance education delivery.

The cost effectiveness review (CER) was completed and endorsed by the Board of Executive Directors in October 1997, and implementation began. The CER implementation is leading to changes in systems and procedures to deliver better services while realizing estimated potential savings in fiscal 1999 through fiscal 2001. These changes, targeting higher productivity in the frontline and generating savings through efficiency gains in the backline, are on track to realize the Strategic Compact's goal of having frontline resources account for 60 percent of the budget while support activities account for 40 percent by fiscal 1999.

To help make the budget an instrument of the Bank's strategy and link resource allocation more closely with institutional priorities, a new more strategic and transparent planning and budgeting process was developed at a strategic forum held in January 1998. Among the outcomes of the forum were:

6. EDI issues it own annual report, which is available from: New Products and Outreach, The Economic Development Institute, The World Bank, 1818 H Street, N.W., Washington, D.C. 20433.

FIGURE 2 IBRD and IDA Commitments, Fiscal Year 1998
(US$ millions)

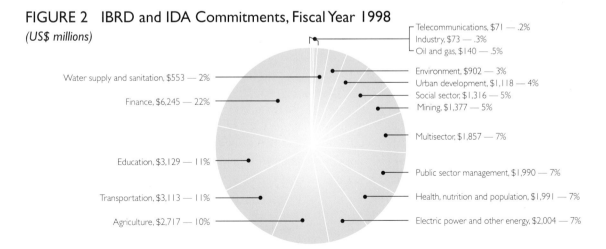

- Telecommunications, $71 — .2%
- Industry, $73 — .3%
- Oil and gas, $140 — .5%
- Environment, $902 — 3%
- Urban development, $1,118 — 4%
- Social sector, $1,316 — 5%
- Mining, $1,377 — 5%
- Multisector, $1,857 — 7%
- Public sector management, $1,990 — 7%
- Health, nutrition and population, $1,991 — 7%
- Electric power and other energy, $2,004 — 7%
- Water supply and sanitation, $553 — 2%
- Finance, $6,245 — 22%
- Education, $3,129 — 11%
- Transportation, $3,113 — 11%
- Agriculture, $2,717 — 10%

TABLE 2. TRENDS IN IBRD AND IDA LENDING, FISCAL YEARS 1996–98

(millions of US dollars)

Sector	1996 IBRD	1996 IDA	1996 Total	1997 IBRD	1997 IDA	1997 Total	1998 IBRD	1998 IDA	1998 Total
Agriculture	973.8	1,105.1	2,078.9	2,810.6	735.9	3546.5	1,480.5	1,236.9	2,717.4
Education	920.8	784.9	1,705.7	762.3	255.1	1,017.4	1,927.8	1,201.5	3,129.3
Electric power and other energy	2,899.2	347.9	3,247.1	1,613.4	275.8	1889.2	1,115.0	889.0	2,004.0
Environment	534.6	348.1	882.7	22.5	224.2	246.7	753.8	148.3	902.1
Finance	1,199.2	231.2	1,430.4	993.7	201.1	1,194.8	6,103.0	141.5	6,244.5
Health, nutrition and population	1,495.2	858.2	2,353.4	245.8	694.1	939.9	911.5	1,079.4	1,990.9
Industry	217.0	31.7	248.7	145.0	50.5	195.5	—	73.0	73.0
Mining	570.8	121.2	692.0	300.0	21.4	321.4	1,369.5	7.0	1,376.5
Multisector	906.3a	759.2	1,665.5	1,373.0	813.0	2,186.0	1,187.7	669.4	1,857.1
Oil and gas	30.0	25.6	55.6	114.0	21.6	135.6	130.0	10.0	140.0
Public sector management	1,036.0	840.2	1,876.2	729.7	190.8	920.5	1,638.5	351.7	1,990.2
Social sector	440.0	554.5	994.5	1,303.7	66.5	1,370.2	933.9	381.6	1,315.5
Telecommunications	35.0	—	35.0	—	—	—	68.1	2.4	70.5
Transportation	2,236.9	535.7	2,772.6	3,224.8	607.0	3,831.8	2,134.7	977.8	3,112.5
Urban development	632.0	236.5	868.5	506.0	162.3	668.3	893.6	223.9	1,117.5
Water supply and sanitation	529.1	80.7	609.8	380.4	302.4	682.8	438.6	114.3	552.9
Total	14,655.9	6,860.7	21,516.6	14,524.9	4,621.8	19,146.7	21,086.2	7,507.7	28,593.9

—Zero.

NOTE: *While single loans may cover several sectors, this classification assigns each loan approved in the fiscal year to a single sector.*

a. *Includes the refinanced/rescheduled overdue charges of $168 million for Bosnia and Herzegovina.*

• agreement on five Bank Group-wide corporate priorities;[7]

• an intensified action program for implementing the internal renewal program; and

• budget allocation principles designed to align resources better with corporate priorities.

Bank management and the Board of Executive Directors monitored progress in reaching the objectives set out in the Strategic Compact to maximize the Bank's effectiveness in the fight against poverty.

In fiscal 1998 the Board of Executive Directors endorsed reform of the Bank's human resources policies to align them with the needs of the new Bank. The new strategy will help the Bank attract and retain the best people from all over the world, treat them fairly over the course of their Bank careers, and foster teamwork, learning, and innovation.

An independent inspection panel established by the executive directors in September 1993 helps to ensure that the Bank's operations adhere to the institution's operational policies and procedures regarding the design, preparation, or implementation of a project. Any group of individuals who may be directly or adversely affected by a Bank-supported project or projects may ask the panel to investigate complaints that the Bank has failed to abide by its policies and procedures. The executive directors decide, on

7. To (i) follow through on the Strategic Compact, CER, and staff survey; (ii) implement the Bankis internal renewal agenda; (iii) respond to the globalization challenge—including the East Asian financial, social, and government crisis; (iv) identify and implement bolder and more aggressive approaches to capacity building, governance, education (especially of girls), and Africa; and (v) develop partnerships with the private sector and civil society.

the recommendation of the panel, whether an inspection will take place.

The Panel continues to receive numerous queries concerning potential requests for inspection. It has received thirteen formal requests for inspection to date, eleven of which were found to be admissible, and seven have been acted upon. [8]

Against this backdrop, Bank and IDA commitments increased significantly: commitments by the IBRD amounted to $21,086.2 million, up $6,561.3 million from fiscal 1997, and commitments by IDA amounted to $7,507.7 million, up $2,885.9 million from fiscal 1997. IBRD disbursements, at $19,232 million, were up $5,234 million compared to fiscal 1997, and IDA's disbursements were $5,630 million, down $349 million from fiscal 1997. Figures 1 and 2 show fiscal 1998 lending by region and by sector, and table 2 shows trends in lending by sector.

During the fiscal year the Republic of Palau became a member of the IBRD, increasing the membership to 181. At the end of the fiscal year, action was pending on membership in the IBRD for the Federal Republic of Yugoslavia (Serbia/Montenegro).

The Republic of Palau also joined IDA in fiscal 1998, bringing total membership to 160. At the end of the fiscal year, action was pending on membership in IDA for Barbados, Ukraine, Venezuela, and the Federal Republic of Yugoslavia (Serbia/Montenegro).

On June 23, 1998, the Board of Governors of the IBRD approved a selective capital increase (SCI) of 23,246 shares for five countries (Brazil, Denmark, the Republic of Korea, Spain, and Turkey) in recognition of discrepancies that had developed over time between these countries' shareholding and their economic positions.

8. Details from the Inspection Panel's *Annual Report*, and at http://www.worldbank.org

The Board of Executive Directors is responsible for the conduct of the general operations of the Bank and performs its duties under powers delegated by the Board of Governors. As provided in the Articles of Agreement, five of the twenty-four executive directors are appointed by the five member governments having the largest number of shares; the rest are elected by the other member governments, who form constituencies in an election process conducted every two years.

The executive directors consider and decide on the IBRD loan and IDA credit proposals made by the president, and they decide policy issues that guide the general operations of the Bank. They are also responsible for presenting to the Board of Governors at the Annual Meetings an audit of accounts, an administrative budget, and an annual report on the operations and policies of the Bank, as well as any other matters that in their judgment require submission to the Board of Governors. During fiscal 1998 the Board of Executive Directors met ninety-two times in formal board meetings and as the Committee of the Whole another sixty-eight times in informal sessions. In addition, most of the executive directors serve on one or more of five standing committees: Audit Committee, Committee on Development Effectiveness, Budget Committee, Personnel Committee, and Committee on Executive Directors' Administrative Matters. The ex-

ecutive directors' Steering Committee, an informal advisory body, also meets regularly. Although a committee cannot make a decision for the entire Board of Executive Directors, the committees increasingly look in depth at Bank policies and practices and report their findings and recommendations to the executive directors.

In addition, workgroups of executive directors and alternate executive directors at times make special trips to borrowing countries to observe Bank-supported operations and the Bank's assistance strategy firsthand. They meet a wide range of people, including staff of the Bank's resident missions or field offices, government officials, project managers, nongovernmental organizations (NGOs), project beneficiaries, and the business community. In fiscal 1998, groups of executive directors visited the Middle East and North Africa (Jordan, Tunisia, West Bank and Gaza, and Yemen) and eastern and southern Africa (Eritrea, Lesotho, and South Africa).

Shaping policy

The Board of Executive Directors' oversight responsibility covers virtually all Bank policy, so its role cannot be clearly separated from most of the Bank's activities and initiatives as described in this *Annual Report*. This oversight responsibility is exercised in part by the executive directors' approval of Bank or IDA lending operations and the annual budget process. The executive directors also exercise

an important role in shaping Bank policy and its evolution. It is in this role that the directors represent the changing perspectives of their shareholder governments vis-à-vis the Bank's role. These policy initiatives normally reflect needs perceived by shareholders and involve a process of consensus building, both among executive directors and with Bank management. Many of the changes in Bank policy grow from initiatives by the executive directors and occur gradually over a period of years, such as the increasing emphasis on social development, gender, environment, and capacity-building issues.

In fiscal 1998, the executive directors approved the introduction of two adaptable lending instruments to add to the Bank's lending toolkit: the Learning and Innovation Loan (LIL) to support small, time-sensitive programs to build capacity and pilot promising development initiatives or to experiment and develop locally based models prior to large-scale interventions; and the Adaptable Program Loan (APL) to provide phased, but sustained, support for the implementation of long-term development programs *(see box 4-1)*. On a pilot basis, the executive directors agreed in principle that IDA be allowed to offer partial risk guarantees to private lenders in IDA-only countries where IBRD enclave guarantees are not available *(see box 3-2)*.

The executive directors have increasingly encouraged closer linking of the operations of the Bank, IFC, and MIGA. In fiscal 1998 the Board of Executive Directors considered eight country assistance strategies prepared jointly by the Bank and the IFC.[1]

The executive directors adopted strategies and guidelines in support of the Bank's commitment to strengthen its efforts to promote good governance and combat corruption. They acknowledged that corruption and weak governance undermined macroeconomic stability, private sector activity, and sustainable development. They agreed that the Bank should be actively involved in responding to member governments' requests to strengthen their institutions and performance in these areas. And they noted that member governments have the primary responsibility for combating corruption and strengthening governance, and underscored the importance of a consistent and even-handed approach to these issues.

Strategic Compact with shareholders

Last year the executive directors unanimously endorsed the Strategic Compact between the Bank and its shareholders—a plan for reform and renewal of the Bank to make it more effective in achieving its overriding goal of poverty reduction. The compact's objective is to transform the way the Bank conducts its business by improving its products, speeding up its processes, lowering its costs, making it more demand driven, and increasing its development impact. The executive directors' committees play a major role in helping directors to discharge their oversight responsibilities in monitoring the compact. The executive directors reviewed two semi-annual reports on the compact and noted that considerable progress has been made in meeting its ambitious objectives. They stressed the need to continue to improve the corporate scorecard, focusing on key performance indicators and strengthening the link to development results.

In early fiscal 1998 the executive directors considered a report on cost effectiveness focusing on aligning resource allocation with strategic priorities, developing clearer standards for policy compliance, simplifying business processes, and reducing overhead. The recommendations of the Cost Effectiveness Review are being imple-

mented within the framework of the Strategic Compact. The executive directors approved far-reaching reforms to the Bank's human resources (HR) policies. The new HR policy framework is a major milestone in the Strategic Compact.

Response to the East Asian financial crisis

Under the executive directors' oversight, the Bank has been very active in responding to the East Asian crisis as part of the international effort to restore confidence and sustainable growth in the region and address the social impacts of the crisis. The Bank has pledged up to $16 billion to underpin programs of structural reform and technical assistance for countries in the region. In a swift response to the crisis, the executive directors approved a record $5,000 million in loans to the Republic of Korea. Together with its partners, the International Monetary Fund (IMF) and the Asian Development Bank (ADB), the Bank is helping several of its Asian client countries address structural issues relating to the current financial crisis.

Heavily indebted poor countries

Last year the executive directors of the Bank and the IMF endorsed a program of action for reducing the debt burden of eligible heavily indebted poor countries (HIPCs) to a sustainable level and established the HIPC Debt Initiative Trust Fund. There has been extensive international cooperation among all partners—multilateral and bilateral—in implementing the initiative for the benefit of the poorest and most indebted countries. Further progress has been made in fiscal 1998 in implementing the initiative to support governments that show strong commitment to reform. Six countries have qualified for assistance—Bolivia, Burkina Faso, Côte d'Ivoire, Guyana, Mozambique, and Uganda. Uganda was the first country to reach the completion point under the initiative.

Country and sector strategies

The country assistance strategy (CAS) is the central tool for reviewing and guiding Bank country programs. It is a key Bank instrument for customizing its poverty reduction strategy,

1. Brazil, Côte d'Ivoire, Egypt, India, Indonesia, Kazakhstan, Mexico, and Poland.

strengthening partnerships with clients, and allocating resources across competing demands. As a result of the executive directors' work, there has been a visible refocusing in the CAS on building on lessons from past performance, consulting civil society, evaluating the impact of Bank efforts and results on the ground, and strengthening the Bank's presence in the field.

In reviewing CASs in fiscal 1998, the executive directors continued their efforts to see poverty reduction—the Bank's overriding objective—more comprehensively integrated into strategies. Directors increasingly recognized considerable progress made in CAS quality. They emphasized the need for increasing country focus to enhance ownership and results on the ground. They agreed that the priorities for further advances in CAS quality are sharper strategic selectivity and enhanced treatment of self-evaluation and monitoring of CAS implementation.

In fiscal 1998 the executive directors approved a sector strategy for health, nutrition, and population—a prototype for a new Bank product intended to complement CASs with a sectoral perspective on the Bank's comparative advantage, effectiveness, and priorities.

Development effectiveness

The Board of Executive Directors' Committee on Development Effectiveness (CODE) oversees the development effectiveness aspects of Strategic Compact monitoring and implementation and tracks the results of Bank operations on the ground. CODE validates and guides the activities of the Operations Evaluation Department (OED) and attests to the adequacy of management responses to OED findings and recommendations. The committee assists the executive directors in assessing the corporate performance scorecard, portfolio management, and quality assurance and in refocusing the development priorities.

In fiscal 1998 the committee continued to montor implementation of strategies for strengthening self- and independent evaluation and developing a coherent evaluation framework. Significant progress has been made on all fronts in renewing and revamping the Bank's evaluation system.

The committee continued to ensure that evaluation results are routinely and rapidly fed back into the formulation of new directions, policies, and procedures. For example, it considered Country Assistance Reviews prepared by OED for Bangladesh, Côte d'Ivoire, Mozambique, and the Philippines and reported its findings to the Board of Executive Directors prior to the discussion of the CASs for those countries. Similarly, the committee reviews draft sector strategies ahead of executive directors' discussions; in fiscal 1998 these included health, nutrition, and population; and energy and the environment. Other areas of the committee's focus in fiscal 1998 included operational policy reform, performance of technical assistance projects, the Africa region's portfolio and capacity-building activities, and the Special Program of Assistance to Africa (SPA).

Selective capital increase

The IBRD 's executive directors recommended, and the Board of Governors approved, a selective capital increase (SCI) of 23,246 shares for five countries—Brazil, Denmark, the Republic of Korea, Spain, and Turkey. The SCI will provide additional callable capital of $2,626 million, paid-in capital of $168.3 million, and additional contributions to IDA of about $250 million. These countries are expected to maintain higher IDA shares in IDA-12 and thereafter.

New auditors

In fiscal 1998 the executive directors' Audit Committee reviewed the effort to enhance the Bank's internal controls environment; the financial policies, including management of portfolio concentration and liquid assets; and the issues related to the generation and allocation of the Bank's net income. In addition, the committee followed the orderly conclusion of the tenure of Price Waterhouse and the transition to Deloitte Touche Tohmatsu (DTT) as the new auditor. The committee agreed to include a management discussion and analysis as a preface to the IBRD's financial statements in the fiscal 1998 *Annual Report*. The committee's recent discussions included the approach to determining the adequacy of the Bank's loan loss provisions and the Bank's procurement function.

AFRICA

Despite cautious optimism about the region's progress, Africa's growth must be boosted if poverty is to be reduced for large numbers of people. The macroeconomic reforms that facilitated positive growth for three years now must be deepened to reshape the role of the state and enhance its effectiveness. In fiscal 1998 the Bank worked closely with African clients to support them in efforts to improve social services and infrastructure and build attractive business environments that will encourage private investment and private sector development. Special attention was given to human development, especially to helping African people take advantage of global communications systems for accessing information. Several countries qualified for assistance under the Highly Indebted Poor Countries (HIPC) Debt Initiative, allowing them to focus scarce resources on development and poverty reduction rather than debt repayment.

For the third year in a row, the average Sub-Saharan African country experienced positive per capita economic growth in 1997. This, combined with improved economic policies and increased political openness, has created greater opportunity for development. As Africa's leaders address the different development needs of their countries and strive for what some are calling an African renaissance, the World Bank has been challenged to find new ways to respond to these opportunities

and to meet the changing needs of its African clients.

The Bank's fiscal 1997 *Annual Report* was optimistic about the region's economic recovery. This is reinforced by the fiscal 1998 results. While the region's gross domestic product (GDP) grew at 3.8 percent, this was heavily influenced by South Africa's growth of 2 percent in 1997; the average African country grew 4.6 percent, slightly lower than in 1996 (4.8 percent). Some thirty-seven countries registered positive per capita GDP growth in 1997, and twenty-one of them grew at 5 percent and more. Exports expanded roughly twice as fast as GDP in recent years and lower fiscal deficits and inflation also boosted growth *(see figure 2-1)*.

But optimism must remain guarded while economic performance falls short of levels needed to reduce poverty substantially and deliver growth to all layers of society. Serious challenges to recent progress must be recognized:

• HIV/AIDS as an economic threat;[1]

• dependence on development assistance;

• the rapid rise of domestic debt in some countries; and

• the potentially dampening effect of the East Asian crisis.

The majority of African economies have responded positively to growing social stability and sound policies, but the plight of Africans in some eight or so countries still severely affected by social and

political instability must not be forgotten. Some, like Angola, show impressive growth figures, but they do not translate into either stability or better living standards.

If growth is to be boosted, the macroeconomic reforms that have facilitated positive growth rates in Africa for three years must be deepened to reshape the role of the state and enhance its effectiveness.

Africa takes charge

The importance of African leadership was underscored when the Bank's president participated in meetings of African leaders in Kampala and Dakar in January and June 1998 respectively. Africa's leaders hold the key to the success of the continent's economic, social, and political growth and stability. But they face a tough challenge: to deepen the macroeconomic stabilization and economic reforms that many have begun and to reshape the role of the state by improving capacity to manage resources, ensuring delivery of social services and

---

1. Life expectancy is decreasing markedly in those countries with high HIV/AIDS prevalence rates: estimates suggest reductions of as much as seventeen years, or down to the levels of the 1950s. There is hope, however: a decline in HIV infection has been observed in Uganda since 1995, with new infection rates falling. The Bank is supporting two ongoing projects in Uganda that focus on safer sex and twenty-six other projects with HIV/AIDS components across the region. Some 42 percent of the Bank's cumulative HIV/AIDS lending between 1986–97 has been in the Africa region.

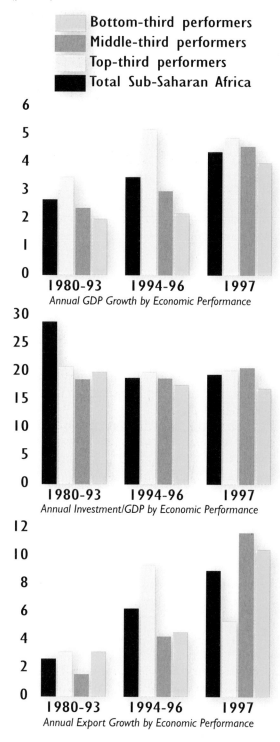

FIGURE 2-1
Sub-Saharan Africa:
Comparative Economic Performance
(percent)

- Bottom-third performers
- Middle-third performers
- Top-third performers
- Total Sub-Saharan Africa

Annual GDP Growth by Economic Performance

Annual Investment/GDP by Economic Performance

Annual Export Growth by Economic Performance

Note: Unweighted country averages.

infrastructure, and creating attractive business environments.

The Bank supported its African clients in these efforts in fiscal 1998. Table 2-1 shows the sectoral distribution of lending to the region for the 1989–98 period. Table 2-2 compares commitments, disbursements, and net transfers to the region for fiscal years 1993–98, and table 2-3 shows operations in the Africa region approved by the Board of Executive Directors during fiscal 1998 by country. See also figure 2-2 for IBRD and IDA commitments by sector.

Deeper-level reforms are underway in Senegal, for example, where a $100 million IDA adjustment credit is supporting power company privatization and petroleum sector liberalization. Up to eighteen African countries will have partly or totally private telecommunications by the end of 1998. The Bank remains involved in the rehabilitation of the Abidjan-Ouagadougou railway link, which is still the only railway concession in Sub-Saharan Africa. Work on the Maputo corridor between Mozambique and its neighbors could soon change that. The Bank has provided technical assistance in the development of designs and the evaluation of the prospective port and rail concessions. Negotiations toward an agreement are well advanced.

As Africa takes charge, a number of its leaders have recognized the stranglehold that corruption has on development efforts. Six countries (Benin, Ethiopia, Malawi, Mali, Tanzania, and Uganda) have requested help from the Bank to establish national anticorruption programs, and, in many cases, the Economic Development Institute's integrity programs are supporting these efforts. When corruption has threatened to undermine development objectives, the Bank has made its views public. In some countries, corruption has been a central feature of country assistance program (CAS) discussions.

Moving forward

Growing evidence that the impact of development assistance is most effective in countries that pursue sound economic policies has guided the Bank to be increasingly selective in its lending. In those countries where policies are conducive to reducing poverty through growth, trade, and investment, lending has increased significantly. In fiscal 1998, a greater number of CASS specifically set out strategies to accelerate growth. For countries yet to embrace stronger policies, the Bank has focused its assistance on policy dialogue and advisory services.

For Africa to build further on its initial successes, trade and private investment must grow. Currently, 61 percent of exports are made up of agricultural products, minerals, and metals, and only 19 percent manufactures; growth remains far too low and undiversified. Long-term private capital flows to Africa have increased from $4 billion in 1996 to $8 billion in 1997[2] but remain a fraction of the $256 billion total flows to developing countries. Africa must attract more investment, not only from foreigners but from Africans themselves: some 37 percent of African assets are held abroad, according to estimates—higher than any other region.

In fiscal 1998 the Bank helped its African clients, such as Malawi and Mozambique, to lower trade barriers and increase competitiveness. In some countries, trade taxes can account for up to 40 percent of fiscal revenue, and in one example of an effort to address this, the Bank and the West African Economic and Monetary Union (WAEMU) are discussing ways to meet the transitional financial costs as fiscal policies are strengthened.

Financial sector reform is critical to Africa's development and competitiveness. At the end of fiscal 1998, thirty financial sector activities were underway in the region, with a loan portfolio of $397 million. Privatization and restructuring projects are underway in Ghana, Togo, and Uganda. At the regional level, the Bank is helping the West African and Central African economic and monetary unions to develop common payments systems and improve banking supervision; and with the Southern African Development Community (SADC), work is ongoing to harmonize payment systems.

As part of the Bank's regional microfinance strategy, raising awareness about principles and methodologies to build sustainable microfinance institutions and develop national microfinance strategies has been a particular focus on nonlending activities such as workshops in Ghana, Mozambique and Uganda. A series of regional seminars—co-sponsored by EDI and

For Africa to build on its successes, trade and private investment must grow. Building a skilled cadre of people will enhance Africa's competitivenes in the global economy.

held in Benin, South Africa, and Zimbabwe —attracted policy makers and financiers from about fifteen African countries. A project in Benin, which transformed a bankrupt cooperative movement into one of Africa's most successful credit union systems, has become a best-practice model and is being replicated in Guinea.

A striking feature of a meeting of the Economic Committee of the Global Coalition for Africa (GCA) in Gaborone was the consensus among all players—governments, donors, and the private sector—on the need for a stable business and macroenvironment and a performing financial sector. There is also greater recognition that the private sector has a significant role to play in assisting Africa reach the sustainable growth rates that will begin to make a difference to people's welfare. While much of the Bank's support for private sector development has been policy-based, promotional activities have been ongoing throughout the year. The Gateway Initiative in Ghana goes beyond this to provide concrete ways in which the private sector can be supported. Developed during fiscal 1998 with techncial assistance from the Japanese

2. World Bank. 1998. *Global Development Finance 1998.* Washington, D.C.

and other trust funds, the project is designed to provide serviced land for exporters, which includes easy access to a port. The site will be privately owned and managed.

The West African Enterprise Network (WAEN), in which the Bank has been a partner for five years, represents some 350 businesses in West Africa. It has been successful in pushing for trade policy reform and investment between countries in the subregion. In fiscal 1998 the Bank sought support from the Development Grant Facility (DGF) to help WAEN achieve full independence and extend the initiative to eastern and southern Africa.

To promote privatization in Africa, the Bank and MIGA created a specialized window within IPAnet, MIGA's Internet-based marketplace for investment opportunities,[3] to launch Privatization Link,[4] profiling investment opportunities arising from privatization. MIGA also supported private investment by issuing guarantees totaling $126 million covering projects in Angola, Cape Verde, Equitorial Guinea, Kenya, Mozambique and Uganda. They facilitated $2.3 billion in foreign direct investment in these countries.

All these efforts in trade and investment are central to promoting agricultural growth, which in turn is the engine of rural development. Positive trends are emerging in Africa's agricultural sector as a result of substantial im-

3. http://www.ipanet.com
4. http://www.privatizationlink.org

TABLE 2-1.   LENDING TO BORROWERS IN AFRICA, BY SECTOR, FISCAL YEARS 1989–98

(millions of US dollars)

Sector	Annual average, FY89–93	FY94	FY95	FY96	FY97	FY98
Agriculture	612.8	152.6	407.1	301.3	193.7	176.9
Education	291.9	286.7	156.6	131.6	75.1	372.3
Electric power and other energy	216.7	90.0	255.3	73.3	163.7	380.3
Environment	40.5	2.6	8.0	38.5	95.4	71.8
Finance	252.0	400.1	7.2	116.9	65.9	—
Health, nutrition and population	174.5	161.6	250.4	158.7	54.9	227.0
Industry	274.1	16.8	—	23.7	23.8	—
Mining	5.4	—	24.8	12.2	21.4	5.0
Multisector	623.7	724.1	420.9	387.8	706.9	404.9
Oil and gas	58.1	186.2	—	—	—	—
Public sector management	107.0	61.0	117.3	592.2	110.7	155.1
Social sector	62.6	85.5	155.7	257.5	—	114.7
Telecommunications	86.0	—	—	—	—	—
Transportation	376.3	501.9	74.8	420.7	52.9	770.1
Urban development	208.1	64.7	158.0	190.0	147.3	85.0
Water supply and sanitation	218.8	74.1	248.2	35.7	25.0	110.7
Total	3,608.5	2,807.9	2,284.3	2,740.1	1,736.7	2,873.8
Of which: IBRD	831.2	127.7	80.7	—	56.0	57.4
IDA	2,777.4	2,680.2	2,203.6	2,740.1	1,680.7	2,816.4

NOTE: *Details may not add to totals because of rounding.*
— *Zero.*

TABLE 2-2. WORLD BANK COMMITMENTS, DISBURSEMENTS, AND NET TRANSFERS IN AFRICA, FISCAL YEARS 1993–98

(millions of US dollars)

Item	Uganda		Côte d'Ivoire		Ethiopa		Total region	
	1998	1993–98[a]	1998	1993–98[a]	1998	1993–98[a]	1998	1993–98[a]
IBRD and IDA commitments	172	919	342	1,604	669	1,388	2,874	15,260
Undisbursed balance	570	570	322	322	467	467	8,984	8,984
Gross disbursements	168	987	215	1,268	72	761	2,506	16,510
Repayments	10	72	147	1,068	16	87	954	6,375
Net disbursements	157	915	68	200	56	674	1,552	10,135
Interest and charges	14	75	85	773	11	61	560	4,459
Net transfer	143	840	-17	-573	45	613	992	5,676

NOTE: *The countries shown in the table are those with the largest borrowings of Bank funds during fiscal 1997–98. Details may not add to totals because of rounding.*

a. *Disbursements from the IDA Special Fund are included through fiscal 1996.*

provements in macroeconomic and agricultural policies. More responsive agricultural extension services have also helped agriculture reach an estimated 3.5 percent growth in 1997 despite drought in some areas. The Bank's rural development portfolio is smaller (118 operations in the portfolio in fiscal 1997 and 100 in fiscal 1998) but has improved in quality.[5] Local governments, the private sector, nongovernmental organizations (NGOs), and other donors have become closer partners in agricultural extension. A village participation initiative, pioneered in Benin in fiscal 1997 and supported by a learning and innovation credit in fiscal 1998, was piloted in a further seven countries (Burkina Faso, Côte d'Ivoire, Guinea, Madagascar, Malawi, Mali, and Uganda) in fiscal 1998. About 1,000 villages are involved in the pilots that are using existing Bank-financed agricultural services projects to launch new working approaches toward integrated rural development. Field staff from extension services and other agencies are helping villagers to plan and implement collective action for rural development.

Africa's richest resource: its people

Lack of capacity cuts across the entire range of challenges to national development, from policy analysis to the effective delivery of basic social services. In fiscal 1998 the African Governors agreed to launch the Partnership for Capacity Building in Africa (PACT), with African governments leading the planning. In addition, capacity building continues to be worked into all elements of Bank activities and has been included as a central theme in CAS documents in Côte d'Ivoire, Ethiopia, Kenya, South Africa, and Zimbabwe, for example. Some older projects have also been restructured in order to better promote capacity building.[6]

Background research undertaken for *World Development Report 1998*[7] reinforced the importance of knowledge and information to successful development. But Africa is in danger of being left behind as global communications systems become increasingly sophisticated. The Bank is

5. Problem projects have dropped from 20.3 percent of the portfolio in 1997 to 17 percent in 1998.

6. Malawi's Second Institutional Development Project, approved in fiscal 1994, now includes an activity to address the country's acute lack of accountants by strengthening a local institution to qualify Malawians in-country rather than abroad. And Tanzania's entire Bank portfolio was examined from a capacity-building dimension, and recommendations are being implemented by the country team.

7. World Bank. Forthcoming. *World Development Report 1998: Knowledge and Information for Development.* New York: Oxford University Press.

TABLE 2-3.   OPERATIONS APPROVED DURING FISCAL YEAR 1998, AFRICA

Country/project name	Date of Approval	Maturities	Principal amount (millions) SDR	Principal amount (millions) US$
Angola				
Post-Conflict Social Recovery Project	Apr 15, 1998	2008/2037	3.70	5.00
Benin				
Borgou Region Pilot Rural Support Project	Jun 15, 1998	2008/2037	3.00	4.00
Social Fund Project	May 19, 1998	2008/2037	12.40	16.70
Burkina Faso				
Second National Agricultural Services Development Project	Jul 1, 1997	2007/2037	30.30	41.30
Cameroon				
Higher Education Technical Training Project	Jun 24, 1998	2008/2038	3.70	4.86
Third Structural Adjustment Credit	Jun 25, 1998	2008/2038	133.50	180.00
Second Structural Adjustment Credit	Dec 15, 1997	2006/2035	12.90	18.10
Cape Verde				
Economic Reforms Support Credit	Dec 23, 1997	2008/2037	21.80	30.00
Chad				
Household Energy Project	Jun 2, 1998	2008/2038	4.00	5.27
Comoros				
Health Project	Feb 26, 1998	2008/2038	6.20	8.40
Social Fund Project	Dec 4, 1997	2008/2037	8.50	11.50
Côte d'Ivoire				
Private Sector Development Capacity Building Project	Jun 25, 1998	2008/2038	8.90	12.00
Transport Sector Adjustment/Investment Program	Jun 23, 1998	2008/2038	130.60	180.00
Education and Training Support Project	May 29, 1998	2008/2038	39.60	53.30
Private Sector Development Adjustment Credit	Dec 15, 1997	2006/2036	26.10	36.60
Urban Land Management and Housing Finance Reforms Technical Assistance Project	Nov 5, 1997	2008/2037	7.30	10.00
Commercial Debt Restructuring Program	Jul 10, 1997	2008/2037	36.00	50.00
Eritrea				
Human Resources Development Project	Jan 15, 1998	2008/2037	39.10	53.00
Health Project	Dec 16, 1997	2008/2037	13.40	18.30
Ports Rehabilitation Project	Nov 18, 1997	2008/2037	22.20	30.30
Ethiopia				
Agricultural Research and Training Project	Jun 9, 1998	2008/2038	44.50	60.00
Education Sector Development Program Project	May 26, 1998	2008/2038	74.30	100.00
Road Sector Development Program Support Project	Jan 15, 1998	2008/2037	224.50	309.20
Second Energy Project	Dec 11, 1997	2008/2037	146.14	200.00
Gambia				
Participatory Health, Population and Nutrition Project	Mar 31, 1998	2008/2038	13.40	18.00
Ghana				
Economic Reform Support Operation	Jun 11, 1998	2008/2038	37.10	50.00
Natural Resource Management Project	Jun 4, 1998	2008/2038	6.90	9.30
Private Sector Adjustment Credit	Dec 15, 1997	2005/2035	1.70	2.40
Health Sector Program Support Project	Oct 21, 1997	2008/2037	25.10	35.00
Guinea				
Microfinance Capacity-Building Project	Jun 25, 1998	2008/2038	3.80	5.00
Public Expenditure Management Adjustment Credit	Dec 16, 1997	2008/2037	50.80	70.00
Guinea-Bissau				
National Health Development Program	Nov 25, 1997	2007/2037	8.60	11.70
Kenya				
Structural Adjustment Credit	Dec 15, 1997	2006/2036	12.50	17.50
Lesotho				
Agricultural Policy and Capacity Building Project	Jun 25, 1998	2008/2038	5.10	6.80
Lesotho Highlands Water Project	Jun 4, 1998	2003/2013	n.a.	45.00

Country/project name	Date of Approval	Maturities	Principal amount (millions)	
			SDR	US$
Madagascar				
Mining Sector Reform Project	Jun 30, 1998	2008/2038	3.80	5.00
Second Community Nutrition Project	Apr 21, 1998	2008/2038	20.40	27.60
Education Sector Development Project	Mar 10, 1998	2008/2037	47.70	65.00
Rural Water Supply and Sanitation Pilot Project	Dec 18, 1997	2008/2037	12.60	17.30
Malawi				
Secondary Education Project	Mar 24, 1998	2008/2038	35.50	48.20
Fiscal Restructuring Deregulation Program Credit	Dec 15, 1997	2006/2036	1.70	2.40
Mali				
Grassroots Initiatives to Fight Hunger and Poverty Project	Apr 7, 1998	2008/2037	15.90	21.50
Mauritania				
Health Sector Investment Project	Mar 31, 1998	2008/2037	17.80	24.00
Public Resource Management Credit	Dec 15, 1997	2006/2036	0.30	0.40
Mauritius				
Environmental Sewerage and Sanitation Project	Feb 12, 1998	2003/2013	n.a.	12.40
Mozambique				
National Water Development I Project	Feb 12, 1998	2008/2038	26.20	36.00
Niger				
Transport Infrastructure Rehabilitation Project	Dec 18, 1997	2008/2037	20.30	28.00
Rwanda				
Transport Sector Project	Dec 18, 1997	2000/2030	33.09	45.00
Senegal				
Energy Sector Adjustment Credit	May 19, 1998	2008/2038	74.00	100.00
Agricultural Export Promotion Project	Dec 9, 1997	2008/2037	5.90	8.00
Urban Development and Decentralization Program	Nov 20, 1997	2008/2037	55.20	75.00
Integrated Health Sector Development Program	Sep 4, 1997	2007/2037	35.90	50.00
Tanzania				
Agricultural Research Project—Phase II	Jan 29, 1998	2008/2037	15.90	21.80
Structural Adjustment Credit	Dec 15, 1997	2007/2037	1.80	2.60
Human Resources Development Pilot Project	Oct 7, 1997	2008/2037	15.00	20.90
Togo				
Public Enterprise Restructuring and Privatization Support Project	Mar 5, 1998	2008/2038	22.00	30.00
Road Transport Project	Sep 11, 1997	2007/2037	36.00	50.00
National Agricultural Services Support Project	Sep 11, 1997	2007/2037	19.20	26.20
Uganda				
El Niño Emergency Road Repair Project	May 7, 1998	2008/2038	20.50	27.60
Nutrition and Early Childhood Development Project	Mar 24, 1998	2008/2038	25.00	34.00
Education Sector Adjustment Operation	Mar 24, 1998	2008/2038	59.20	80.00
Road Sector Institutional Support Technical Assistance Project	Sep 9, 1997	2008/2037	21.60	30.00
Zambia				
Power Rehabilitation Project	Feb 19, 1998	2008/2037	55.10	75.00
Road Sector Investment Program Support Project	Oct 14, 1997	2007/2037	51.50	70.00
Zimbabwe				
Park Rehabilitation and Conservation Project	Jun 2, 1998	2008/2033	46.30	62.50
Agricultural Services and Management Project	May 29, 1998	2008/2033	6.60	8.80
Community Action Project	May 19, 1998	2008/2033	45.00	60.00
Total			2,064.58	2,873.73

n.a. = not applicable (IBRD loan).

FIGURE 2-2 Africa: IBRD and IDA Commitments by Sector, Fiscal Year 1998

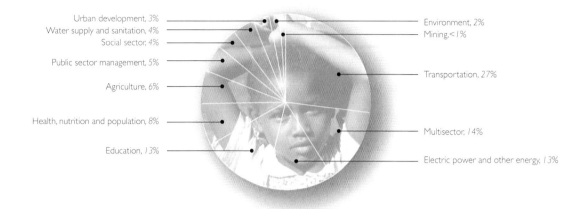

Urban development, *3%*
Water supply and sanitation, *4%*
Social sector, *4%*
Public sector management, *5%*
Agriculture, *6%*
Health, nutrition and population, *8%*
Education, *13%*

Environment, *2%*
Mining, *<1%*
Transportation, *27%*
Multisector, *14%*
Electric power and other energy, *13%*

helping address the challenge with support for several information projects:

• AfricaDev, piloted in fiscal 1998, which connects development practitioners in Africa with the Bank's expertise;

• Africa Live Data Base, which provides economic and social indicators via the Internet;[8]

• Africa Virtual University, which offers degree programs in science, engineering, and continuing education; and

• EDI's World Links for Development program, which has already connected sixty-four schools in six African countries via the Internet with partner schools in the industrialized world.

Among the toughest tasks for African countries is building a skilled cadre of people in order to compete in the global economy. The challenges are in the very bedrock: in education for example, the region faces an alarming deficit with the lowest school enrollment ratio in the world and only 53 percent of adults literate. In fiscal 1998 the Bank significantly increased its support for education with $372 million from IDA to enhance the quantity and quality of education in Cameroon, Côte d'Ivoire, Ethiopia, Madagascar, Malawi, Tanzania, and Uganda. There were similar increases in lending for health, nutrition, and population with projects in nine countries totaling $227 million. New commitments for the social sectors had been reduced in recent years, while critical policy and absorptive-capacity issues were addressed to speed disbursements. With reforms in place, new loans now stand a better chance of success.

Partners in African development

In acknowledging the greater role of Africans in deepening their own development agenda, the Bank has been challenged to reinvigorate its partnerships in the Africa region. The Economic Commission for Africa (ECA) celebrated its 40th anniversary with a conference in which the Bank was a key partner. Entitled "African Women and Economic Development," it established plans to achieve one of the Bank's core ambitions—bringing women into the mainstream of the development agenda. With the African Development Bank, partnership has moved beyond project cofinancing. Côte d'Ivoire, Mozambique, and Senegal were agreed upon as pilot countries, and joint work will be developed.

Partnerships with Africa's regional institutions—such as the Economic Community of West African States (ECOWAS), the East African Community (EAC), and at a continental level, the Organization of African Unity (OAU)—are of growing importance because the success of African countries lies in their ability to work together. The first subregional CAS was developed for southern Africa,[9] based on consultations with individual countries and subregional structures like SADC. The CAS emphasizes the

8. http://www.worldbank.org/html/extpb/Publications.html

BOX 2-1. GETTING PAST DEBT

By the early 1990s the crippling debt repayments that were undermining the development efforts of very poor countries—many of them in Africa—gained widespread attention. As churches and religious groups around the world called for efforts to ease this burden, the Bank and the International Monetary Fund (IMF) developed a special initiative to help. The goal was to enable poor countries with sound economic policies to escape their unsustainable debt in order to focus their energies on development and reducing poverty. The resulting Heavily Indebted Poor Countries (HIPC) Debt Initiative is a commitment by the international community, including creditors, to reduce eligible countries' debt to manageable levels. The HIPC Trust Fund provides debt relief by prepaying a portion of debt owed to multilateral institutions, or purchasing and canceling a portion of the debt, or paying debt service as it comes due. April 1998 was a landmark month for the HIPC Debt Initiative, as Uganda became the first beneficiary with a debt-service relief package of $650 million, and the decision was reached to provide nearly $3,000 million in relief to Mozambique. Burkina Faso, Côte d'Ivoire, and Mali all qualified for HIPC assistance during fiscal 1998. During fiscal 1998 decisions were taken to provide HIPC debt relief to Burkina Faso, and Côte d'Ivoire, amounting to an estimated total debt service relief of $1,000 million, while preliminary debt relief packages in the order of $900 million were considered for Guinea-Bissau and Mali.

need for regional growth in trade and investment, infrastructure development, and stronger and more efficient financial sectors.

NGOs continue to be partners for the implementation of some crucial elements of the Bank's work in the field. For example, in Mali a project that supports development priorities as identified by local communities involves NGOs in literacy and managerial training. In Madagascar, NGOs are helping implement a village-level nutrition program.

The Special Program of Assistance for Africa (SPA) continues to be a primary mechanism for donor coordination of policies and programs in support of African economic reforms. To evaluate the SPA's effectiveness, its members undertook a review of its framework in fiscal 1998 and requested that the Bank's Operations Evaluation Department (OED) undertake an independent assessment. While the importance of the SPA has been reaffirmed, a number of ideas are under consideration by the partnership for improving its mechanisms and strengthening the participation of, and consultation with, African stakeholders, including governments, regional institutions, and civil society.

As part of the United Nations (UN) Special Initiative for Africa, the Bank is spearheading sector investment programs (SIPs) in coordination with UN agencies and the donor community. The use of the SIP instrument through which African countries can direct their priorities in particular sectors is being demonstrated to good effect in Ethiopia, where a $100 million credit is supporting the country's $1,800 million Education Sector Development Program, and in Ghana, where an initial $35 million credit is supporting its $824 million health sector program.

Meeting client needs

Bank commitments dropped in fiscal 1997 while the Bank focused on improving the quality of the existing portfolio and its clients focused on getting necessary policy decisions in place. With the achievement of these goals, commitments bounced back in fiscal 1998 to reach $2,874 million.

To ensure it is meeting clients needs, the Bank undertook client surveys in ten Sub-Saharan countries in fiscal 1998. While clients were generally satisfied with Bank staff and products, and noted improvements since the previous survey in 1995, they challenged Bank staff to adapt their considerable knowledge to countries' specific needs and to be more flexible in developing true partnerships with African nations.

9. Angola, Botswana, Democratic Republic of Congo, Lesotho, Malawi, Mauritius, Mozambique, Namibia, Seychelles, South Africa, Swaziland, Tanzania, Zambia, and Zimbabwe.

Responding to the economic and financial crisis dominated the Bank's assistance program to the East Asia and Pacific (EAP) region in fiscal 1998. The Bank supported countries in their efforts to restructure their financial sectors, reform corporate governance, and provide social safety nets in the face of mounting unemployment, declining incomes and public expenditures, and rising prices for staple commodities, which primarily affect the poor. The Bank pledged some $16 billion, in addition to its regular lending program, to address the extra demands that arose from the crisis. By the end of the fiscal year, $565,000 million of this had been disbursed. Parallel to this effort, the Bank continued its regular operations, supporting clients with programs to promote economic and social reforms, reduce poverty, and build institutional capacity. In response to natural disasters, emergency assistance was extended to China, Indonesia, Papua New Guinea, and Vietnam.

The unprecedented improvement in living standards and poverty reduction experienced by many countries of the East Asia and Pacific (EAP) region during the past two decades was brought to a halt by the economic and financial crisis in fiscal 1998. Massive currency depreciation, liquidity shortage, the compression of investment and consumption, and the industrial and financial restructuring necessary to respond to the crisis cur-

tailed the short-term growth prospects of all countries, though with varying degrees of magnitude. Many of the region's people, who were brought above the poverty line over the last several decades as a result of successful development, again fell below it.

The East Asian crisis was triggered by large-scale movement of funds out of domestic financial markets, beginning in Thailand and quickly spreading to neighboring countries as investor sentiment deteriorated. While the chief factors contributing to the crisis differed from country to country, there were common characteristics:

• failure to contain demand and a boom in lending resulted in large current account deficits and property and stock market bubbles;

• the rigid nature of currency regimes encouraged foreign borrowing (to take advantage of lower interest rates) leading to imprudent exposure to foreign exchange risk by banks and corporations; and

• lax prudential rules and supervision of financial sectors led to sharp deterioration in the quality of banks' loan portfolios.

These factors were compounded by shortcomings in the way countries allocated their resources, including state-directed lending, nepotism, skewed industrial structures, and limits on foreign participation and competition.

While developments in the industrialized economies and in global financial markets con-

tributed to the crisis, they were not its fundamental cause. Weak economic growth in Japan and Europe since the early 1990s led to accommodating monetary policies and low interest rates. These factors, combined with international investors' aggressive search for high returns in emerging markets, led to a situation in which not only more investment flowed into the region's economies than could be profitably employed at a reasonable risk, but also inefficient allocation resulted from structural weaknesses in countries' financial systems.

Economic outlook

Two conflicting developments are shaping the region's economic outlook. First, current account balances are moving into positive territory. If sustained and combined with significant official financial support, this adjustment will help improve investor confidence, lift foreign investment, and build the basis for a recovery. Second, sharp cutbacks in investment spending—owing to the decline in foreign financing, weak banking systems, and tight monetary and fiscal policies—are countering positive trade developments and threatening the prospects for early economic recovery. Investment spending in the region before the crisis was high at 37 percent of gross domestic product (GDP), and a resumption of investment is crucial for recovery and growth. Even so, growth recovery will probably be somewhat slower than initially anticipated, and East Asia's growth rates are unlikely to reach their pre-crisis level without a quick rebound in investment.

Restoring investor confidence is critical and requires effective implementation of sound programs to restructure corporate debts and banking sectors. Addressing the severe credit crunch and high interest rates will be elemental for recovery and resumption of economic growth in the region. But an auspicious external environment is equally important—in particular, stronger economic recovery in Japan, maintenance of open markets by Europe and the United States, and continued efforts by China to stimulate its economy and stabilize exchange rates. These, combined with the availability of enhanced facilities for trade and working capital financing, could stimulate exports and support recovery. Asian countries must also avoid competitive currency devaluation to avert a new round of financial difficulties.

By the end of the fiscal year the Republic of Korea and Thailand had begun to make significant progress on their stabilization and reform programs—particularly financial sector, competition policy and corporate restructuring, and there were encouraging signs that these reform programs were beginning to take hold.

World Bank response

The Bank's core mandate of poverty reduction and sustainable development—together with its traditional focus on better health and

TABLE 2-4. LENDING TO BORROWERS IN EAST ASIA AND THE PACIFIC, BY SECTOR, FISCAL YEARS 1989–98

(millions of US dollars)

Sector	Annual average, FY89–93	FY94	FY95	FY96	FY97	FY98
Agriculture	848.7	1,570.4	373.0	844.9	1,265.0	1,058.7
Education	382.3	436.6	526.5	437.9	645.0	103.5
Electric power and other energy	888.1	1,048.5	1,383.0	1,683.0	1,131.4	783.7
Environment	134.9	381.5	308.1	170.7	—	278.4
Finance	364.7	100.0	—	49.0	28.4	5,420.0
Health, nutrition and population	131.9	160.0	242.2	296.0	58.9	146.5
Industry	204.4	—	175.0	217.0	60.0	—
Mining	—	—	—	35.0	—	—
Multisector	257.0	82.7	167.0	130.0	—	315.0
Oil and gas	82.2	266.0	245.0	—	—	—
Public sector management	78.1	—	88.0	—	—	230.0
Social sector	—	9.7	267.5	40.0	—	10.0
Telecommunications	182.7	250.0	325.0	—	—	34.5
Transportation	746.2	1,380.0	1,032.5	916.9	1,243.7	1,110.0
Urban development	181.5	349.0	486.0	542.7	265.0	45.1
Water supply and sanitation	197.4	—	75.0	57.0	168.6	87.8
Total	4,680.1	6,034.4	5,693.8	5,420.1	4,866.0	9,623.2
Of which: IBRD	3,770.1	4,623.8	4,592.6	4,252.2	4,074.4	8,847.0
IDA	910.0	1,410.6	1,101.2	1,167.9	791.6	776.2

NOTE: Details may not add to totals because of rounding.
— Zero.

education, environmental cleanup and protection, infrastructure development, and institution building—provided the basis for its response to the new challenges presented by the East Asian crisis and underpinned the Bank's lending and advisory services to the region during fiscal 1998. Table 2-4 shows the sectoral distribution of lending to the region for the 1989–98 period. Table 2-5 compares commitments, disbursements, and net transfers to the region for fiscal years 1993–98, and table 2-6 shows operations in the EAP region approved by the Board of Executive Directors during fiscal 1998 by country. Figure 2-3 shows IBRD and IDA commitments by sector.

A two-pronged, rapid and substantial lending program was directed primarily at financial- and corporate sector restructuring and preserving social services, and a complementary program of technical assistance and advisory services strengthened implementation of the lending program.

First, to help countries restructure their financial and corporate sectors, the Bank designed and began to implement programs to put in place needed legal and institutional frameworks. These included establishing bankruptcy and foreclosure laws; reforming governance structures for banks and corporations; strengthening

supervision; and building financial sector capacity. The Bank also helped to design and assess work-out schemes for financial institutions and a process for soundly and transparently disposing of assets of those institutions to be closed. The IFC augmented the Bank's lending program by providing equity and credit to support banks and corporations.

Second, the Bank focused on helping its clients manage the social consequences of the crisis by protecting and improving the quality of social services and public expenditures targeted to help the poor. This included designing and financing social funds and strengthening social security systems for the elderly and unemployed.

To further enhance governments' ability to cope with the crisis, the Economic Development Institute (EDI) conference, "East Asia: The Unfinished Agenda," brought together the region's policymakers to discuss the economic turbulence, identify structural problems, and evaluate development priorities for the aftermath of the crisis.

MIGA supported private investment through guarantee contracts totaling $50 million in coverage for agribusiness, infrastructure and manufacturing projects in China.

TABLE 2-5. WORLD BANK COMMITMENTS, DISBURSEMENTS, AND NET TRANSFERS IN EAST ASIA AND THE PACIFIC, FISCAL YEARS 1993–98

(millions of US dollars)

	China		Indonesia		Korea		Total region	
Item	1998	1993–98[a]	1998	1993–98[a]	1998	1993–98[a]	1998	1993–98[a]
IBRD and IDA commitments	2,616	17,643	703	6,384	5,000	5,975	9,623	37,207
Undisbursed balance	10,906	10,906	4,728	4,728	434	434	20,026	20,026
Gross disbursements	2,094	12,156	659	6,014	5,167	6,267	9,375	30,460
Repayments	395	1,983	749	6,345	292	2,614	2,189	16,354
Net disbursements	1,698	10,173	-90	-331	4,875	3,652	7,186	14,105
Interest and charges	574	2,802	663	5,023	237	1,092	1,945	12,381
Net Transfer	1,124	7,371	-753	-5,354	4,638	2,560	5,241	1,724

NOTE: *The countries shown in the table are those with the largest borrowings of Bank funds during fiscal 1997–98. Details may not add to totals because of rounding.*

a. *Disbursements from the IDA Special Fund are included through fiscal 1996.*

TABLE 2-6. OPERATIONS APPROVED DURING FISCAL YEAR 1998, EAST ASIA AND PACIFIC

Country/project name	Date of Approval	Maturities	Principal amount (millions) SDR	Principal amount (millions) US$
Cambodia				
Urban Water Supply Project	Feb 17, 1998	2008/2037	22.70	30.96
China				
Tri-Provincial Highway Project	Jun 23, 1998	2004/2018	n.a.	230.00
Hunan Power Development Project	Jun 18, 1998	2004/2018	n.a.	300.00
Irrigated Agriculture Intensification II Project	Jun 18, 1998	2004/2018	n.a.	300.00
Guangxi Urban Environment Project [a]	Jun 16, 1998	2003/2018	n.a.	72.00
Guangxi Urban Environment Project [a]	Jun 16, 1998	2008/2033	14.90	20.00
Tarim Basin II Project [a]	Jun 9, 1998	2004/2018	n.a	90.00
Tarim Basin II Project [a]	Jun 9, 1998	2008/2033	44.60	60.00
Third National Highway Project	May 29, 1998	2004/2018	n.a	250.00
Second Inland Waterways Project	May 29, 1998	2004/2018	n.a	123.00
Guangzhou City Center Transport Project	May 29, 1998	2004/2018	n.a	200.00
Hebei Earthquake Rehabilitation Project	May 29, 1998	2008/2033	21.10	28.40
Forestry Development in Poor Areas Project[a]	May 27, 1998	2008/2033	74.30	100.00
Forestry Development in Poor Areas Project[a]	May 21, 1998	2005/2014	n.a.	100.00
Basic Health Service Project	May 19, 1998	2008/2033	63.00	85.00
Sustainable Coastal Resource Development Project	May 19, 1998	2004/2018	n.a.	100.00
State Farms Commercialization Project	Mar 31, 1998	2003/2018	n.a.	150.00
East China (Jiangsu) Power Transmission Project	Mar 26, 1998	2003/2018	n.a.	250.00
Energy Conservation Project	Mar 26, 1998	2003/2018	n.a.	63.00
Shandong Environment Project	Oct 28, 1997	2003/2018	n.a.	95.00
Indonesia				
Kecamatan Development Project	Jun 2, 1998	2002/2014	n.a.	225.00
Coral Reef Rehabilitation and Management Project	Mar 31, 1998	2001/2013	n.a.	6.90
Maluku Regional Development Project	Mar 31, 1998	2001/2013	n.a.	16.30
Northern Sumatra Region Road Project	Mar 31, 1998	2002/2013	n.a.	234.00
West Java Basic Education Project	Mar 31, 1998	2001/2013	n.a.	103.50
Bengkulu Regional Development Project	Mar 3, 1998	2001/2013	n.a.	20.50
Banking Reform Assistance Project	Dec 4, 1997	2001/2013	n.a.	20.00
Information Infrastructure Development Project	Nov 18, 1997	2001/2013	n.a.	34.50
Safe Motherhood Project: A Partnership and Family Approach	Jul 1, 1997	2001/2012	n.a.	42.50
Korea				
Structural Adjustment Loan	Mar 26, 1998	2003/2013	n.a.	2,000.00
Economic Reconstruction Project	Dec 23, 1997	2003/2008	n.a.	3,000.00
Lao People's Democratic Republic				
Southern Provinces Rural Electrification Project	Mar 17, 1998	2008/2037	25.70	34.70
Malaysia				
Economic Recovery and Social Sector Loan	Jun 18, 1998	2002/2014	n.a.	300.00
Mongolia				
Fiscal Technical Assistance Project	Jun 2, 1998	2008/2038	3.80	5.00
Ulaanbaatar Services Improvement Project	Jul 1, 1997	2007/2037	12.30	16.70
Papua New Guinea				
El Niño Drought Response Project	Apr 21, 1998	2001/2013	n.a.	5.00
Philippines				
Community-Based Resources Management Project	Mar 24, 1998	2003/2018	n.a.	50.00
SZOPAD Social Fund Project	Mar 24, 1998	2003/2018	n.a.	10.00
Early Childhood Development Project	Mar 24, 1998	2003/2018	n.a.	19.00
Water Districts Development Project	Sep 9, 1997	2003/2017	n.a.	56.80
Thailand				
Economic Management Assistance Project	Feb 26, 1998	2001/2013	n.a.	15.00
Finance Companies Restructuring Loan	Dec 23, 1997	2001/2013	n.a.	350.00
Financial Sector Implementation Assistance Project	Sep 11, 1997	2001/2013	n.a.	15.00
Vietnam				
Agricultural Diversification Project	Jun 23, 1998	2008/2038	49.60	66.85
Transmission, Distribution and Disaster Reconstruction Project	Jan 20, 1998	2008/2038	144.40	199.00
Debt and Debt Service Reduction Credit	Jan 6, 1998	2008/2037	25.20	35.00
Inland Waterways and Port Rehabilitation Project	Nov 4, 1997	2008/2037	53.70	73.00
Forest Protection and Rural Development Project	Oct 30, 1997	2008/2037	15.90	21.50
Total			571.20	9,623.11

n.a. = not applicable (IBRD loan).

a. "Blend" loan/credit.

FIGURE 2-3 East Asia and the Pacific: IBRD and IDA Commitments by Sector, Fiscal Year 1998

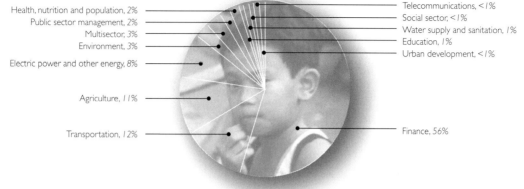

Health, nutrition and population, *2%*
Public sector management, *2%*
Multisector, *3%*
Environment, *3%*
Electric power and other energy, *8%*
Agriculture, *11%*
Transportation, *12%*

Telecommunications, *<1%*
Social sector, *<1%*
Water supply and sanitation, *1%*
Education, *1%*
Urban development, *<1%*
Finance, *56%*

Restructuring financial and corporate sectors

While problems in the region's financial and corporate sectors had been building up for some years, they were masked by rapid economic growth and, in some cases, by lack of transparency in accounting. In fiscal 1998 the Bank played an active role in helping the three countries facing the most serious problems—Indonesia, the Republic of Korea, and Thailand—deal with immediate financial and corporate distress *(see box 2-2)*. The Bank's support for the design and implementation of financial and corporate restructuring included liquidating and restructuring troubled institutions, establishing effective legal and regulatory systems, improving corporate governance, and, more broadly, improving the transparency and quality of information flows.

The region's financial crisis underscored an important and urgent task: the need to strengthen domestic financial sectors and corporate governance across the region. Thus, in addition to those countries directly affected by the crisis, the Bank provided advisory and technical assistance services, including an economic mission and special workshops and conferences to help other client countries deepen their policy and institutional capacity for economic management in an increasingly global environment. Together with the International Monetary

Fund (IMF), for example, the Bank prepared a reform program for the Philippines financial sector that will be supported by a banking sector adjustment loan.

In March 1998 a partnership of the Asian Development Bank, the governments of Japan and the Philippines, and the Bank's EDI organized a timely conference in Manila—the Asian Development Forum. The forum brought together local and regional experts to examine the causes and implications of the financial crisis and facilitated exchange of information and views on the crisis for the region's government officials. Together with the Chinese authorities, the Bank organized a number of workshops to examine the implications and lessons of the East Asian crisis, which led to advances in China's reform programs in the state banking and enterprise sectors.

In response to a request from Malaysia, which has not taken advantage of the Bank's assistance for several years, the Bank prepared a comprehensive Country Economic Memorandum, with particular emphasis on financial sector issues. The Economic Recovery and Social Sector Loan was approved by the Board of Executive Directors and technical assistance for banking reforms developed. A seminar on privatization of state enterprises and a workshop on the financial crisis were conducted in Vietnam to help authorities better understand policy options. EDI conducted commercial banking training programs for China and an economic management program in Cambodia to help the region's transitional economies build appropriate institutions.

Protecting people in the face of crisis and natural disaster

The East Asian crisis put at risk the most remarkable achievement in poverty reduction in modern history. Despite this unprecedented progress, just prior to the crisis some 350 million people in the region were still living on less than one dollar a day and tens of millions just above the poverty line. Furthermore, most countries in the region had little or no social safety net, unemployment insurance, or provision for old-age pension insurance.

The most immediate social effect of the crisis was job loss—particularly for workers in urban areas. The difficulties facing the poor are further aggravated by rising prices for food and other essentials because of the huge depreciation of currencies—especially in Indonesia—combined with likely cutbacks in social expenditures due to declining fiscal revenues. These declining revenues resulted from economic slowdown, increased costs for debt service, and financial sector and corporate restructuring.

To respond to the social consequences of the financial crisis, the Bank stressed the importance of the human dimensions of the crisis, especially protecting the poor, in its discussions with member governments and other partners; and it worked with clients to safeguard budgetary expenditures for social protection. Assistance to design and implement social protection schemes, such as workfare programs, social

---

BOX 2-2   WORLD BANK SUPPORT FOR FINANCIAL AND CORPORATE RESTRUCTURING IN INDONESIA, THE REPUBLIC OF KOREA, AND THAILAND

The $1,000 million Policy Reform Support Loan was prepared to support Indonesia's policy reforms in trade, investment, the financial sector, public finance, the social sector and the environment. To support banking and corporate reform, the operation will include measures to deal with nonperforming portfolios and insolvent banks, audit state banks to improve efficiency and capital adequacy, strengthen credit appraisal and risk management, improve bank supervision, and provide better laws governing bankruptcy, disclosure, and ownership. A $20 million technical assistance loan is helping to improve management and supervision of the banking sector.

The $3,000 million Economic Reconstruction Loan to the Republic of Korea was prepared and approved in a record three weeks. This rapid intervention contributed to international efforts to provide liquidity and helped to lay the framework for policy changes in the financial sector, corporate governance, competition policy, and the labor market. The subsequent $2,000 million Structural Adjustment Loan advanced and deepened the reform program in the corporate and financial sectors. Technical assistance programs are helping the Korean government to strengthen its capabilities for stabilizing, restructuring, and supervising the financial sector; facilitate

corporate restructuring, driven by lead creditor banks; and enhance corporate governance through reform of accounting and auditing, company law, the insolvency system, and securities markets.

Late in the fiscal year, the IFC's Board of Executive Directors approved three projects, marking a resumption of its investment activities in the Republic of Korea for the first time since 1988. The projects will help recapitalize and restructure Korean corporations and financial institutions and promote international best practice models. The investments also are intended to attract other lenders and investors.

In Thailand the Bank helped establish a financial restructuring agency to deal with the creditors and depositors of suspended finance companies, set up an asset management company to recover assets in an orderly and economically sound process, and implement policies to reduce restrictions on foreign equity participation. Bank support included a finance company restructuring loan; a structural adjustment loan to reform the corporate and financial sectors; and technical assistance operations to improve the government's capacity for economic management and enable it to better address financial sector weaknesses and evaluate and improve company competitiveness.

East Asia's financial crisis profoundly affected poor and vulnerable people. The World Bank helped put social safety nets in place to deal with the surge in unemployment and to help minimize the effect that cutbacks in public expenditure might have on the poor.

vestment loan to provide assistance to the unemployed and poor affected by the crisis. A $1,000 million structural adjustment loan, for Indonesia, prepared in fiscal 1998, will include a social protection component and measures to reform forestry policies. Loans were also prepared for rural and urban poverty reduction, and some of the existing portfolio was restructured to redirect funding and encourage more vigorous implementation of existing projects in support of employment, child development, safe motherhood, health, and education. A $400 million agricultural reform support loan is being developed to help finance initial imports of food grain while strengthening farm productivity, food grain markets, and distribution systems. The Bank also chaired a special donor meeting for Indonesia to address the social implications of the crisis and solicit support for the social sectors.

The Bank is helping Korean authorities to reform the country's pension system and design a modern social safety net. The $2,000 million Structural Adjustment Loan included a component to extend unemployment insurance to cover employees in small-scale enterprises. And the Second Structural Adjustment Loan, which is under preparation, will help deepen reforms in the social safety net. EDI's global and regional conferences on pension reform, co-sponsored with the International Social Security Association, are helping governments across the region to strengthen social protection for the elderly.

In Cambodia, the Lao Democratic Republic, Papua New Guinea, the Philippines, and other smaller economies, such as the Solomon Islands, Bank studies on the effects and implications of the region's financial crisis are helping governments put appropriate policies in place to reduce adverse effects on the poor and on their overall economies.

The Bank also responded promptly to natural disasters in the region, with four emergency operations to combat the consequences of an El Niño-induced drought in Indonesia and Papua New Guinea, an earthquake in China's Hubei Province, and an unusually severe typhoon in Vietnam.

funds, unemployment insurance, and social security systems, was intensified, and financial support helped supplement resources to protect the poor.

In Thailand a social and poverty assessment provided a better understanding of the social consequences of the crisis and supported the design and implementation of a social sector in-

Meeting clients' changing needs

The East Asian financial crisis precipitated a wholesale restructuring of the composition of the Bank's fiscal 1998 lending program: ten adjustment and/or technical assistance and emergency operations were added, while four investment loans were deferred to fiscal 1999. Strong efforts were launched to ensure timely implementation of projects and maintenance of the portfolio quality. Improvement measures were initiated, including selective project restructuring in China, Indonesia, and Vietnam; cancellation of sluggish project components; and rebalancing of project costing in the face of shortages in counterpart funding.

The regional office continued to maintain a strong portfolio through intensified supervision, increasingly undertaken by field offices; six of the region's eight country management units were operating in the field at the end of the fiscal year.[10] A flatter management structure was adopted at headquarters, with eleven functional units responsible for delivering services to client countries, managing the project portfolio, and preparing new projects jointly with clients. In fiscal 1998 the Bank's new management and organizational structure allowed closer interaction with clients and faster responses to the urgent needs on the ground, including dealing with natural disasters.

10. China, Indonesia, Republic of Korea, the Philippines, Thailand, and Vietnam.

The South Asia (SAS) region continued to demonstrate economic progress and remained relatively unscathed by the financial and economic crisis in neighboring East Asia. The crisis emphasized the urgency of financial sector reforms to which the Bank and its clients were already committed. In fiscal 1998, World Bank loans, technical assistance, and policy advice focused especially on helping its South Asia regional clients reduce poverty by strengthening economies, developing private sectors, and investing in people through socially and environmentally sustainable development. To help improve the Bank's operations and make them more responsive to client needs, about half of the staff who work with South Asian countries did so from one of the region's five field offices.

In spite of the financial turmoil in neighboring East Asia, most of the countries of South Asia continued to record satisfactory gross domestic product (GDP) and export growth in 1997. Foreign investment in the region continued to grow, with net long-term resource flows reaching the highest level on record. Nonetheless the region still receives just 3.6 percent of net private long-term flows to developing countries, accounts for only 1 percent of world trade, and is home to roughly 40 percent of the world's poor.

At 5.2 percent in 1997, South Asia's GDP growth was down almost 1 percent from 1996, mainly due to sluggish demand and stagnation in India's industrial sector and low cotton output in Pakistan. Estimated growth rates in fiscal 1998 are 5.5 percent in Bangladesh, 5.1 percent in India, 5.4 percent in Pakistan, and 5.8 percent in Sri Lanka.

The fiscal deficit in India rose to an estimated 6.1 percent of GDP compared to fiscal 1997's deficit of 4.9 percent, despite continued efforts by the government to reduce spending. Estimates indicate that Bangladesh's fiscal deficit remained unchanged from fiscal 1997, at 5.3 percent of GDP; Pakistan's fell to 5.4 percent from 6.3 percent of GDP the previous year; and Sri Lanka's to 6.5 percent from 7.6 percent of GDP in fiscal 1997.

Largely due to increased disbursements from official creditors, the region's long-term external debt rose by 3 percent, reaching $142 billion in 1997. Official debt continued to account for the bulk of the region's long-term liabilities. A 9 percent rise in export revenues led to an improvement in the debt-to-export ratio, which fell from 194 percent in 1996 to 183 percent in 1997. Despite this decrease, the ratio still exceeds the average for all developing countries (136 percent in 1997). Short-term external debt remained low, a factor that may have helped prevent spillover from the East Asian financial crisis. Financial sector regulations, which prohibited banks from fueling large credit booms, and small current account deficits also helped the region avoid financial crisis.

Growth in private capital flows leveled off in 1997 after jumping from an average of $5 billion between 1990–95 to $9 billion in 1996. India continued to attract the bulk, with net foreign direct investment flows rising to $3 billion in 1997, a 20 percent increase over the previous year. The World Bank continued to support clients in the region as they met the challenge of reducing poverty, stimulating faster economic growth, and focusing on a range of important development initiatives. Table 2-7 shows the sectoral distribution of lending to the region for the 1989–98 period. Table 2-8 compares commitments, disbursements, and net transfers to the region for fiscal years 1993-98, and table 2-9 shows operations in the South Asia region approved by the Board of Executive Directors during fiscal 1998 by country. Figure 2-4 shows IBRD and IDA commitments by sector.

Uncertainty about the economic prospects of the region increased, following the detonation of nuclear devices by India and Pakistan in May 1998 and the resulting imposition of economic sanctions by several industrial countries. At the request of some executive directors, consideration of several non-basic human needs loans, which were scheduled to be presented in the last quarter of fiscal 1998, was postponed.

Building a stronger economic environment

The Bank continued its support of structural reforms with timely and relevant lending and nonlending services specifically geared to individual country needs and assistance strategies. The Economic Development Institute (EDI) and the Central Bank of Sri Lanka sponsored the seminar "South Asia Beyond 2000: Policies for Sustained Catch-up Growth," held in Colombo, Sri Lanka, where a policy agenda that will allow the region to meet its full development potential into the next century was identified. More than sixty policymakers and academics from the region participated and produced an initiative to continue similar gatherings in the future. The

Bank continues to conduct research to support the region's development. This year a study[11] identified the main environmental effects related to the expansion of electric power generation in India and presented a menu of options to mitigate those effects.

Financial sector. The financial crisis in neighboring East Asia highlighted the dangers of weak banking institutions: they can impede growth through low-quality lending and may

11. World Bank. 1998. "India: Environmental Issues in the Power Sector: National Synthesis." Energy Sector Management Assistance Program. Washington, D.C.

TABLE 2-7. LENDING TO BORROWERS IN SOUTH ASIA,
BY SECTOR, FISCAL YEARS 1989–98

(millions of US dollars)

Sector	Annual average, FY89-93	FY94	FY95	FY96	FY97	FY98
Agriculture	553.3	387.8	551.3	420.6	409.0	876.1
Education	339.0	220.0	423.7	499.8	—	718.2
Electric power and other energy	801.9	230.0	250.0	700.0	24.2	295.0
Environment	103.3	14.7	168.0	263.9	64.8	—
Finance	234.3	—	916.0	205.0	105.0	—
Health, nutrition and population	270.5	233.1	257.9	376.7	593.8	626.4
Industry	198.5	250.3	3.2	—	—	—
Mining	2.4	—	—	63.0	—	532.0
Multisector	269.5	—	—	—	—	—
Oil and gas	301.0	—	120.8	—	—	—
Public sector management	33.0	296.8	—	92.0	31.7	250.0
Social sector	111.5	—	—	—	—	543.2
Telecommunications	22.4	—	—	35.0	—	—
Transportation	246.0	491.3	—	—	684.5	23.5
Urban development	8.3	246.0	39.0	21.5	—	—
Water supply and sanitation	145.9	—	275.8	251.6	98.6	—
Total	3,640.8	2,370.0	3,005.7	2,929.1	2,011.6	3,864.4
Of which: IBRD	1,728.6	474.0	1,584.8	1,161.6	626.5	1,318.0
IDA	1,912.3	1,896.0	1,420.9	1,767.5	1,385.1	2,546.4

NOTE: *Details may not add to totals because of rounding.*
— *Zero.*

TABLE 2-8. WORLD BANK COMMITMENTS, DISBURSEMENTS, AND NET TRANSFERS IN SOUTH ASIA, FISCAL YEARS 1993–98

(millions of US dollars)

Item	Bangladesh 1998	Bangladesh 1993–98[a]	India 1998	India 1993–98[a]	Pakistan 1998	Pakistan 1993–98[a]	Total region 1998	Total region 1993–98[a]
IBRD and IDA commitments	646	2,155	2,142	11,419	808	3,229	3,864	17,597
Undisbursed balance	1,147	1,147	8,578	8,578	2,053	2,053	12,423	12,423
Gross disbursements	331	1,858	1,375	9,701	606	3,539	2,441	16,104
Repayments	63	272	1,147	6,226	243	1,359	1,479	7,991
Net disbursements	269	1,586	228	3,475	363	2,180	962	8,113
Interest and charges	45	257	706	4,950	211	1,329	984	6,668
Net transfer	224	1,329	-478	-1,475	152	851	-22	1,445

NOTE: *The countries shown in the table are those with the largest borrowings from the World bank in fiscal 1997–98. Details may not add to totals because of rounding.*

a. Disbursements from the IDA Special Fund are included through fiscal 1996.

initiate or propagate a crisis if a bank run is provoked by low confidence. To respond to such weaknesses in the South Asia region, analytical, technical, and financial support was extended to several client countries to help them speed up financial sector reforms. Financial sector reviews were conducted in Bangladesh and Sri Lanka. A banking sector adjustment loan to Pakistan supported reforms that have arrested the flow of bad loans and put in place appropriate financial regulations, as well as increased the efficiency of financial intermediation and strengthened the legal framework and judicial processes. To complement this work, EDI directed training at high- and medium-level managers of the State Bank of Pakistan to help upgrade the country's prudential regulation and supervision system. The course provided participants with an understanding of macroeconomic policy analysis and financial programming, the roles of the financial and commercial sectors, and fiscal and exchange rate policy. Bank-supported technical assistance also helped establish an electronic clearing and settlement system for India's National Stock Exchange.

Private sector development. Developing a larger role for the private sector is an important ingredient for South Asia's rapid, sustained economic growth. In addition to its support for the pri-

vate financial sector, the Bank engaged in projects to expand the private sector's role in developing infrastructure. For example, technical, financial, and advisory assistance was extended to Bangladesh for the Private Sector Infrastructure Development Project. The project is establishing a fund to catalyze much needed long-term debt finance for private sector subprojects in basic infrastructure, such as power generation and transmission, toll roads, telecommunications, and others.

Because economic growth and foreign direct investment have been hampered by insufficient power supply, the IFC has invested funds for electricity expansion in South Asia's underdeveloped areas. In fiscal 1998 the IFC led a private sector coalition that invested in Nepal's Upper Bhote Koshi Hydroelectric Power Project. The second project of its kind undertaken by the private sector in Nepal, it is expected to increase the country's power supply by 10 percent.

MIGA is also helping to expand private sector investment in South Asia. In fiscal 1998, MIGA issued its first guarantee for a project in India. The $9.6 million guarantee covers a project to establish a mobile cellular network. In addition, MIGA issued guarantees to cover a power plant in Sri Lanka and two banking projects in Pakistan.

Infrastructure. The Bank supported increased public investment in South Asia's infrastructure in fiscal 1998. For example, a loan to Nepal is helping bring down transportation costs associated with trade by establishing an inland container depot for rail transfers, upgrading depots, and streamlining trade and transit procedures.

The Bank's new adaptable program loan (APL) was utilized to provide front-end support for the early stages of India's Haryana Power Sector Restructuring Project. The first phase is building the foundation of a long-term lending partnership with Haryana by helping remove the most critical impediments to power transmission and improving the quality of power supply to remote areas. Future support will be governed by the pace of reform implementation and adapted to meet specific investment requirements.

Rural development. Because the majority of the region's poor live in rural areas, support for rural development remained high on the Bank's agenda. In partnership with the government of Pakistan, the Asian Development Bank, and the Overseas Economic Cooperation Fund of Japan, Pakistan's National Drainage Program was one

TABLE 2-9. OPERATIONS APPROVED DURING FISCAL YEAR 1998, SOUTH ASIA

Country/project name	Date of Approval	Maturities	Principal amount (millions) SDR	Principal amount (millions) US$
Bangladesh				
Health and Population Program Project	Jun 30, 1998	2008/2038	185.50	250.00
Primary Education Development Project	Apr 9, 1998	2008/2038	111.00	150.00
Silk Development Project	Nov 18, 1997	2008/2037	8.30	11.35
Private Sector Infrastructure Development Project	Oct 28, 1997	2007/2037	168.60	235.00
Bhutan				
Second Education Project	Mar 3, 1998	2008/2038	10.10	13.69
India				
Uttar Pradesh Diversified Agriculture Support Project [a]	Jun 30, 1998	2004/2018	n.a.	79.90
Uttar Pradesh Diversified Agriculture Support Project [a]	Jun 30, 1998	2008/2033	37.20	50.00
Orissa Health Systems Development Project	Jun 29, 1998	2008/2033	56.80	76.40
Woman and Child Development Project	Jun 29, 1998	2008/2033	222.50	300.00
Andhra Pradesh Economic Restructuring Project [a]	Jun 25, 1998	2004/2018	n.a	301.30
Andhra Pradesh Economic Restructuring Project [a]	Jun 25, 1998	2008/2033	179.40	241.90
Kerala Forestry Project	Mar 24, 1998	2008/2033	28.80	39.00
National Agricultural Technology Project [a]	Mar 17, 1998	2008/2033	73.80	100.00
National Agricultural Technology Project [a]	Mar 17, 1998	2003/2018	n.a.	96.80
Haryana Power Sector Restructuring Project	Jan 15, 1998	2003/2018	n.a.	60.00
Uttar Pradesh Forestry Project	Dec 9, 1997	2008/2032	39.00	52.94
Uttar Pradesh Second Basic Education Project	Dec 4, 1997	2008/2032	43.70	59.40
Third District Primary Education Project	Dec 4, 1997	2008/2032	111.80	152.00
Coal Sector Rehabilitation Project [a]	Sep 9, 1997	2003/2017	n.a.	530.00
Coal Sector Rehabilitation Project [a]	Sep 9, 1997	2008/2032	1.50	2.00
Nepal				
Multimodal Transit and Trade Facilitation Project	Nov 25, 1997	2008/2037	17.00	23.50
Irrigation Sector Project	Nov 25, 1997	2008/2037	58.70	79.77
Agricultural Research and Extension Project	Aug 26, 1997	2007/2037	17.50	24.30
Pakistan				
Second Social Action Program Project	Mar 24, 1998	2008/2033	184.50	250.00
Banking Sector Adjustment Loan	Dec 9, 1997	2003/2018	n.a.	250.00
National Drainage Program Project	Nov 4, 1997	2007/2032	198.60	285.00
Northern Education Project	Oct 30, 1997	2008/2032	16.40	22.80
Sri Lanka				
Mahaweli Restructuring and Rehabilitation Project	Apr 14, 1998	2008/2038	41.70	57.00
Second General Education Project	Dec 9, 1997	2008/2037	51.40	70.30
Total			1,863.80	3,864.35

n.a. = not applicable (IBRD loan).

a. "Blend" loan/credit.

FIGURE 2-4 South Asia: IBRD and IDA Commitments by Sector, Fiscal Year 1998

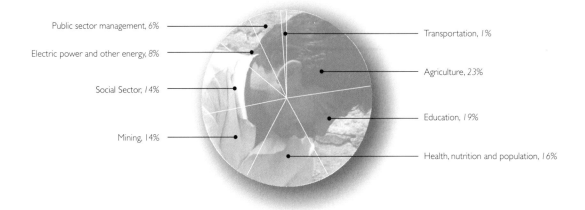

Public sector management, 6%

Electric power and other energy, 8%

Social Sector, 14%

Mining, 14%

Transportation, 1%

Agriculture, 23%

Education, 19%

Health, nutrition and population, 16%

such program to receive support in fiscal 1998. Conceived and developed by the government of Pakistan in 1995 in response to an ongoing crisis in the Indus Basin irrigation system, the project is improving irrigation and drainage infrastructure and decentralizing the management of the irrigation and drainage system. Recognizing the importance of stakeholder involvement in devising solutions to the crisis, the Bank and its partners engaged in widespread consultations with the affected communities, which also helped win support for the reform program.

Bank support for encouraging environmentally sustainable growth in rural areas took an innovative turn this year as a Bank loan, together with Global Environment Facility (GEF) funds, was extended to aid the Sri Lankan government's efforts to conserve medicinal plant populations. Medicinal plants are an essential component of health services in South Asia, especially for the rural poor. The project is establishing five medicinal plant conservation areas for managing and researching sustainable methods and levels of harvesting.

Investing in the region's people

Reflecting the Bank's commitment to poverty reduction by enhancing human development, ten Bank projects in the South Asia region focused on improving countries' social sectors in fiscal 1998. These included a record seven education projects in the region. Because rapid expansion of education has occurred at the ex-

pense of high-quality teaching and learning in recent years, the Bank's support this year emphasized improving the quality of primary education. With Bank support, governments are involving their local communities in designing and implementing education projects so that beneficiary needs are better met (*see box* 2-3).

Malnutrition and poor health not only diminish people's potential for growth and learning, but inhibit nations' economic development potential and poverty reduction efforts. In South Asia some 50 percent of children under five are malnourished. India's Woman and Child Development Project is illustrative of Bank initiatives to address this problem and to improve access to health care—especially for children up to age six, and pregnant and breastfeeding mothers from the poorest sections of society. The project is supporting the government's Integrated Child Development Program in the states of Kerala, Maharashtra, Rajasthan, Tamil Nadu, and Uttar Pradesh, bringing improved health services to about 18 million women and children.

The Bank-led Second Social Action Program Project (SAPPII) in Pakistan is a multidonor project that is improving overall social services. It follows the success of the First Social Action Program Project launched by the government in fiscal 1993, which resulted in an increase in spending for social services from 1.8 percent to 2.1 percent of GDP between 1994–97 and an increase in the speed with which the government releases funds for social services. SAPPII is helping

BOX 2-3 IMPROVING EDUCATION THROUGH COMMUNITY PARTICIPATION

The benefits of universal primary education have been well documented, and South Asian countries are intensifying their efforts to achieve "education for all" early in the next century. Unfortunately, the push to increase the quantity of education has sometimes come at the expense of quality, which can reduce demand. In addition, many parents in poor or rural areas cannot afford to forgo the income or assistance provided by the work children do outside or inside the home.[1] To increase enrollment and encourage children to stay in school, the Bank is supporting schools that local communities have helped to plan and operate. This has not only mobilized local support, but has also increased the quality of education.

Since fiscal 1993 the Bank has supported five state-level education projects in India that utilize community participation to increase demand for education, especially among girls and other disadvantaged children. The first Uttar Pradesh Basic Education Project generated a much higher than expected enrollment; total enrollment has jumped by 32 percent since fiscal 1992. The Uttar Pradesh Second Basic Education Project was approved in fiscal 1998. Early assessments indicate that Village Edu-

cation Committees (VECs), established to involve the community in the construction and operation of local schools, have been an important component in increasing the demand for education. VEC-sponsored education awareness campaigns have been especially effective in encouraging parents to send their children to school—and to keep them there.

In fiscal 1998 the Bank undertook its first education project in the state of Bihar, where school enrollment and literacy rates are well below the national averages. Targeted at seventeen educationally disadvantaged districts, the Third District Primary Education Project is establishing VECs for each school. These committees are acting as monitors, recording teacher and student participation and school effectiveness. The project will enable the state of Bihar to enroll more than 5.5 million extra children over the next five years.

1. The Bank is concerned about child labor from both a development and humanitarian point of view, and in fiscal 1998 issued a framework for addressing child labor issues (see section three). There is compelling evidence that the long-run solution to child labor problems comes from reducing poverty, improving the situation of women, and increasing access to good-quality education.

to upgrade and expand basic social services to under-served portions of the population with a focus on governance improvements in the public sector service delivery system and encouraging NGO and private sector participation in delivering social services.

Improving Bank operations

To facilitate a closer relationship with clients and to better understand the cultural, political and social dimensions of the region, about half of the Bank staff working with South Asian countries now do so from one of the region's five field offices.[12] Management of both lending and nonlending services has been more evenly divided between headquarters and the field offices, with over 20 percent of economic and sector work and 40 percent of the lending portfolio in fiscal 1998 managed by staff in the field (*see figure 2-5*).

Village immersion programs[13] are increasing Bank staff understanding of the region's develop-

ment challenges, facilitating interaction between Bank staff and local communities, and exposing Bank staff to community initiatives that have successfully reduced poverty. Fifty-seven staff went to five different South Asian countries this year, bringing the total number of program graduates in the region to eighty-eight.

By working more closely with the IFC and MIGA, the Bank is working to provide a full menu of services to countries in the region. The 1998 country assistance strategy (CAS) for India, for example, which was conducted in close consultation with the government, NGOs, and civil society, was prepared jointly with the IFC and in close consultation with MIGA.

12. Colombo, Dhaka, Islamabad, Kathmandu, and New Delhi.

13. These programs are a part of the Bank's Executive Development Program, which is equipping Bank managers to broaden their perspective and enhance their managerial and leadership skills.

Improvements in portfolio management have resulted from incorporating monitorable performance indicators, agreed with borrowers, into new lending operations in recent years. The number of problem projects has subsequently fallen from forty-five in the beginning of fiscal 1997, to twenty-six by the end of fiscal 1998. Thirteen projects have been upgraded from problem status since the beginning of fiscal 1998, including the Karachi Water and Sanitation Project in Pakistan. The project had been unable to meet its financial covenants in recent years, but agreements for the implementation of 30 percent tariff increases, plus actions to improve collection performance and to reduce public sector arrears owed to the Karachi Water

and Sanitation Board (KWSB), will bring the project close to compliance in fiscal 1999. The KWSB has also reduced its staff by about 4,500, achieved an almost clean audit opinion over three years, and reduced wasteful expenditure by implementing an internal audit review. Moreover, much of the project construction is approaching completion, and certification of works and operation of the system are expected at the end of the year.

Efforts to help clients battle corrupt practices are addressed through project design and supervision. Two examples: (i) Political interference in staff appointments was addressed in one project by making approval of additional civil works contingent upon the removal of

South Asian countries are working to achieve education for all children early in the next century. Educating girls is a critical component: educated women are less likely to die in childbirth and more likely to have smaller, healthier families and raise children who are immunized, well nourished, educated, and well cared for.

FIGURE 2-5
Percentage of Projects Managed in South Asian Field Offices, Fiscal Years 1996–98

(percent)

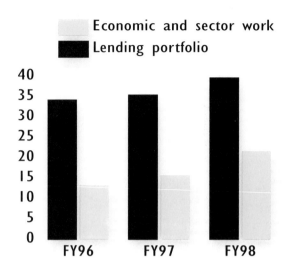

Economic and sector work
Lending portfolio

nonqualified staff; and (ii) corruption in a construction program was addressed by making the fiscal 1998 construction conditional on management by two private architectural and engineering firms. Support for improving the efficiency and transparency of procurement in Bank-financed projects, complemented by improvements in the audit and monitoring functions of Bank-financed projects, is also helping. And the Bank is helping implementing agencies to shorten contract award times through remedies included in the Bank's procurement guidelines.[14] Ex-post reviews of procurement awards have been intensified with the engagement of external auditing firms, and field offices have been strengthened to provide in-country expertise to assist implementing agencies in all aspects of procurement, disbursement, and auditing.

14. World Bank. 1995. *Guidelines: Procurement under* IBRD *Loans and* IDA *Credits.* Washington, D.C.

Countries in the Europe and Central Asia (ECA) region continued to meet the challenges of transition with varying degrees of progress. Many Central European and Baltic countries are now sustaining growth and attracting external capital and investment. With support from the Bank and its partners, they are focusing on policies and institutional changes that will allow them to sustain growth while gradually meeting European Union (EU) membership requirements. In Eastern Europe, Caucasus, and Central Asia, countries are still facing the challenges of sustained stabilization and making further progress in privatization, liberalization, and preservation of basic safety nets. In these countries the Bank is both promoting reform and providing balance of payments support. The Bank is also assisting some countries with the difficult tasks of reconstruction after conflict. The quality and effectiveness of Bank operations across the region improved in fiscal 1998, as portfolio management was enhanced and client focus sharpened.

Stabilization and liberalization efforts are beginning to pay off in the transitional countries.[15] In 1997, ten of the Eastern Europe and Central Asia (ECA) region's client countries grew at 5 percent or more, and fourteen at more than 3 percent. Yet underlying the region's general economic improvement is uneven progress among countries.

Many have made considerable progress toward meeting the initial challenges of transition—establishing macroeconomic stability, liberalizing markets, and privatizing assets while maintaining social safety nets—and are now confronting a second stage of reform. Now the challenge for these countries includes:

• moving from a focus on reducing the fiscal deficit and inflation to improving the composition of public expenditures and overhauling the tax system;

• complementing mass privatization programs with improvements in corporate governance through increased competition, protection of shareholder and creditor rights, and enhanced prudential regulation and supervision of financial systems;

• moving from preventing the collapse of key infrastructure to expanding the supply and quality through private sector provision; and

• shifting from attempting to prevent the collapse of basic social safety nets to making pension and transfer systems fiscally sustainable and better targeted.

Central Europe and the Baltics

Most Central European countries have experienced several years of growth, and private sector investment and consumption have started to expand. In some countries this growth is associated with increased current account deficits, financed partly by foreign direct investment and partly by borrowing from abroad. A lesson from the East Asian crisis is that under these circumstances, countries must establish good prudential and supervisory frameworks to avoid the risk of collapse of their financial systems. The Bank is supporting these efforts.

Joining the European Union (EU) is a major objective for Central European and Baltic countries. In partnership with others the Bank is coordinating strategies and sectoral approaches to help its clients meet the challenges *(see box 2-4)*. The Bank is working closely with countries to identify high-priority policy reforms that enhance economic growth prospects and facilitate EU accession, as well as to devise strategies for minimizing the costs of expensive reforms—such as the adoption of EU environmental standards.

Most of the Central European countries that experienced crises in early 1997 are showing strong signs of recovery. In Albania, major civil disturbances in early 1997 followed the collapse of "pyramid schemes," but the new government moved

15. Albania, Armenia, Azerbaijan, Belarus, Bosnia and Herzegovina, Bulgaria, Croatia, Czech Republic, Cyprus, Estonia, Former Yugloslav Republic of Macedonia, Georgia, Hungary, Kazakhstan, Kyrgyz Republic, Latvia, Lithuania, Moldova, Poland, Romania, Russia, Slovakia, Slovenia, Tajikistan, Turkmenistan, Ukraine, and Uzbekistan.

BOX 2-4 WORLD BANK SUPPORT FOR EUROPEAN UNION ENLARGEMENT

One of the key economic events of 1997 was the European Union (EU) decision to invite ten of the Bank's client countries in Central and Eastern Europe—Bulgaria, Czech Republic, Estonia, Hungary, Latvia, Lithuania, Poland, Romania, Slovakia, and Slovenia—to initiate the process for eventual EU membership. The European Commission (EC) Agenda 2000, issued in July 1997, set out the terms and conditions under which candidate countries would be able to join the EU. While the EU is prepared to mobilize significant financial resources to assist candidate countries to meet the accession requirements, Agenda 2000 recognizes that during the accession period substantial assistance will also be required from other partners—including the EU's own bank, the European Investment Bank (EIB); the European Bank for Reconstruction and Development (EBRD); and the World Bank. In October 1997 the Bank joined the EC, EIB, and EBRD in a joint working group to reflect on how

best the four institutions can coordinate their respective interventions in the candidate countries. Their Memorandum of Understanding spelling out the modus operandi among the concerned institutions was signed in March 1998.

The Bank already had held intensive discussions with most of the candidate countries to determine how best it could assist them in meeting membership requirements. This dialogue is reflected in country assistance strategies, which are the guiding principles of the Bank's assistance. In addition, Country Economic Memoranda were issued in fiscal year 1998 for Estonia, Poland, and Slovakia with the theme of "the challenge of EU accession;" reports dealing with particular EU accession issues were also prepared for Lithuania and Slovenia. Similar reports will be undertaken next fiscal year for the Czech Republic and Hungary.

quickly to restore stability with support from the Bank and other international donors. Gross domestic product (GDP) growth in 1998 is projected at around 10 percent. Bulgaria's seven years of mixed efforts at stabilization and structural reform spiraled into a macroeconomic crisis that culminated in 1997 in the adoption of a currency board arrangement and a reform program that rapidly stabilized the economy. And while Romania's ambitious and wide-ranging reform program made a good start in 1997, as prices were liberalized and directed credit ended, by early 1998 progress faltered as political commitment wavered. Still the Bank continued to support investments in key areas to underpin long-term development.

Eastern Europe, Caucasus, and Central Asia

Eastern Europe and Caucasus experienced positive growth in 1997 for the first time since the transition began. Moldova posted its first year of positive growth, while Armenia and Georgia continued to grow. In Russia, output growth is expected to be positive after zero growth in 1997. Performance was more mixed

in Central Asia, with the Kyrgyz Republic demonstrating the best performance.

Though significant progress was made on reducing inflation, the fiscal situation in both Russia and Ukraine remained fragile. High interest rates on short-term debt became a major burden on public finances in the latter part of the fiscal year. To restore market confidence and reduce interest rates—important ingredients for restoring growth—structural reforms aimed at sustained and predictable reductions in fiscal deficits are necessary.

In the face of these diverse country situations, the Bank's fiscal 1998 assistance strategy reflected its regional clients' unique needs and their progress in meeting the challenges of transition. Table 2-10 shows the sectoral distribution of lending to the region for the 1989–98 period. Table 2-11 compares commitments, disbursements, and net transfers to the region for fiscal years 1993–98, and table 2-12 shows operations in the ECA region approved by the Board of Executive Directors during fiscal 1998 by country. Figure 2-6 shows IBRD and IDA commitments by sector.

TABLE 2-10.   LENDING TO BORROWERS IN EUROPE AND CENTRAL ASIA, BY SECTOR, FISCAL YEARS 1989–98

(millions of US dollars)

Sector	Annual average, FY89-93	FY94	FY95	FY96	FY97	FY98
Agriculture	291.3	502.9	202.0	185.8	771.7	149.5
Education	48.0	59.6	40.0	5.0	137.8	592.4
Electric power and other energy	309.8	164.8	191.7	325.4	504.9	545.0
Environment	19.0	80.0	123.0	30.1	—	43.9
Finance	218.2	280.0	147.0	638.9	290.3	82.0
Health, nutrition and population	89.2	—	220.4	350.4	95.5	27.0
Industry	108.9	375.0	—	—	111.8	10.3
Mining	—	—	—	540.8	300.0	800.0
Multisector	710.6	506.3	2,085.0	656.8[a]	1,227.0	1,119.5
Oil and gas	172.0	691.3	226.3	10.0	135.6	10.0
Public sector management	164.8	270.0	70.9	505.6	109.1	587.4
Social sector	33.4	10.9	127.5	212.0	935.2	358.6
Telecommunications	60.0	153.0	—	—	—	30.0
Transportation	271.2	352.0	486.0	868.0	312.7	356.0
Urban development	97.0	171.0	418.0	44.3	56.0	358.4
Water supply and sanitation	83.9	109.6	161.0	21.5	67.3	154.4
Total	2,677.3	3,726.4	4,498.8	4,394.6	5,054.9	5,224.3
Of which: IBRD	2,648.2	3,533.3	3,953.8	3,918.2	4,560.9	4,462.3
IDA	29.1	193.1	545.0	476.4	493.9	762.0

NOTE: *Details may not add to totals because of rounding.*
— Zero.

a. Includes the refinanced/rescheduled overdue charges of $168 million for Bosnia and Herzegovina.

Reconstructing after conflict

Supporting reconstruction after conflict remained a major Bank activity in a few countries. With internationally supported reconstruction efforts underway in Bosnia and Herzegovina, the Bank's support increasingly focused on macroeconomic institution building and the reforms needed for transition to a market economy. An adjustment loan that focused on fiscal management and private sector development was complemented by a line of credit for enterprise reconstruction support for the agriculture, education, electric power, forest management, gas, housing, transport, and water sectors.

The government of Tajikistan formally ended its civil war with the signing of a peace agreement in July 1997. And in fiscal 1998, IDA extended two credits to support economic recovery.

Accelerating structural reforms

Although most countries have sharply reduced fiscal deficits, tax and public expenditure reform remains critical. With Bank support, both Kazakhstan and Russia are improving tax administration and budget management. Russia took several major steps to improve tax collection, including the termination of non-cash arrangements for clearing arrears and actions against large high-profile tax debtors. Bank-financed adjustment operations in Armenia, Azerbaijan, Georgia, and Russia are increasing payment rates in power and energy sector public utilities.

Social insurance, especially pensions, accounts for a large share of public spending in many countries, and often is not affordable over the long run. New loans are supporting Azerbaijan, Bosnia and Herzegovina, Georgia, and Macedonia in the first phase of pension reform and Hungary and Kazakhstan in implementing comprehensive pension reforms that include mandatory contributions to private pension funds.

To combat corruption and improve public sector performance, the Bank is helping governments in Albania, Georgia, Latvia, and Ukraine to formulate anticorruption strategies, collect data to define problems, and assist with in-country workshops to develop anticorruption strategies and action plans. The strategies typically include accelerating specific policy reforms—including deregulation and tax simplification, civil service, public procurement and auditing, legal and judicial reform, and strengthened public oversight mechanisms. These reforms reduce the incentives for corruption, side payments, and rentseeking.

To help governments improve municipal functioning, the Bank initiated a major program of analytical work and project preparation in the Baltic countries, Hungary, Poland, Russia, and Ukraine. This work will help improve the predictability and transparency of intergovernmental fiscal relations. It will provide appropriate incentive frameworks at national levels and help build the management capacity of municipalities and other subnational entities, which are often responsible for key investment decisions, environmental management, and delivering social services. The Municipal Finance Initiative, a joint undertaking of the Bank Group—including EDI and the IFC—is helping subnational entities tap financial markets.

Accelerating privatization and financial sector reform continues to be a regional priority. Introducing more flexible pricing mechanisms in auctions has speeded up privatization in some countries where it had stalled. Adjustment loans are supporting small-scale privatization in Moldova and accelerating privatization of medium- and large-scale enterprises in Armenia, Azerbaijan, Georgia, and Russia. Also in Russia, a structural adjustment loan is facilitating more transparent, open, and competitive case by case

TABLE 2-11. WORLD BANK COMMITMENTS, DISBURSEMENTS, AND NET TRANSFERS IN EUROPE AND CENTRAL ASIA, FISCAL YEARS 1993–98

(millions of US dollars)

Item	Romania 1998	Romania 1993–98[a]	Russia 1998	Russia 1993–98[a]	Ukraine 1998	Ukraine 1993–98[a]	Total region 1998	Total region 1993–98[a]
IBRD and IDA commitments	131	1,842	1,629	9,792	216	2,222	5,224	26,694
Undisbursed balance	1,387	1,387	4,103	4,103	934	934	11,630	11,630
Gross disbursements	352	1,448	2,172	5,967	168	1,238	4,854	19,461
Repayments	46	61	29	29	0	0	2,271	8,680
Net disbursements	306	1,387	2,143	5,938	168	1,238	2,583	10,780
Interest and charges	78	281	233	540	66	133	1,095	5,803
Net transfer	228	1,106	1,910	5,398	102	1,105	1,488	4,977

NOTE: *The countries shown in the table are those with the largest borrowings of World Bank funds during fiscal 1997–98. Details may not add to totals because of rounding.*

a. *Disbursements from the IDA Special Fund are included through fiscal 1996.*

smuggling, and bans on advertising and promotion. The Bank and partners in other UN agencies—especially UNICEF and WHO—governments, and nongovernmental organizations are enhancing efforts to promote effective tobacco control.

The Bank's assistance to client countries seeking to achieve widespread and equitable coverage of health, includes loans and nonlending services, such as policy guidance, technical advisory services, and national capacity-building services. In fiscal 1998 the Economic Development Institute's (EDI) support of these efforts included the successful pilot training course "Health Sector Reform and Sustainable Financing," which will now be offered each year in Washington as well as at regionally based partner institutes throughout the world.

Education

The Bank's support of education aims to help client governments improve the access and equity of education. Education lending increased significantly in fiscal 1998 with thirty-six education loans to twenty-eight countries totaling $3,129 million. Cumulative education loans total $26,815 million for about 610 projects in more than 116 countries.

School education represents the main thrust of Bank support, with primary and general secondary accounting for half of lending to the sector. The Ugandan government's Universal Primary Education Policy, supported by the Bank and linked to the Heavily Indebted Poor Countries (HIPC) Debt Initiative, is illustrative. The project is expanding access to primary education to the poorest by offering families free schooling for up to four children. Response to the initiative has been enthusiastic, and primary school enrollment has increased from about 2.7 million to about 5.3 million. Primary education's high social returns will make a significant difference for this group.

The Bank is increasingly supporting sectorwide approaches to education in recognition of the interdependence between subsectors. One example is the Bank's support for the first

---

BOX 3-1   SECTORWIDE APPROACHES TO HEALTH, NUTRITION, AND POPULATION

Sectorwide approaches (SWAPs) to improving health, nutrition, and population (HNP) services allow client countries to focus attention on the highest priority programs and help to build broader ownership of reform efforts. Bangladesh, Ghana, Pakistan, and Zambia already have SWAPs underway and several other countries, including Tanzania and Uganda, are planning them.

SWAP operations have highlighted the need for clients to hire workers based on merit rather than influence, to decentralize services toward communities, and to increase expenditures on non-salary recurrent items, such as medicines. SWAPs can help encourage expenditures on areas that will have the highest impact on the greatest number of people but that have traditionally been neglected—such as improving women's health or arresting the spread of tuberculosis—while constraining more expensive tertiary care that reaches fewer, mostly richer, people.

And SWAPs facilitate an important shift in the relationship between country and donor, from "clientship" to partnership, which offers greater op-portunity for effective change than more narrowly focused projects do.

A SWAP *in Bangladesh*

Bangladesh spends $4 per person per year of public funds on health. Yet, the country faces high infant and maternal mortality rates, 80 percent of children are malnourished, and communicable disease is widespread (half the population test positive for tuberculosis, for example). The Bank helped Bangladesh develop a SWAP to set its HNP sector priorities more effectively. As a result, the government has given top priority to defining and delivering essential basic services, aimed at improving maternal and child health and family planning, and addressing the most pressing communicable diseases. The government initiated fundamental reforms in program design and management to strengthen these essential services while curtailing less essential programs. Substantial donor assistance, coordinated by the Bank, is enhancing this effort.

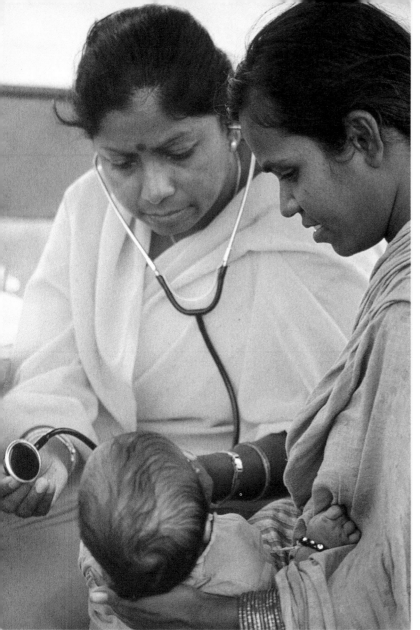

1998 marks the tenth anniversary of the Safe Motherhood Initiative. The consequences of maternal deaths extend into the next generation: when a mother dies, her children are three to ten times more likely to die within two years than children whose mothers survive.

phase of the Ethiopian government's Education Sector Development Program (ESDP) covering 1997–2001, which aims to increase the extremely low rates of school enrollment as part of a longer-term program to achieve universal primary education. The program gives priority to increasing access to, and improving the quality of, primary education, particularly for children in rural areas and for girls. Its scope is sectorwide, comprising primary, secondary, tertiary, technical-vocational, adult literacy, and nonformal education. Under the ESDP, the central government is providing a policy framework and broad guidelines, and regional governments are developing their own plans based on specific

regional goals and conditions. The details of the program have been developed through a partnership between central and regional governments. Donors are coordinating their support and advisory roles.

Egypt's Education Enhancement Program (EEP), part of the government's comprehensive education reform program, is a prime example of successful donor, client government, and Bank partnership and cooperation. EEP is cofinanced by the European Union (EU), and its interventions target enrollment of rural girls, better-quality student learning, and a more efficient education system. This unique program introduces a strategic framework whereby multiple donors can fund priority education activities.

Partnerships have been strengthened with outside organizations including the International Program for the Improvement of Educational Outcomes (IPIEO), the United Nations Educational, Scientific, and Cultural Organization (UNESCO), and UNICEF. The IPIEO partnership with UNESCO is providing the empirical basis for education reform and policy advice for poor countries to improve education. The Bank's Development Grant Facility (DGF) Council endorsed the first year of a multiyear program to support UNICEF's education programs; in fiscal 1998 a $1.2 million grant supported small-scale innovative programs at the community and local levels to increase girls' enrollment rates. A multi-agency partnership between the Rockefeller Foundation, the United Kingdom's Department for International Development, and UNICEF is working to examine factors that hinder or facilitate the effective implementation of girls' education projects and initiatives. And the Bank provided technical assistance to the EU to develop a grant-funded project to increase basic education enrollment rates of girls and minority groups in Gansu, China's poorest province.

Development of the Bank's education knowledge management system progressed in fiscal 1998. It includes best-practice information on access and equity in education, early childhood development, effective schools and teachers, the economics of education, post-basic education,

education system reform and management, project design and implementation, and education and technology. The early child development Web site is available to the Bank's partners and clients.[6]

Training and operational support in education technology has been a high priority in fiscal 1998 as the Bank's emphasis on knowledge management as a means to increase development effectiveness has grown. Distance education activities, using technology to enhance teaching and learning in the classroom, included a conference on distance education for training teachers, held in Addis Ababa and attended by representatives from eight African countries.

Social protection

Social protection measures are essential if governments are to help the poor cope with economic hardship and change. The Bank is supporting its clients in their efforts to:
- protect working people against loss of income through old age or unemployment;
- help unemployed people find jobs through job placement, training, or public works programs;
- ensure that the labor market provides gainful employment; and
- provide social assistance to those who either cannot work or fall beneath the poverty level.

In fiscal 1998 Bank support included:
- technical assistance support and lending for pensions reforms (public and private; funded and unfunded; and mandatory and voluntary);
- technical assistance and lending for policy reform in programs that provide benefits in cash or kind (maternity, child, sick pay, and other social assistance benefits);
- social funds, where Bank loans are passed on as grants to local groups for locally generated social development efforts;
- policy reform in labor markets, such as vocational training programs, unemployment benefits, and severance payments; and
- special income support for displaced workers and policies to improve the functioning of the labor market and enhance labor supply while eliminating abusive forms of labor.

Social protection[7] is of increasing importance in the Bank's lending portfolio and also a signifi-cant component of other Bank projects. In fiscal 1998 thirteen loans totaling $1,316 million supported social protection and a further fourteen loans in other sectors—mostly multisector and public sector management—had clearly separable social protection components totaling $2,044 million. An estimated $400 million additional financing for social protection is concealed in multisectoral components of other loans.

Bank lending for social protection in fiscal 1998 was dominated by efforts to mitigate the impact of the East Asian financial crisis on the poor: existing social protection infrastructure was enhanced with support for pensions, labor markets, social assistance, and social funds. This included $1,000 million to the Republic of Korea for social protection components and $10 million for a social fund in the Philippines.

Bank loans also supported social protection in all other regions in fiscal 1998. In Eastern Europe and Central Asia, a coal sector loan to Russia included a $160 million component for social protection, and a separate social protection implementation loan of $28.6 million was also approved. In addition, pension reform was supported with a $300 million loan to Kazakhstan; and a $20 million social fund was approved for Georgia. Social funds, common in Africa and Latin America, were used for the first time in Eastern Europe this year with Bank assistance.

In Latin America pension reform was supported in Mexico and Uruguay, labor restructuring in Argentina and public works in Bolivia. In Sub-Saharan Africa support included financing for social funds in the Comoros and a microfinance project in Guinea. In the Middle East and North Africa activities that received Bank support included pension reform in Morocco and vocational training in Jordan and Lebanon. In South Asia, support for Pakistan's Social Action Program includes significant financing for social protection.

The World Bank recognizes that safe, productive, and environmentally sound working conditions are key to economic and social progress

6. www.worldbank.org/children
7. The Bank's social protection Web site is available at: www.worldbank.org/hddsp

everywhere, including in its client countries, and works closely with other international organizations, most notably the International Labour Organization (ILO), in this area. It assists member governments to help reduce the adverse effects that shifts in trade patterns and capital flows have on workers by supporting change in labor policies as part of general economic reforms—when such a change is deemed to raise productivity and economic growth and reduce poverty. The Bank's policy advice has focused on setting fair workers' incomes, reducing health and safety risks, and setting standards for workers' conditions—including the improvement of labor standards. In preparing the Republic of Korea's structural adjustment loan, for example, the Bank engaged in a constructive dialogue with labor unions and supported a number of reforms to labor markets and social safety nets, including the expansion of labor standards to all workers; previously these were not applied to firms with fewer than five workers.

To help improve knowledge and expertise on effective pension systems, the Bank completed a pensions primer of up-to-date implementation advice for policymakers undertaking pension reform.[8] The primer includes guides to setting up a regulatory structure for a multi-pillar pension system and financing the transition costs of moving from one type of pension system to another. Case studies of recent reformers are provided, including Bolivia, Latvia, Mexico, and Poland. In addition, a pension simulation model based in EXCEL was developed that helps policymakers determine the health of their current pension system and simulates the impact of proposed reforms. Training was provided to Bank staff and clients in the use of this model. In addition, EDI's pension program is fostering research, dissemination of information, and best practices in pension reform, as well as helping government officials analyze, design, and implement new pension systems. In fiscal 1998, in partnership with the Harvard Institute for International Development (HIID), an EDI workshop brought together leading experts in pension reform from government, academia, international organizations, and public- and private-sector pension funds from twenty-two Bank client countries.

In fiscal 1998 the Bank and the ILO worked jointly on vocational education and training issues and labor in export processing zones; undertook an evaluation of labor market policies in Eastern Europe; and completed a study of labor market policies of the CFA franc zone.[9] This year, ILO staff briefed Bank staff on core labor standards and follow-up discussions are planned to facilitate a joint study of core labor standards and their economic implications.

The Bank expanded its support for intraregional networking among social funds in Africa and Latin America and supported the first such efforts in Europe and the Middle East. This direct "South-South" learning is an important new development in the social assistance field. The continuing success of these projects emphasizes the potential for partnerships among international agencies, governments, and civil society.

Child labor. Research shows that poverty is a major cause of child labor. Thus, the Bank's continuing emphasis on poverty reduction and social sector investments contributes to a general decline in child labor. The Bank also supports initiatives to address the problems of working children, including their need to get an education while working. In India, for example, the government recently directed its district primary education project managers—who already target disadvantaged children—to target working children, too. Further, the Bank and the government are exploring specific steps to get children out of work and into school, while taking into account the need to help families increase their incomes to offset the loss of children's wages. And in Brazil the Bank is working with local communities on a pilot program to address the problems of street children by providing vocational training to improve their living standards and increase their future ability to earn a living.

Specific interventions to address child labor are relatively new for the Bank. Thus it is working in close cooperation with experts including

8. The Pension Reform Options Simulation Toolkit (PROST).
9. Dar, Amit, and P. Zafiris Tzannatos. 1998. "World Bank Lending for Labor Markets 1991-1996." World Bank, Washington, D.C.

To support initiatives that are people-centered, participatory, and respectful of country context and social conditions, the Bank is including participatory processes and techniques in project design and implementation.

international organizations such as the ILO and UNICEF. In fiscal 1998 a World Bank paper set out a framework for ways in which the Bank can do more to address child labor issues in a direct and effective way within its overall poverty reduction mandate.[10] The Bank's role includes:

- integrating child labor issues into Bank programs, including CASs and lending programs;
- improving education opportunities;
- providing financial support for poor families; and
- identifying problems and solutions to child labor issues.

A primer on child labor is being developed that will provide advice to clients and Bank staff on the design of cost-effective interventions to reduce the incidence of harmful child labor practices.

Collaborating with nongovernmental organizations

Because nongovernmental organizations (NGOs) and civil society often work most closely with, and most effectively represent the interests of, poor and marginalized groups, the Bank continues to advance its partnerships with them to achieve development that is equitable, inclusive, and sustainable. A paper, discussed with the executive directors in fiscal 1998, set out an approach to strengthen the quality and understanding of the Bank's partnerships with such organizations.[11]

Work with NGOs continues to be brought into the mainstream of Bank activities and examples of NGO involvement in Bank work can be found throughout the pages of this *Annual Report*. As table 3-2 illustrates, with 50 percent of operations approved in fiscal 1998 involving NGO participation in some capacity, the level of NGO involvement in Bank-supported operations

10. Fallon, Peter, and Zafiris Tzannatos. 1998. *Child Labor—Issues and Directions for the World Bank.* Washington, D.C.: World Bank.

11. World Bank.1998. "The Bank's Relations with NGOs— Issues and Directions." Washington D.C.

continued to grow.[12] NGOs also played a greater role in economic and sector work and other policy-related work. The executive directors reviewed a country assistance strategies study in fiscal 1998, for example, which highlighted an increase in civil society participation in CASs.[13]

But while the Bank increasingly recognizes and capitalizes on the positive role that strong and independent local NGOs can play in economic and social development, the capacities of NGOs and the legal and cultural environments in which they operate vary tremendously from country to country. Thus, the Bank, working with client governments, is increasing its efforts to build effective partnerships on the ground facilitated by sixty-three NGO specialists working from resident missions.

The NGO–World Bank Committee, which has helped to guide NGO-Bank relations since the early 1980s, took steps to decentralize in fiscal 1998. While broad areas of work on participation and southern NGO capacity building continue to be guided at the central level, greater emphasis is being placed on regional meetings, where region-specific issues and strategies for effective cooperation can best be identified and implemented.

The First Global Forum on the Structural Adjustment Participatory Review Initiative (SAPRI), held in July 1997 in Washington, D.C., demonstrates the Bank's commitment to engage in open and frank discussions with civil society and NGOs on the impact of adjustment lending and policy advice.[14] The program provides a framework for the World Bank, governments, and a global network of civil society organizations to discuss ways to improve mutual understanding of policy impacts on the poor and explore improvements in economic reform programs.

The SAPRI program was developed collaboratively by Bank staff and an NGO and civil society network of over 500 NGOs. Seven countries are participating: Bangladesh, Ecuador, Ghana, Hungary, Mali, Uganda, and Zimbabwe. Civil society and NGO participation on the national steering committee has been determined by a broad and inclusive selection process led by local organizations. And a series of public forums have spread the news about SAPRI.

NGOs continue to engage the Bank in constructive dialogue and collaborative partnership on issues from privatization to forest policy. In October 1997, for example, the Bank's Finance and Private Sector and Infrastructure (FPSI) network organized the first international dialogue between civil society organizations and the World Bank Group on privatization. In addition, a meeting between leaders of religious faiths entitled "World Faiths and Development," co-chaired by the Archbishop of Canterbury and the Bank's president in fiscal 1998, resulted in agreement on joint work to identify areas for future cooperation.

In the face of the East Asian financial crisis, Bank staff held meetings with NGOs and representatives of civil society in several Asian countries to discuss and learn about the impact the region's economic crisis was having on the poor. The Bank's president met with a number of these groups during a visit to the region. He also met with representatives from a number of trade unions in Singapore and Washington to discuss the social consequences of the crisis, particularly on labor.

The Small Grants Program (SGP) channels an average of $700,000 annually to institutions (including NGOs) in developing countries to strengthen their capacities to promote dialogue and disseminate information about international and local development issues.

12. Figures are based on a desk review of project appraisal documents for projects approved by the executive directors at the end of the fiscal year. As such, they often reflect intended involvement of NGOs and community-based organizations, as well as actual involvement in the design stage. The extent to which the intended involvement is carried out during implementation is not yet known. Moreover, involvement can take many forms ranging from quick consultation to major responsibility for implementation of project components. In future years, the Bank intends to focus greater resources on identifying and monitoring high-level involvement by NGOs.

13. The preparation of over half of all full CASs in fiscal 1997 and the first half of fiscal 1998 included consultations with civil society and NGOs. About 20 percent of the CASs involved broad and substantial participation, including a major outreach into rural or high-poverty areas or civil society involvement in planning the consultations. By comparison, in fiscal 1996 only one quarter of CASs had any consultation, and less than 10 percent had a high level of participation.

14. Information on the SAPRI program is available at: www.worldbank.org/html/prddr/sapri/saprihp.htm.

TABLE 3-2. PATTERNS IN WORLD BANK–NGO OPERATIONAL COLLABORATION, FISCAL YEARS 1987–98

	Total 1987–95		1996		1997		1998	
	No.	%	No.	%	No.	%	No.	%
By region[a]								
Africa	680	34	53	55	49	61	59	54
East Asia and Pacific	378	20	46	44	37	32	45	51
South Asia	239	33	21	76	19	84	25	73
Europe and Central Asia	225	16	61	38	67	24	69	37
Latin America and the Caribbean	443	24	54	48	52	60	68	51
Middle East and North Africa	180	12	21	38	17	41	20	52
Total	2,145	25	256	48	241	47	286	50
By sector								
Agriculture	443	41	33	88	45	82	47	74
Education	190	29	29	52	18	56	36	63
Electric power and energy	165	5	19	21	17	18	15	40
Environment	74	42	13	69	9	100	18	78
Finance	109	2	17	12	13	23	17	6
Health, population and nutrition	134	66	23	57	15	60	24	79
Industry	86	27	4	25	5	40	2	33
Mining	16	12	8	63	2	50	4	100
Multisector	190	4	19	37	21	10	19	30
Oil and gas	53	26	3	33	5	20	2	—
Public sector management	141	7	27	15	20	5	28	24
Social sector	60	92	17	82	17	65	12	80
Telecommunications	37	—	1	—	—	—	3	—
Transportation	233	7	24	21	28	29	27	71
Urban development	113	37	10	70	13	46	19	55
Water supply and sanitation	101	16	9	67	13	69	13	62
Total	2,145	25	256	48	241	47	286	50

—Zero

a. Refers to percentage of NGO-involved projects in all World Bank-approved projects in the region.

Incorporating social development

Since the World Summit on Social Development held in Copenhagen in 1995, the Bank has worked to make its activities more inclusive and effective and to improve the understanding of the social underpinnings of development. Significant Bankwide progress was made in fiscal 1998 to refocus the development agenda and support initiatives that are people-centered and participatory, respectful of country context and social conditions, and contribute to sustainable economic and social development.

Bankwide initiatives to increase lending for the social sectors, reduce debt, target the poor, and emphasize rural development are consistent with the summit's recommendations. In addition, the Bank took a number of new steps to mainstream attention to social concerns in fiscal 1998, including provision of additional funds under the Strategic Compact to incorporate social development more firmly into the development activities of the Bank and its clients.

A major emphasis was to mainstream social analysis, participation, and gender considerations into Bank-supported projects through social assessments (SAs); over 125 SAs were either completed or underway in fiscal 1998. SAs have made projects more inclusive by involving key stakeholders, including the poor, and taking account of diversity and gender issues. SAS have also made projects more socially sound and more effective and sustainable, by increasing local ownership of project goals and using institutional arrangements better suited to country conditions and local realities.

Eleven CASs were selected for special attention to social development issues in fiscal 1998—Albania, Bangladesh, Bolivia, Guatemala, Kenya, Mongolia, Nepal, Papua New Guinea, Tajikistan, Vietnam, and Yemen. An increasing number of CASs involved key stakeholders in the preparation process as well, such as in Colombia. The Colombian government welcomed consultations and participated in the CAS design and some fifty leaders, representing broad segments of civil society, helped define its strategic priorities. The coincidence of views between civil society and government in placing peace and coexistence as the main development challenge for Colombia led the Bank to include it as a CAS priority. A committee of representatives of governments, NGOs, and the Bank was established to monitor progress in carrying out the CAS commitments, which include promoting public institution building with the participation of local communities and civil society and developing conflict resolution capacity at the local level.

Increased attention to important social development issues is evident in many fiscal 1998 operations. For example, in East Asia, attention was given to the social consequences of the financial crisis and in Latin America and the Caribbean, to the problems of crime and violence. In Eastern Europe and Central Asia, precedence was given to the social dimensions of reform, while the focus in Africa was on poverty and gender, and post-conflict reconstruction and development. The priority in South Asia was on the challenge of creating inclusive and fair institutions at the local level. All regions expanded their interactions with stakeholders in both the government and civil society. And the new Adaptable Program Loans (APLS) and Learning and Innovation Loans (LILS) are supporting social development activities. In El Salvador, for example, an APL to support education reform is addressing the problems of rising youth alienation and violence—which threatens the

country's newly established and politically integrated civic society and the improving economy—by funding activities, to be defined by the students themselves, to increase their participation in their own schooling experience and encourage them to stay in school.

Some of the poorest nations are post-conflict countries in which both physical and social infrastructure have been destroyed. Following board approval of a post-conflict framework, the new Post-Conflict Unit was established in fiscal 1998 to provide critical operational support and policy guidance and to undertake strategic operational partnerships. It also acts as the secretariat for a small post-conflict fund supported under the Development Grant Facility (DGF). In fiscal 1998 post-conflict assistance is underway in a number of countries, including Afghanistan, Angola, Azerbaijan, Bosnia and

FIGURE 3-2
World Bank Lending for Environment Projects, Fiscal Years 1986–98
(US$ millions)

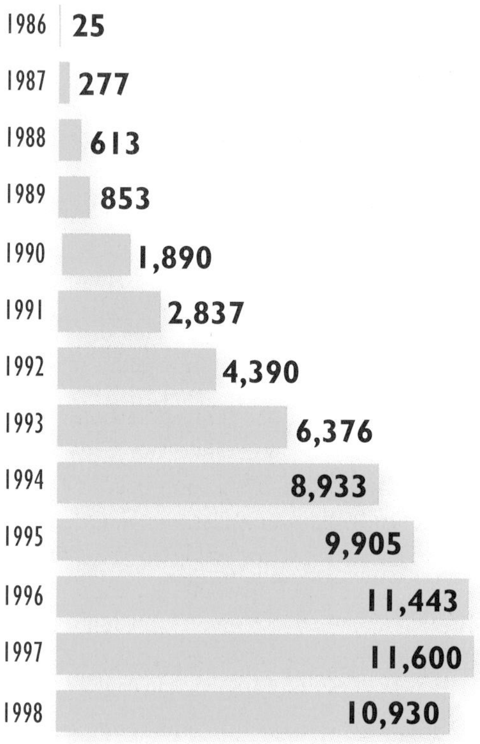

Year	Amount
1986	25
1987	277
1988	613
1989	853
1990	1,890
1991	2,837
1992	4,390
1993	6,376
1994	8,933
1995	9,905
1996	11,443
1997	11,600
1998	10,930

Note: Environment projects approved since FY86 and that are currently active.

Herzegovina, Cambodia, Croatia, Rwanda, and Tajikistan.

Broadening the environmental agenda

Eighteen stand-alone environmental projects amounting to $902 million, and ten agriculture, water, or urban development projects with a strong environmental focus totaling $590 million, were approved in fiscal 1998. Cumulative active environmental projects—including investment projects to reduce pollution, protect ecosystems, and build environmental management capacity—leveled off in fiscal 1998 after years of sharp increases (see figure 3-2). The leveling off of the cumulative active portfolio reflects environmental projects approved in earlier years that have reached completion. This trend is expected to continue as many earlier projects are heading toward completion.

The Bank's environmental agenda continued to broaden in 1998, embracing the concept that sustainable development can only be achieved if activities are sustainable at the global as well as the local level. The direct and significant linkage between domestic welfare and poverty alleviation and the degradation of the global commons is well-established. In 1998 the Bank engaged in some new partnerships and strengthened others.

Environmental sustainability is the core of local and regional economic development. Helping countries improve environmental management capacity and mainstream environmental sustainability principles into their development programs is at the core of the Bank's business. A Bank loan to support the development of environmental policy and legal and regulatory frameworks in the Dominican Republic—the Environmental Policy Reform Project—is illustrative. Other projects are testing new instruments for environmental management, such as in Uganda where the Institutional Capacity Project for wildlife and tourism is using innovative approaches to institutional strengthening, staff training, and public/private partnerships to promote ecotourism. In fiscal 1998 the executive directors approved diverse support for natural resources management, from a project in Vietnam to protect forests and promote sustainable rural development to one in Indonesia

to manage and protect coral reefs. Operations to promote energy efficiency and pollution control included a household energy project in Chad and pollution abatement projects in Argentina, China, and Egypt.

The Bank continues to develop tools and methodologies to help integrate environmental principles into development planning. It has developed a set of social and environmental "safeguard policies" designed to protect people and natural resources from any adverse impacts of development projects.[15] In the field of "green accounting," indigenous efforts to develop resource and environmental accounts in Mongolia and South Africa have been the focus of technical assistance efforts in fiscal 1998, with first results from Mongolia feeding into the CAS. Joint work was initiated with China's State Environmental Protection Administration to develop sustainable development indicators at the provincial and city level, and with Mexico's Ministry of Environment, Natural Resources, and Fisheries to construct program impact indicators.

EDI conducted subregional and national learning programs such as the "Economic Globalization and Environmental Sustainability" program held in Central America, South Asia, and Southern Africa. In Central America, separate workshops were held for regional journalists and the National Councils of Sustainable Development of Belize, El Salvador, Guatemala, and Nicaragua. And a program on national policy design in Costa Rica examined the positive impacts of appropriate water pricing on the management of protected areas.

The global agenda

In line with measures outlined at the United Nations General Assembly Special Session (UNGASS) on the Environment in June 1997, the Bank continued to develop a forward-looking strategy to support the objectives of the global

---

15. A compliance monitoring unit is being established in the Environmentally and Socially Sustainable Development (ESSD) Vice Presidency to ensure that Bank projects fully comply with these policies.

environment conventions,[16] integrate global environmental concerns into CASs and economic and sector work, and, where appropriate, set measurable corporate targets for activities to protect and improve the global environment. Global overlay theme papers indicating how global environment issues can be incorporated into sector policy and investment planning have been completed for the agriculture, energy, forestry, and transport sectors. These are being applied in nine country and sector-specific operations, such as the Nepal Land Resources Management Study, which is identifying how land and forest management practices can be adjusted to better conserve the rich biodiversity of Nepal's mountain forests.

A sector strategy paper on energy and the environment was under preparation during fiscal 1998 using a consultative process with external stakeholders via an open forum on the World Wide Web. When completed, the strategy paper is intended to lead to a better understanding of policy and lending priorities and to serve as the basis for the development of country-specific assistance programs. With the government of Russia and clorofluorocarbon (CFC) producers, the Bank has developed a new initiative to phase out CFC production in Russia by 2000—which is crucial to curbing the supply of CFCs and ensuring success of phase-out activities for other ozone-depleting substances funded under the Global Environment Facility (GEF) and the Multilateral Fund for the Montreal Protocol (MFMP).

Implementation of the 1993 Water Resources Management Policy[17] continued as a Bank priority in fiscal 1998. The policy stresses three principles: dealing with water comprehensively; ensuring the participation of all stakeholders, especially communities, NGOs, and the private sector; and managing of water as an economic good. The Bank is an active participant in the Global Water Partnership, a broad-based coalition focusing on improving the quality and nature of technical assistance and cooperation in water. The Bank was a prime player, along with International Union for the Conservation of Nature (IUCN), in the formation of the World Commission on Dams. The commission brings together a wide range of stakeholders tasked with

defining the circumstances under which large dams are appropriate investments and, when they are, with setting globally acceptable standards on how they should be planned, designed, built, and operated.

At the UNGASS meeting in June 1997, the Bank renewed its commitment to help reverse the global trend of forest loss and degradation and announced an international alliance with the World Wide Fund for Nature (WWF).[18] In partnership with others, the alliance will work together to support countries to achieve (i) an additional 50 million hectares of effective new forest protected areas, plus a comparable area of existing reserves under effective protection; and (ii) 200 million hectares of the world's production forests under independently certified sustainable management by the year 2005.

The cooperation of the global timber industry is needed if these ambitious targets are to be met. Thus, in fiscal 1998 the Bank's president convened the first meeting of chief executive officers of the world's largest timber companies to exhort them to take the lead in improving the management and conservation of the world's remaining forests. As a result, joint research and planning is being undertaken by industry and conservation leaders to identify ways to reduce forest loss and degradation.

The Bank also embarked on an implementation review of its 1991 forest policy paper[19] in 1998. It will continue through fiscal 1999 and will involve a wide consultation and strategy formation process.

The Global Environment Facility and the Montreal Protocol. The Bank serves as an implementing agency for both the GEF and the MFMP. It shares this responsibility with the United Nations Development Programme (UNDP) and the United Nations Environment Programme (UNEP)

16. The Convention on Biological Diversity; the Convention to Combat Desertification; the Framework Convention on Climate Change; the UN Convention on the Law of the Sea; and the Vienna Convention for Protection of the Ozone Layer.

17. World Bank. 1993. *Water Resources Management: A World Bank Policy Study.* Washington, D.C.

18. WWF is known as the World Wildlife Fund in the United States and Canada.

19. World Bank. 1991. *The Forest Sector.* Washington, D.C.

and, in the case of the MFMP, with the United Nations Industrial Development Organization (UNIDO). The two programs cover four focal areas: biodiversity, climate change, ozone depleting substances, and international waters.

By the end of fiscal 1998, World Bank management approved eighteen GEF projects for a total of $939 million in GEF resources, which are leveraging another $4,100 million in cofinancing. The GEF's second replenishment, agreed by the GEF Council in March 1998, will make available a further $2,750 million for eligible projects for global environment management over the next three years.

By the end of June 1998, Bank management had approved 379 investment subprojects totaling $270 million of MFMP funding: of these, 51 subprojects totaling $42 million were approved in fiscal 1998. Projects approved during fiscal 1998 will phase out 15,000 tons of ozone depleting substances, bringing the cumulative phaseout of the ozone-depleting potential, accomplished with MFMP support through the Bank, to 30,000 tons. This represents about 15 percent of total CFCs consumed in all developing countries in 1994. Of special note is a $62 million program to phase out the production and consumption of halons in China (the world's largest producer of such substances).

Revitalizing rural development

In fiscal 1998 the Bank published its new rural strategy paper,[20] and selected rural development as one of the top six areas of emphasis for the next few years. Nearly three quarters of poor people in developing countries live in rural areas so it is essential to focus on rural economies if poverty is to be reduced. Effective rural development also contributes to food security and helps protect the environment by making land and water use more efficient. This is critical if the world is to feed a rapidly growing population—estimates suggest population could grow by 45 percent over the next thirty years.

The revitalization of the Bank's work on rural development is showing demonstrable results. The Operations Evaluation Department (OED) evaluations show that projects are now performing much better than in recent years, with 72 percent of completed projects being judged satisfactory in fiscal years 1995–97 compared with just 52 percent in 1989–91. The goal is to achieve an 80 percent satisfactory rating by 2002.

Bank-supported rural strategies are raising the emphasis of rural development particularly in the twenty-two focus programs, which are intended to accelerate rural development by leveraging incremental activities (assisted by $6.5 million funded under the Strategic Compact). These activities in 1998 included rural strategies for India, Morocco, and Vietnam; a water management strategy in the Middle East and North Africa region; and analysis of cross-country agricultural policy issues by countries seeking admission to the EU.

Demand for Bank support for rural projects is growing: the pipeline for agricultural and rural development projects for fiscal 1997-99 average some fifty-seven new projects per year, up from forty-six per year in fiscal 1994-96. In fiscal 1998, lending for rural development projects totaled $3,162 million, and included projects supporting rural transport and rural water supply and sanitation.

Collaboration among partners is stronger and richer, and many new alliance-building initiatives were launched or strengthened in fiscal 1998:

• *Land Reform Network.* The Bank, the Food and Agriculture Organization (FAO), and the International Fund for Agricultural Development (IFAD) are supporting a network for countries with programs of negotiated or market-assisted land reform. It provides a forum for exchanging ideas and information and finding solutions to common problems.

• *Integrated Pest Management Facility.* Jointly sponsored by the Bank, FAO, UNDP, and UNEP, the facility is providing experts to help design projects using innovative pest management techniques that limit farmers' exposure to harmful chemicals and protect the environment.

• *Fisheries research.* Established at the FAO in Rome with Bank support, research is yielding ways to conserve and manage marine and inland

20. World Bank. 1997. *Rural Development: From Vision to Action.* Washington, D.C.

fishery resources, increase fish productivity, understand the dynamics of fishing communities, and the socioeconomic consequences of government fishery policies.

• *Decentralization and rural development.* An international network—with FAO, the German Agency for Technical Cooperation (GTZ), IFAD, the Swiss Development Corporation, the United Nations Capital Development Fund (UNCDF), and UNDP—provides a forum for practitioners, policymakers, and scholars to share experiences and coordinate activities in support of rural development using decentralized participatory strategies.

• *Popular Coalition to Eradicate Poverty and Hunger.* Hosted by IFAD with Bank participation, the coalition has been formed to support activities to improve the ability of poor people to gain or protect their access to productive resources (land, water, and forests) and the tools and processes to manage them.

In fiscal 1998 the Decentralization, Fiscal Systems and Rural Development Research Program was completed, and the results were presented at the Technical Consultation for Decentralization at the FAO. The research was carried out to understand the impact of decentralization on rural service delivery, economic growth, and poverty reduction, and to identify which programs and strategies work best. The research indicated positive results from decentralization: it can increase participation, improve the accountability and responsiveness of government, and lead to programs and projects that better match local preferences and are, therefore, more sustainable. It also indicated that to work well, programs must include strong enforceable systems of monitoring and evaluation by citizens and central governments, and mechanisms to ensure participation of the rural poor—not just the rural elite. Lessons learned are being used to design more effective rural development programs.

The report *Integrated Pest Management: Strategies and Policies for Effective Implementation*[21] released in fiscal 1998 examined the impacts of policies and regulations on farmers' decisions and set out an approach for encouraging farmers to adopt environmentally friendly ways of controlling insect damage.

The Consultative Group on International Agricultural Research

The Consultative Group on International Agricultural Research (CGIAR)[22] exists to mobilize the best in agricultural science on behalf of the world's poor and hungry. It fulfills its mission through a network of sixteen international agricultural research centers.

Fifty-seven developing and developed countries, private foundations, and regional and international organizations, including the Bank, collectively support the CGIAR. In 1997,[23] CGIAR contributions totaled $320 million, up from the previous year's $304 million. New Zealand, Peru, Portugal, and Thailand joined the CGIAR in 1997.

The CGIAR's research is critical to supporting the Bank's commitment to environmentally and socially sustainable development and its renewed focus on rural development. Some 300 research projects are aimed at finding ways to increase agricultural productivity (40 percent); strengthen national agricultural research systems (21 percent); protect the environment (17 percent); improve policies (11 percent); and save biodiversity (11 percent).

A review of the CGIAR system began last year and will be completed by the end of 1998.

Promoting finance, private sector, and infrastructure development

The finance, private sector, and infrastructure development programs of the World Bank Group (the Bank, IFC, and MIGA) were strengthened in fiscal 1998 to improve client service through stepped up delivery of assistance—for financial sector development, private sector development, energy, mining, telecommunications,

21. Schillhorn van Veen, Tjaart, Douglas Forno, Steen Joffe, Dina Umali-Deininger, and Sanjiva Cooke. 1997. *Integrated Pest Management: Strategies and Policies for Effective Implementation.* Environmentally and Socially Sustainable Development Studies and Monographs Series 13. Washington, D.C.: World Bank.

22. The CGIAR issues its own annual report which can be obtained from the CGIAR Secretariat, 1818 H Street, NW, Washington, D.C. 20433; tel: (202)473-8951; fax: (202)473-8110. For more information, see: www.cgiar.org

23. The CGIAR's fiscal year is from January 1–December 31.

FIGURE 3-3 IBRD and IDA Lending to Sectors with Potential for Private Sector Involvement, Fiscal Year 1998

(US$ millions)

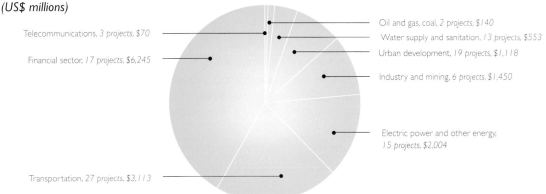

Telecommunications, *3 projects, $70*

Financial sector, *17 projects, $6,245*

Transportation, *27 projects, $3,113*

Oil and gas, coal, *2 projects, $140*

Water supply and sanitation, *13 projects, $553*

Urban development, *19 projects, $1,118*

Industry and mining, *6 projects, $1,450*

Electric power and other energy, *15 projects, $2,004*

transport, urban development, and water supply. Operations in these sectors were designed to help client countries strengthen their policy environment to facilitate private sector development, encourage private sector participation in infrastructure and social sectors, and build technical and managerial capacity. Bank assistance to these sectors increased by almost two-thirds in fiscal 1998, largely because of the Bank's response to the East Asian financial crisis, but also because of increased demand for energy, industry and mining, and urban development support *(see figure 3-3)*.

The Quality Assurance Group (QAG) reviewed project quality in the FPSI sectors in two studies during the fiscal year. The first, on projects at risk, found some improvement—about 5 percent—with increases in quality for the financial sector, oil and gas, urban development, and water and sanitation. The second, a study of 100 projects out of 247 projects approved by the executive directors in calendar 1997, showed that project quality at entry was somewhat higher in the FPSI sectors than in other sectors of the lending program. Fully 90 percent of the FPSI projects were judged to be good to satisfactory in this study. Attention to quality is not only pursued through ex-post reviews of this kind, but also through better knowledge management that imparts lessons learned in the timely way to Bank staff developing new projects.

IFC loans, lines of credit, quasi-equity and equity investments also facilitate private sector growth in client countries; in fiscal 1998, new investment approvals totaled $3,417 million, with an additional $2,513 million in loan syndications and underwriting Major efforts were undertaken at the country level to take advantage of IFC-World Bank synergy, especially in infrastructure privatization, mining, oil and gas, and telecommunications.

MIGA's political risk insurance, covering equity and debt investments in companies, and MIGA's investment promotion work are frequently utilized in conjunction with other Bank operations, guarantees, and technical assistance. MIGA issued $830.8 million in total coverage in fiscal 1998, its highest level yet, facilitating about $6,100 million in foreign investment in twenty-six member countries. MIGA's Board of Executive Directors also approved a recommendation for a $1 billion recapitalization package to the Council of Governors. The funding consists of an $850 million general capital increase ($150 million paid-in and $700 million callable capital) and a grant transfer from the IBRD, which will enable further expansion of MIGA's activities.

Guarantees

The World Bank's partial risk and partial credit guarantees help catalyze private investment for priority investment projects. The product continues to be integrated into the Bank's CASs and operations, complementing the risk mitigation products offered by MIGA and IFC.

In 1998 the active pipeline of more than thirty projects showed more diversity than the earlier focus on the power sector, by including water and transportation projects. A large pipeline is critical in the project finance business because of the complexity of transactions and the high attrition rate. The East Asian financial crisis, and its effects on other emerging markets, slowed project finance significantly in 1998 and delayed some of the Bank's guarantee operations. The Bank's board approved an innovative guarantee operation for the Jorf Lasfar Power Project in fiscal 1998, the first independent power project in Morocco. Selected as one of the fifteen best project finance deals of the year by *Project Finance* magazine, the partial risk guarantee supports a DM 313 million commercial bank syndicate by protecting against the political risk of nonpayment of various contractual obligations.

The executive directors also approved two new applications of the guarantee program: (i) the IBRD Enclave Guarantee for IDA-Only Countries; and (ii) the IDA Guarantee for IDA-Only Countries *(see box 3-2)*. Many IDA-only countries have undertaken successful macroeconomic reforms and have improved their business environments, which have increased their appeal for private investors.

In fiscal 1998 the Bank increased project finance advisory services on structuring specific transactions and enhancing creditworthiness in Brazil, China, and Turkey. It also supported and advised the governments of Colombia and the Philippines on ways to better manage their contingent liabilities and establish guarantee frameworks for infrastructure projects.

Private sector development

Helping clients develop vibrant private sectors is one of the Bank's principal development goals as it provides jobs to fast-growing working populations, creates fiscal space for poverty reduction programs, and helps client countries compete in the rapidly changing global economy.

The Bank is helping improve business environments by supporting economic policy reform, promoting strategies for country competitiveness, and encouraging private sector involvement in the operations of state companies through concessioning, management contracting, partial privatization, and mass privatization programs. Microfinance and small- to medium-scale enterprise development that encourage small business development also are rapidly expanding elements in the Bank's menu of assistance.

In Eastern Europe, for example, the Bank is helping client countries handle difficult second-generation privatization challenges including addressing the lack of managerial capacity in small, newly privatized businesses; weak corporate governance; and lack of financial sector transparency. In fiscal 1998 the Bank provided technical assistance—often in partnership with other donor grant funds and with client country government resources—to Belarus, Russia, and Uzbekistan to finance local consulting services to small businesses still unsure of their strategy, direction, and operating procedures. Lines of credit and grants are being made available on a matching basis to business owners to hire local advisers to assist in a full range of business topics including strategic planning, financial accounting, and marketing. In Lithuania a dozen local consulting firms sprang up to provide business administration services to about 100 companies under a $5 million Bank loan.

Bank services to support privatization in fiscal 1998 included preparation and dissemination of competitiveness benchmarks for use by clients seeking intercountry comparison, training for utility regulators (over 300 regulators from fifty countries) and loans, such as that which supports the Colombia Regulatory Reform Project to strengthen the legal and regulatory framework governing a number of major utilities.

The new Business Partners for Development was launched this year with private sector partners. This alliance enables private companies to set up locally based, development-oriented projects in four thematic areas (education, natural resources, water and sanitation, and youth development) in Bank client countries. Projects are funded by the private sector, the Bank, and other official donors. Under the program, natural resource companies in Angola's mining region are funding a series of social sector com-

munity development projects with the local
government and local NGOs.

Through a new infrastructure privatization
program funded by the government of Japan,
country infrastructure assessments are being
prepared, such as in India, and freestanding
technical assistance is being provided, such as an
awareness-raising workshop on privatization for
parliamentarians in Uganda. The facility, jointly
managed with the IFC, helps countries quickly to
identify feasible privatization opportunities and
bring global experience to bear on implementing them.

Other partnerships have expanded and
matured, including the Consultative Group for
Assistance to the Poorest (CGAP) involving
twenty-five donor countries. The success of

microfinance programs has impressed international as well as client country institutions, both
public and private. Conservative estimates
project that eighteen retail microfinance institutions working with CGAP in 1997 will expand
their outreach from 180,000 very poor clients
in 1996 to 500,000 in 1999. And they expect to
be financially sustainable and capable of leveraging commercial capital over the next one to
four years. The CGAP Secretariat facilitates sharing of global best practice through seminars,
publications, and local training programs; helps
create supportive policy environments; coordinates donor activities; and monitors the progress
of microfinance programs worldwide.

To date, the CGAP Secretariat has funded fifty-
eight innovative programs: they include the
Foundation for International Community Assistance (FINCA)'s technical assistance hubs in Latin
America and East Africa, which reach more
than 70,000 clients, and the Kenya Rural Enterprise Program (K-REP) that is being transformed
into a commercial bank to serve poor clients.
Another group, the Society for Helping Awak-
ening Rural Poor through Education (SHARE) in
India plans to more than double its outreach to
11,000 poor clients.

Another partnership, the Japan-sponsored
Privatization Trust Fund, supporting technical
assistance, is successfully operating in fifty countries. Some twenty-five projects initiated in
fiscal 1998 cover air transport privatization,
municipal privatization, privatization implementation services—such as support to
Sri Lanka's Public Enterprise Reform Commission—and small farm commercialization
in Africa.

Financial sector development

Assistance to the financial sector intensified
dramatically during fiscal 1998 as the East Asian
financial crisis unfolded. The Bank provided
crisis-related lending to Indonesia, the Republic
of Korea, and Thailand totaling $5,400 million
(see box 2-2) and provided extensive technical
assistance on financial sector policies, bank asset
resolution, and corporate governance issues related to the crisis.

At the 1997 World Bank Annual Meetings in

Hong Kong, the Bank described the issues raised by the East Asia crisis, the basis for related IMF-World Bank coordination and additional actions planned. These included:

- systematic monitoring and in-depth analysis of countries at risk;
- commitment of additional budget resources to assist countries at risk;
- increased emphasis in country assistance strategies (CASs) on financial sector work;
- recruitment of more financial sector specialists;
- enhanced training of Bank staff on financial sector issues;
- better mechanisms for deploying staff and resources to financial crises; and
- greater use of expert staff from member countries.

Subsequently, at the G-8 Summit in Birmingham, U.K., in May 1998, the heads of state or government of the eight major industrialized countries expressed concern about the impact of the regional crisis on the poor and most vulnerable. They agreed that economic and financial reforms should be matched with actions and policies by the countries concerned to help protect these groups from the worst effects of the crisis; and the heads of state welcomed the support of these efforts by the World Bank, the Asian Development Bank, and bilateral donors and the increased emphasis on social expenditure in programs agreed to by the IMF.

Staff and resources for support of the financial sector were severely stretched as the Bank responded to the needs of East Asia while also supporting countries in other regions facing financial sector vulnerabilities. The executive directors therefore authorized up to an additional $25 million annually, for two years, to establish the Special Financial Operations Unit to concentrate exclusively on crisis countries. To date, Indonesia, the Republic of Korea, and Thailand have been so covered. In addition, the resources are helping to expand the Bank's assistance to vulnerable countries for crisis prevention assistance and longer-term financial strengthening.

The Bank's expanding assistance for the financial sector features a number of distinct products, including highly focused and action-oriented rapid financial sector assessments, which analyze financial sector vulnerability. The assessments provide the framework for an enhanced policy dialogue and increase the level and quality of the Bank's policy-level interactions with the client. In many countries this analysis is followed by an essential technical assistance package (ETAP), culminating in the preparation of technical assistance support. Client countries facing financial crisis may also need follow-on lending to address urgent policy and institutional requirements for financial sector strengthening. The Bank is also intensifying its monitoring of financial sectors to help identify emerging problems.

The Capital Market Development Program, which aims to promote rapid growth of debt markets and other capital markets that are essential for reducing financial sector vulnerability, is a major new dimension in the Bank's financial sector assistance program. The objective is to help accelerate development of local long-term debt and equity markets to mobilize domestic savings and reduce countries' reliance on volatile foreign capital, particularly short-term bank loans. Instruments to mobilize capital for long-term project financing, secondary-debt market liquidity, and asset-based securitization are included. The Bank also strengthened its capital markets institutional assistance program—with efforts underway this fiscal year in Brazil, India, the Republic of Korea, Mexico, the Philippines, Romania, and Thailand.

Other elements of the Bank's financial sector assistance program are:

- Joint technical assistance, with support from the government of Japan's Policy and Human Resource Development (PHRD) Fund, for financial sector assistance in Asian countries; country programs have been approved for Indonesia, the Republic of Korea the Philippines, and Thailand.
- The Asia-Europe Meeting (ASEM) Trust Fund—a collaborative response to the East Asian financial crisis by European donors. Contributions will be split roughly 50–50 between support for financial and social sector assistance programs.
- The Toronto International Leadership Centre for Financial Sector Supervision—a joint government of Canada-World Bank center that

TABLE 3-3. WORLD BANK PPI OPERATIONS, FISCAL YEARS 1988–98

Instrument	Africa	East Asia and Pacific	South Asia	Europe and Central Asia	Latin America and the Caribbean	Middle East and North Africa	Total
Adjustments: Single Sector	5	0	0	2	1	1	9
Adjustments: Multisector	2	1	0	4	7	1	15
Technical assistance	6	2	1	1	16	0	26
Investment lending	44	31	21	25	34	10	165
Guarantees	0	4	2	0	1	2	9
Total	**57**	**38**	**24**	**32**	**59**	**14**	**224**
of which: increase in FY98	*(9)*	*(9)*	*(3)*	*(13)*	*(11)*	*(3)*	*(48)*

offers specialized short-term training programs for senior financial managers from member countries, and agencies and organizations concerned with the financial sector.

• The EDI's activities, such as the "Preventing Bank Crises: Lessons from Recent Global Failures" workshops—which share lessons of experience with central bank, finance ministry officials, and bank executives (workshops were held in the United States and Singapore in fiscal 1998)—and work to help set up training and research centers on financial issues (such centers in Buenos Aires and Abidjan are delivering training and research on local regulatory problems).

Private provision of infrastructure (PPI)

About 15 percent of infrastructure project investment in Bank client countries comes from the private sector. But a major jump in private participation is required to meet the more than $250 billion needed for investment in infrastructure over the next decade. The Bank's lending program supports this evolution by working with countries to build private sector participation elements into the infrastructure projects it finances. In fiscal 1998, forty-eight Bank-supported projects included PPI components *(see table 3-3)*.

Examples of pathbreaking PPI operations approved during fiscal 1998 include:

• The Haryana Power Sector Restructuring Project in India that establishes a new legal, regulatory and institutional framework for the power sector; initiates the privatization of power distribution; and resolves some of the most critical bottlenecks in commercial and technical services to customers. One of the largest state power distribution companies is being privatized under this operation.

• The São Paulo Integrated Urban Transport Project in Brazil that is helping transfer the transport company's operations to a private concessionaire to improve efficiency, expand suburban service, and establish more effective regional transport coordination.

• The Cesme-Alacati Water Supply and Sewage Project in Turkey that provides for hiring and monitoring the performance of a private operator, which will improve water and sewage services; this is a first, but important, step in privatization. The project also improves the municipality's capacity to limit adverse environmental effects.

The World Bank Group (the Bank, IFC and MIGA) work closely so that programs are consistent, and duplication and gaps are avoided in meeting client needs for technical assistance and project finance. Joint support for infrastructure development was particularly notable in fiscal 1998 *(see box 3-3)*. The new public-private venture, the Solar Development Corporation is illustrative. This equity investment by the Bank Group and major U.S.-based foundations will result in a retail market for photovoltaic solar home systems in developing countries. The venture is being prepared for eventual ownership by private investors. The Bank and the IFC have also mounted joint efforts to evaluate private power development options in Bangladesh and Panama. An IFC-World Bank study on environmental issues in India's power sector was also prepared. And support for privatizing Panama's electric power distribution company includes Bank-funded technical assistance, while the IFC is taking equity and managing the sale of the company to private investors.

The sector strategy paper on energy and environment that was under preparation during fiscal 1998 was an IFC-World Bank effort. One outcome of the strategy will be increased attention to energy and environment issues in the CAS process. China's Energy Conservation Project, approved in fiscal 1998, reflects the strategy's emphasis on making markets work effectively as a means of improving energy efficiency and reducing demand for energy—thus reducing the associated pollution that excess energy use causes. Under the project, innovative energy management companies have been set up to make self-sustaining energy efficiency investments through energy performance contracting, especially in industrial enterprises. Similar energy efficiency projects are being prepared in Argentina and Brazil and a number of energy-environment reviews will be undertaken with financial support from the Energy Sector Management Assistance Program.

Both the IFC and CGAP invested in the Kenya Rural Enterprise Program (K-REP): the IFC invested $1 million and CGAP provided $750,000 for a management-employee stock ownership plan to enable K-REP to convert to a bank. The Bank and the IFC cooperated to support corpo-rate restructuring in Indonesia and the Republic of Korea.

The Foreign Investment Advisory Service (FIAS). In fiscal 1998 FIAS[24] completed forty-six new advisory projects in thirty-eight countries. Projects focused on poorer countries and countries reorienting their economies toward greater openness. The trend toward reform and the realization that foreign direct investment (FDI) can provide tangible benefits to the host economy is illustrated by the use of several FIAS products:

• Projects aimed at developing and/or strengthening strategies for national investment promotion agencies were completed for eight countries ranging from Fiji to Croatia to the Dominican Republic.

• Analyses of the legal environment for foreign investment and incentive regimes were requested by more than ten countries.

• An initiative to assist small island economies continued, with seven projects completed in individual Pacific Forum countries and regional training programs implemented through the Forum Secretariat.

• Egypt, Indonesia, Mali, and the Philippines sought assistance to identify administrative bar-

---

24. FIAS is a joint IFC-World Bank program that provides advisory services to governments to help them improve the policy and institutional environment for foreign private direct investment. The program is funded by the Bank, the IFC, other donors, and paying customers from the countries that receive advice.

BOX 3-3   JOINT WORLD BANK GROUP SUPPORT FOR INFRASTRUCTURE DEVELOPMENT

By working together, the World Bank and the IFC more effectively support client needs. In the case of infrastructure development and privatization, a number of innovative joint programs were underway in fiscal 1998:

   • *collaboration on rail concessioning in Brazil;*

   • *Bank-financed technical assistance helping prepare a concession for a Buenos Aires water utility and the IFC subsequently investing in the company;*

   • *continued Bank support to develop Argentina's regulatory capacities, along with investment in smaller cities not yet viable for IFC investments;*

   • *joint work advocating private participation in the water sector, disseminating good practice examples, and holding seminars worldwide;*

   • *IFC inputs sought early to ensure that potential private investors' or lenders' concerns were taken into account at the beginning of the privatization process such as in Ecuador; and*

   • *a jointly financed study and advisory services to the newly privatized Air Afrique, which provided background on the status and perspectives of air transport in the region.*

The private sector is the engine of long-term growth. To encourage private entrepreneurs to invest and flourish, the Bank is helping countries establish stable and open business climates with access to credit and sound financial systems.

riers to investment, hoping to pave a smoother road to greater levels of FDI.

• Indonesia, the Philippines, and Thailand received advice on investment promotion schemes for specific regions within those countries.

• FIAS participated in the post-conflict rehabilitation of Bosnia and Herzegovina by assisting the state and entity governments to draft a foreign investment policy that sets the foundation for bringing investment back to that region.

Managing private capital flows

The rapid increase in private capital flows to developing countries during the 1990s has been accompanied by a high degree of volatility, particularly in the case of portfolio flows. This was witnessed in Mexico in 1995 and East Asia in 1997.

The Bank's specific interventions to respond to the East Asian financial crisis are discussed in more detail in Section Two. But the crisis has significant implications for emerging markets outside of the region as well. The Bank moved rapidly to assess these implications and to position itself to deal with the global consequences of the crises by:

• Strengthening its financial sector capacities by establishing a Special Financial Operations Unit to deal with crises situations; preparing financial sector assessments in countries with weak financial systems; and expanding efforts to build staff expertise.

• Helping client countries manage the social consequences of the crisis by protecting public expenditures targeted for the poor; enhancing the quality of social services; improving the design and financing of social funds; and strengthening social security systems for the unemployed and the elderly.

• Strengthening collaboration with the IMF, in both crisis and noncrisis countries. Recognizing the increasing interlinkages between macro- and microeconomic dimensions of the crisis, and between short- and long-term development, the Bank will undertake strengthened and regular assessments of structural policies and governance at the sector and corporate levels to complement the IMF's surveillance at the macroeconomic level. Country assistance strategies (CASS) will be stronger as a result and will help the Bank respond in crisis situations and help prevent future crises.

• Undertaking jointly with its partners, including the IMF, analysis of lessons learned from

TABLE 3-4. ADJUSTMENT LENDING RISES IN RESPONSE TO THE CRISIS IN EAST ASIA

	FY96 $ Million	FY96 Percent	FY97 $ Million	FY97 Percent	FY98 $ Million	FY98 Percent
Adjustment commitment by region						
Africa	1,138	25	693	14	818	7
East Asia and Pacific	130	3	10	0	5,685	50
Middle East and North Africa	710	16	195	4	180	2
Latin America and Carribean	1,028	23	1,011	20	1,589	14
Europe and Central Asia	1,500	33	3,174	62	2,768	25
South Asia	3	0	3	0	250	2
Adjustment commitment by sector						
Finance	570	13	895	18	6,067	54
Multisector	1,410	31	1,906	37	1,803	16
Other	2,530	56	2,285	45	3,420	30
IBRD *and* IDA *adjustment commitments*						
Debt reduction loan	30	1	183	4	85	1
Rehabilitation import loan	65	1	120	2	10	0
Sector adjustment loan	3,325	74	2,671	53	2,051	18
Structural adjustment loan	1,090	24	2,112	42	9,143	81
IBRD *and* IDA *adjustment commitments*						
IBRD	2,830	63	4,138	81	9,935	88
IDA	1,679	37	948	19	1,354	12
Total adjustment loans	4,509	100	5,086	100	11,289	100
Total World Bank commitments						
IBRD	14,656[a]		14,525		21,086	
IDA	6,861		4,622		7,508	
Total IBRD + IDA	21,517		19,147		28,594	
Share of adjustment loans		21		27		39

a. Includes the refinanced/rescheduled overdue charges of $168 million for Bosnia and Herzegovina.

the East Asian crisis with special attention to the relationship between public, financial, and corporate sectors.

• Increasing commitments and disbursements under adjustment loans to help countries respond to the crisis *(see table 3-4)*.

Strengthening public governance

The East Asian financial crisis drew attention to the close linkages between corporate governance mechanisms and public sector governance. Failures and lack of accountability in the private and public sectors often go hand in hand and can result in widespread corruption. Controlling corruption requires matching the role of government with its capability; adopting sound legal and regulatory frameworks for private sector activity; establishing a strong and motivated civil service; setting up sound budgeting and financial management systems; putting effective watchdog institutions in place; and providing a capacity to detect, investigate, and prosecute fraud and corruption when it occurs.

The board of Executive Directors approved a new anticorruption strategy in fiscal 1998.[25] The Board noted that corruption must be addressed as part of a broad and integrated strat-

25. World Bank. 1998. "Helping Countries Combat Corruption: The Role of the World Bank." Washington, D.C., Public Sector Management Department

egy for improving public sector performance and economic and sector policies. The strategy guides Bank activities at four levels: preventing fraud and corruption in Bank financed projects; helping countries that request Bank assistance in efforts to reduce corruption; taking corruption more explicitly into account in CASS; and adding voice and support to international efforts to reduce corruption. However, success in dealing with corruption depends on whether there is a strong demand for reform.

In 1998 the Bank helped countries diagnose the size and nature of problems using survey data and new diagnostic tools. It is helping countries:

• improve financial management and procurement in Bank-financed projects to ensure that opportunities for fraud and corruption are minimized and resources are used efficiently to achieve their intended purposes;

• develop anticorruption strategies (underway in some nineteen countries) and integrate them into broader public sector reform programs;

• implement broader public sector reforms in borrower countries such as Ecuador, Russia, and Venezuela; and

• assess the costs of corruption and build a consensus for concerted action, drawing on experience in countries that have successfully combated corruption.

In many countries central governments are decentralizing some of their political, fiscal, and/or administrative responsibilities to lower-level governments and to the private sector. Decentralization is particularly widespread in developing countries for a variety of reasons: the advent of multiparty political systems in Africa; the deepening of democratization in Latin America; the transition from a command to a market economy in Eastern Europe and the former Soviet Union; the need to improve delivery of local services to large populations in the centralized countries of East Asia; and the challenge of ethnic and geographic diversity in South Asia (see box 3-4).

Supporting Bank programs through research

The World Bank's activities and lending programs are grounded in knowledge about development processes that is gathered and distilled from research of client experience. This research is periodically evaluated to assess to what extent it has increased the Bank's understanding of development, supported its research capacity building in client countries, improved policy advice, and supported operations.

Following up on earlier reports of the external impact of Bank research and research capacity building, in fiscal 1998 the Bank conducted a comprehensive evaluation of the contribution

BOX 3-4   WORLD BANK SUPPORT FOR DECENTRALIZATION

Whatever its origins, decentralization can have significant repercussions for resource mobilization and allocation, macroeconomic stability, service delivery, and equity.

A growing number of Bank-funded projects are supporting sectoral decentralization strategies. Twelve percent of all projects completed between fiscal years 1992 and 1997 involved decentralizing reponsibilities to lower levels of government: some 43 percent of urban development projects, 27 percent of health projects, 26 percent of social funds, and 16 percent of environment projects. Projects with decentralization components are most prevalent in the

Africa region at 19 percent, and least prevalent in the East Asia and Europe and Central Asia regions at 6 percent.

In addition to sector specific support, the executive directors have agreed that the Bank may support decentralization through loans to subnational governments. Although such loans will necessarily be guaranteed by the central government, the loans would otherwise be negotiated and undertaken by independent local governments whose capital markets would eventually permit them to borrow directly. Such loans can be both project-specific and state-level structural adjustment loans.

its research makes to Bank operations and advisory capacity. Focus group discussions, structured interviews, and surveys revealed that Bank research is widely used in discussions with clients, in preparing economic or sector analyses, and at all stages of project development and implementation. It showed that Bank operations staff want research to show them how to identify best policies and how to implement them. They also want more research on social issues, political economy and institutional development, public sector and civil service reform, and implementing privatization and liberalization in different sectors.

Financial sector liberalization, without the requisite institutional development and regulatory reform, contributed to the central challenge facing the Bank and its members in fiscal 1998: the financial crisis in East Asia. The problems underlying the crisis were addressed in two major research efforts. The annual *Global Development Finance* (*GDF)* provides comprehensive information on international capital flows. Research underlying *GDF 1998*[26] shows that high savings and low inflation rates in East Asian countries diverted attention from lax financial sector regulation, disclosure, and supervision, which encouraged and obscured the growth of high-risk investments and mismatches between the maturities of assets and debts. *Private Capital Flows to Developing Countries 1997*[27] reviews the causes and effects of increased financial integration and instability, and analyzes the role of macroeconomic and domestic financial sector reform in attracting and managing capital inflows.

The process and effects of global integration range far beyond financial markets, however. *Global Economic Prospects 1998*[28] investigates the adjustment costs of liberalization, the effects of globalization of production, and the implications of predicted rapid growth in the largest developing countries.

Much World Bank assistance since the 1980s was made contingent on the recipient countries'

adoption of structural adjustment programs—programs widely criticized for increasing poverty, inequality, and unemployment. The Structural Adjustment Participatory Review Initiative (SAPRI) is a study unprecedented in the composition of its research team, combination of traditional economic approaches and techniques from political economy, and participatory processes. SAPRI is being conducted with national governments and the World Bank by a broad network of some 500 NGOs and civil society organizations—many vehemently critical of structural adjustment. In the seven subject countries, information disclosure policies have been adopted, national steering committees formed, and national forums conducted. And voices are being heard that were previously silent.

Bank research published in fiscal 1998 illustrated how the AIDS epidemic also is forcing governments and donors to deal directly with groups that society not only does not hear, but usually shuns. The importance of early prevention, and directing prevention efforts to sex workers and those who inject drugs, are the central conclusions of the major research program on HIV/AIDS, which is detailed in *Confronting AIDS Public Priorities in a Global Epidemic.*[29] Although 90 percent of all HIV infections occur in developing countries, half of the population in the developing world live in countries in which there is still time to prevent widespread epidemics. But, as the major message conveyed by this research shows, early action is urgent.

26. World Bank. 1998. *Global Development Finance 1998.* Washington D.C.

27. World Bank. 1997. *Private Capital Flows to Developing Countries 1997.* New York: Oxford University Press.

28. World Bank. 1998. *Global Economic Prospects 1998.* Washington D.C.

29. World Bank. 1997. *Confronting AIDS: Public Priorities in a Global Epidemic.* New York: Oxford University Press.

Fiscal 1998 was marked by continued improvement in the quality and quantity of the Bank's operational work, including greater development effectiveness by the Bank and better products and services for clients. Highlights for the year include:

• The satisfactory outcome rate for Bank operations rose from 68 percent for operations evaluated in fiscal 1997, to 72 percent for operations evaluated in fiscal 1998.

• The percentage of problem projects declined slightly from 14.8 percent to 14.2 percent;

• The time between project appraisal and Board approval declined from 7.8 to six months;

• Decentralization progressed; 22 country directors were based in the field at the end of fiscal 1998.

• Country assistance strategies (CAS)s were delivered with higher standards of quality in terms of country ownership, strategic focus, candor, and participation; and

• A number of new products were developed *(see box 4-1)*.

Development effectiveness

The World Bank has long been notable among multilateral development banks for its scrutiny of its activities to draw lessons from experience and use them to improve effectiveness. Improved performance measurement and increased capacity to monitor and evaluate work programs—

to utilize the lessons of experience and signal the need for corrective action in a timely manner—are at the center of the Strategic Compact. Therefore, work to improve monitoring and evaluation and disseminate evaluation findings took high priority in fiscal 1998.

Operations evaluation. Under the aegis of the executive directors' Committee on Development Effectiveness (CODE), the independent Operations Evaluation Department (OED) promotes learning and accountability in World Bank operations by identifying what works and what doesn't and by disseminating lessons of experience *(see also section one for a discussion of* CODE*'s activities in fiscal 1998)*. OED evaluates the Bank's global development effectiveness in terms of the results of Bank programs. At the country level it assesses progress toward sound implementation of Bank-financed operations, agreed policy reforms, and institutional development objectives.

In December 1997, CODE endorsed OED's new strategy, which places greater emphasis on the utilization of evaluation results and on capacity building—for borrowers and within the Bank for self-evaluation. The new approach establishes closer links between resource management and evaluation and emphasizes "just in time" production of studies in line with the policy calendar.

In fiscal 1998, OED reviewed 288 implementation completion reports prepared by regional offices; issued project performance audits for seventy-two completed operations; and completed impact evaluation reports for eight projects and nine sectors, along with four sector policy evaluations.[1] These products are used as building blocks for major evaluation studies: (i) process reviews carried out in fiscal 1998 included assessments of the Bank's appraisal practices and grants; (ii) thematic evaluations included public expenditure, involuntary resettlement, and adjustment lending in Sub-Saharan Africa; (iii) country assistance reviews included those for Albania, Bangladesh, Bolivia, Côte d'Ivoire, Mozambique, and the Philippines; and (iv) country assistance notes included Indonesia, Jamaica, Kenya, Malawi, Thailand, and Togo.

OED's *Annual Review of Development Effectiveness (ARDE)*[2] will complement the new corporate scorecard by assessing long-term performance trends. It synthesizes the evaluation findings of the past year, while the "Annual Report on Operations Evaluation" attests to the adequacy of evaluation processes Bankwide.

1. Topics include post-conflict reconstruction; finance; health, nutrition, and population; and follow-up on resettlement.
2. Evans, Alison, and William G. Battaile, Jr. 1998. *1997 Annual Review of Development Effectiveness.* World Bank, Washington, D.C.

BOX 4-1 NEW PRODUCTS TO RESPOND BETTER TO CLIENT NEEDS

To improve the Bank's responsiveness to clients' needs, several products were developed in fiscal 1998:

Adaptable lending. *Approved by the executive directors in September 1997, this type of lending proved immediately popular with borrowers. The package consists of two new lending options: the Learning and Innovation Loan (LIL) and the Adaptable Program Loan (APL). LILs are designed to (i) support small, time-sensitive programs that build capacity and/or pilot promising initiatives, or (ii) to experiment and develop locally-based models prior to larger-scale interventions. Management's authority to approve the LILs, which are modest in size—not exceeding $5 million—is a key feature of the instrument.*

APLS provide funding for long-term development programs where there is clear agreement on long-term objectives but where the path to achieve them requires a significant degree of learning from results. A sequence of APLS starts with a first loan to fund the initial set of activities; subsequent funding is provided when agreed milestones and benchmarks for realizing the program's objectives are met. The executive directors approve the first APL, along with the program, and delegate approval of subsequent loans to management. Eleven APLS and fifteen LILs were approved in fiscal 1998.

New knowledge products and services. *One of the most notable is EducationNet, which makes available development knowledge and best practice information on a variety of development topics to clients through the Internet.*

Guarantee instruments. *Two new guarantee instruments for IDA-only countries also were approved in fiscal 1998 (these are described in box 3-2).*

Loan terms flexibility. *The Bank continued to offer the expanded range of terms for new IBRD loan commitments introduced in June 1996. It also successfully concluded the offer of currency choice for existing IBRD loans introduced in September 1996, which allowed IBRD borrowers to amend the terms of their existing currency-pool loans, made since 1980, to reflect the offered currency of their choice. These popular initiatives provide borrowers flexibility to select loan terms that are consistent with their debt management strategy and suited for their debt servicing capacity. An extensive information campaign was undertaken to support borrower decisionmaking, which in turn promoted a strategic dialogue among developing countries on sovereign debt management issues and created opportunities for countries to share and learn from each other.*

Borrowers selected the new loan terms for 95 percent of fiscal 1998 loan commitments. Of new commitments totaling $21,086.2 million, borrowers selected LIBOR-based single-currency loans for $15,434 million and fixed-rate single-currency loans for $4,626 million. In addition, borrowers from 34 countries elected to convert $14,703 million of existing currency-pool loans into single-currency loan (SCL) terms.

The ARDE concludes that the Bank may reach the goal of 75 percent satisfactory ratings for Bank operations by the year 2000 and that a longer-term goal of 80 percent or higher is feasible. The proportion of projects with satisfactory outcomes, as evaluated by OED at the fiscal year of exit, increased from an average 67 percent for fiscal 1990–95 to 71 percent in fiscal 1996 and, based on a partial (about half) sample, to 76 percent in fiscal 1997. OED found that borrower performance—the demonstrable assumption of ownership rights and responsibilities by the borrower for a project—is the most important factor contributing to the recent improvement in portfolio performance. The next most important determinants of success are the Bank's own performance and country economic conditions. Country policies and the overall quality of the institutional environment are also important for project success.

Evaluation has been influential in the redesign of Bank processes and policies:

• An OED study on large dams in fiscal 1998 led to the creation of an international commission that will set global standards for identifying, designing, constructing, and operating large dams.

• An evaluation of the Bank's post-conflict reconstruction activities led to the establishment of a new sector-specific policy.

- An evaluation of financial sector reform activities informed the recasting of the Bank's financial intermediary lending policies.

- At the initiative of the director general (DGO), OED, and the managing directors for operations, a Bankwide working group reviewed the process for implementation completion reports prepared by operational staff to find ways to make them more cost-effective and timely.

- An OED evaluation of the Special Program of Assistance for Africa (SPA), a fifteen-member donor partnership chaired by the Bank, contributed to a mid-term review of the partnership by SPA members.

OED strengthened its partnerships and evaluation capacity-building activities in fiscal 1998. Highlights include:

- OED and the Operations Evaluation Group of the IFC launched a joint evaluation of Foreign Investment Advisory Service activities in the private sector.

- OED continued to provide leadership to the multilateral development banks' Evaluation Cooperation Group and is supporting efforts by the Development Assistance Committee (DAC) of the Organisation for Economic Co-operation and Development (OECD) to strengthen and improve evaluation.

- With the Bank's Learning and Leadership Center and the Poverty Reduction and Economic Management (PREM) network, OED organized a seminar on evaluating public sector performance, which was attended by representatives from seven multilateral agencies and eight donor and borrower countries. In-country workshops and presentations for borrowers and country teams located in the field—some utilizing videoconferencing—are also becoming a standard dissemination and learning feature of OED's work.

Self-assessment. Using methodologies developed in consultation with OED, the Quality Assurance Group (QAG) encourages quality in Bank performance by monitoring the portfolio, undertaking assessments of a sample of the Bank's work, and catalyzing changes in Bank policies, programs, and processes based on assessment results. QAG has a small core staff and operates mainly through expert panels, which

are customized for each assignment and are drawn from Bank managers and staff as well as experts from outside the Bank.

The *Annual Report on Portfolio Performance (ARPP)* for fiscal 1997, prepared by QAG, indicated a turnaround in portfolio health over the past couple of years. The change reflected improved economic management in a number of borrowing countries, more proactive portfolio management, and greater selectivity in lending decisions. The ARPP signaled the importance of consolidating and furthering these gains by maintaining close attention to priority problem areas, improving the quality of supervision and reporting, and enhancing further quality at entry.

During fiscal 1998, QAG supported these goals primarily through the portfolio improvement program (PIP) and by ensuring the quality of Bank products through assessments of quality at entry, supervision, and economic and sector work.

The PIP targeted risky countries, sectors, and instruments for increased management attention. These included eighteen country management units, five sectors or subsectors, two lending instruments (technical assistance and financial intermediary lending), and thirty-nine operations at risk. Several targeted country portfolios have shown significant improvement (Guinea, Jamaica, Madagascar, Nigeria, Turkey, Venezuela, and Yemen). Portfolio management tools were further refined in fiscal 1998, including the concept of "projects at risk," which identifies projects that may not achieve their objectives; a realism index, which is a measure of the accuracy of self-reporting on project quality; and a proactivity index, which reflects timely response to problem projects. The level of projects at risk declined and the proactivity index improved during the year.

The quality assessment program covered about 15 percent of the portfolio and initiated reviews of economic and sector work. The introduction of rapid assessments covering about 250 ongoing projects and about 100 recently approved projects provided more information on portfolio quality and a baseline for future monitoring. These assessments found about 30 percent of projects with less than satisfactory supervision, and about 20 percent with less than satisfactory quality at entry. The rapid assessments will be undertaken annually to assess progress in achieving the goal of 100 percent satisfactory quality at entry and supervision.

In addition, in-depth assessments of quality at entry undertaken before board presentation covered about twenty projects. Thematic quality reviews of projects under implementation covered about twenty-five projects including biodiversity and education projects in Africa and public sector management projects in Europe and Central Asia, among others. The quality of about thirty economic or sector reports was assessed. The results of these assessments were shared with country and network managers and staff in order to improve ongoing and future operations.

Performance indicators. The initial set of performance indicators developed in fiscal 1997 was aggregated into a performance scorecard,

and indicators were refined and modified as the Bank gained experience with them through fiscal 1998. While the entire portfolio was retrofitted with indicators in fiscal 1998, work to improve them and assist borrowers in their use intensified.

A framework for the new scorecard has been developed. When completed, the scorecard will link the ultimate development outcomes ("why" the Bank is in the development business) through the effectiveness of Bank assistance strategies ("what" the Bank decides to undertake) with business processes and capacity ("how" the Bank is carrying out its business). The scorecard will summarize performance on about twelve dimensions based on qualitative and quantitative indicators, and it will be monitored, together with corporate priorities, through an information system. The Bank is examining additional indicators to those proposed by the DAC *(see box 2 in Overview section)*, with a view to adding greater specificity and clarity to development outcomes. Income growth,

Figure 4-1. IBRD and IDA Commitments and Disbursements, Fiscal Years 1994–98
(US$ millions)

Note: Excludes guarantees and loans to the IFC.
IBRD data for 1996 includes the refinanced/rescheduled overdue charges of $168 million for Bosnia and Herzegovina.

for example, will be included in the Bank scorecard because of its fundamental role in poverty reduction.

The scorecard also includes indicators that measure the Bank's responsiveness to clients and collaboration with partners. This is being done through surveys in coordination with CAS cycles. Operational effectiveness and responsiveness will continue to be measured by indicators of the timeliness, volume, and quality of Bank products and services. New approaches are also being developed to evaluate the Bank's knowledge management and human resource development efforts.

Commitments and guarantees

World Bank commitments (IBRD and IDA combined) increased by 49.3 percent to reach $28,593.9 million in fiscal 1998 (*see figure 4-1*). One World Bank guarantee, totaling $184 million, was approved by the executive directors.

Adjustment lending amounted to 39 percent of Bank commitments, (compared to the previous year's 26.5 percent). The fiscal 1998 adjustment total includes $10 million in rehabilitation import loans and $85 million in debt reduction loans (*see table 4-1*).

Two projects in the West Bank and Gaza, totaling $20.7 million and funded from the Trust Fund for Gaza and the West Bank, were approved.

Assisting the poorest. In fiscal 1998 assistance to the poorest countries, those with a per capita gross national product (GNP) of $786 or less (in terms of constant 1997 U.S. dollars) totaled $7,847.5 million—$1,386.1 from the IBRD, and $6,461.4 from IDA (*see figure 4-2*).

Some 40.1 percent of total Bank investment lending during the year was directly targeted to the poor compared to 29 percent the year before. These projects supported activities to increase the productivity of and economic opportunities of the poor, develop their human resources, and provide social safety nets (*for a description of each such targeted projects, turn to the Project Summaries*).

In fiscal 1998, total commitments from IDA (including grant commitments of $75 million) reached $7,583 million (*see figure 4-1*), $2,961 million higher than in fiscal 1997 and 33 per-

cent above the fiscal 1995–1997 average. Most of the increase took place in Africa and South Asia, mainly reflecting significant policy improvements in some African countries and greater implementation capacity in large South Asian countries with overall good policy performance. Another important factor was the completion of the Bank's renewal process, which had resulted in inevitable delays in the pace of commitments in fiscal 1997.

In addition to regular IDA lending commitments, the first IDA heavily indebted poor countries (HIPC) grant for $75 million was approved in fiscal 1998 as part of the Uganda Education Sector Adjustment Operation, which also included an $80 million credit. IDA grants are one of the instruments used to support the HIPC Debt Initiative during a country's "interim period."[3] The Uganda education grant represents a reduction in that country's debt of $27 million in net present value terms.

The Debt-Reduction Facility for IDA-Only Countries provides grant funds to heavily indebted IDA-eligible countries, which use these funds to buy back their commercial debt at a deep discount. Three operations (Côte d'Ivoire, Togo, and Vietnam) were completed in fiscal 1998 under the Facility's auspices. Of these, Côte d'Ivoire and Vietnam were Brady-type debt and debt-service reduction (DDSR) operations, and Togo was a cash buy-back operation. The operations for Côte d'Ivoire and Togo utilized $25.1 million in IBRD resources from the Facility and $154.9 million in cofinancing to extinguish a total of $769.4 million in eligible principal debt. The Facility contributed $1 million toward the advisory services for the

3. Under the HIPC Debt Initiative, the "interim period" is the three-year period between the "decision point," the point at which a country's eligibility for relief under the initiative is confirmed by a debt sustainability analysis, and the "completion point," the point at which a country has achieved a sustainable debt situation through debt rescheduling and stock-of-debt reductions from multilateral and bilateral creditors. During the interim period, a country undertakes a broad-based program of adjustment and reform in partnership with the Bank and the International Monetary Fund (IMF), which includes maintaining sound macroeconomic management, improving the quality of public expenditure, strengthening institutional capacity, and enhancing the delivery of social services.

TABLE 4-1. WORLD BANK ADJUSTMENT OPERATIONS, FISCAL YEAR 1998

(amounts in millions of US dollars)

| Country | Project | World Bank financing | | |
		IBRD	IDA	Total
Sector adjustment loans				
Bolivia	Capitalization Program Adjustment Credit (IDA reflows)	0.0	2.9	2.9
Cape Verde	Economic Reforms Support	0.0	30.0	30.0
Côte d'Ivoire	Private Sector Development Adjustment	0.0	36.6	36.6
Côte d'Ivoire	Transport Sector Adjustment/Investment Program	0.0	180.0	180.0
Guyana	Private Sector Development (IDA reflows)	0.0	1.5	1.5
Mauritania	Public Resource Management Credit (IDA reflows)	0.0	0.4	0.4
Mexico	Second Contractual Savings Development	400.0	0.0	400.0
Morocco	Contractual Savings Development Loan	100.0	0.0	100.0
Nicaragua	Financial Sector Adjustment Credit	0.0	70.0	70.0
Russia	Coal Sector Adjustment Loan II	800.0	0.0	800.0
Pakistan	Banking Sector Reform	250.0	0.0	250.0
Uganda	Education Sector Adjustment Operation	0.0	80.0	80.0
Uruguay	Contractual Savings Structural Adjustment Loan	100.0	0.0	100.0
Structural adjustment loans				
Albania	Rehabilitation Project	0.0	25.0	25.0
Argentina	Pension Reform Adjustment Loan (Salta)	75.0	0.0	75.0
Argentina	Pension Reform Adjustment Loan (San Juan)	50.0	0.0	50.0
Argentina	Pension Reform Adjustment Loan (Rio Negro)	75.0	0.0	75.0
Argentina	Pension Reform Adjustment Loan (Tocuman)	100.0	0.0	100.0
Armenia	Structural Adjustment Credit II	0.0	60.0	60.0
Azerbaijan	Structural Adjustment Credit	0.0	70.0	70.0
Bosnia and Herzegovina	Public Finance Structural Adjustment Credit	0.0	63.0	63.0
Bulgaria	Financial and Enterprise Sector Adjustment Loan	100.0	0.0	100.0
Cameroon	Second Structural Adjustment Credit (IDA reflows)	0.0	18.1	18.1
Cameroon	Third Structural Adjustment Credit	0.0	180.0	180.0
Georgia	Structural Adjustment Credit II	0.0	60.0	60.0
Ghana	Private Sector Adjustment	0.0	2.4	2.4
Ghana	Economic Reform Support Operation	0.0	50.0	50.0
Guinea	Public Expenditure Management Adjustment Credit	0.0	70.0	70.0
Honduras	Public Sector Modernization Structural Adjustment Credit (IDA reflows)	0.0	14.2	14.2
Hungary	Public Sector Adjustment Loan	150.0	0.0	150.0
Kazakhstan	Public Sector Resource Management Adjustment Loan	230.0	0.0	230.0
Kazakhstan	Pension Reform Adjustment Loan	300.0	0.0	300.0
Kenya	Structural Adjustment Credit	0.0	17.5	17.5
Korea, Republic of	Emergency Assistance Loan	3,000.0	0.0	3,000.0
Korea, Republic of	Structural Adjustment Loan	2,000.0	0.0	2,000.0
Malaysia	Economic Recovery and Social Sector Loan	300.0	0.0	300.0
Mexico	Health System Reform	700.0	0.0	700.0
Moldova	Structural Adjustment Loan II	55.0	45.0	100.0
Russia	Structural Adjustment Loan II	800.0	0.0	800.0
Senegal	Energy Sector Adjustment Credit	0.0	100.0	100.0
Tanzania	Structural Adjustment Credit I (IDA reflows)	0.0	2.6	2.6
Thailand	Finance Companies Restucturing Loan	350.0	0.0	350.0
Yemen, Republic of	Financial Sector Adjustment Credit	0.0	80.0	80.0
Debt-reduction loans				
Côte d'Ivoire	Commercial Debt Restructuring Program	0.0	50.0	50.0
Vietnam	Debt Reduction Loan	0.0	35.0	35.0
Rehabilitation-import loans				
Tajikistan	Post-Conflict Rehabilitation Credit	0.0	10.0	10.0
Total		9,935.0	1,354.2	11,289.2

Vietnam operation, which provided debt relief of 50 percent and addressed approximately $800 million of debt; an IDA DDSR credit of $35 million was used to cofinance the operation.

Disbursements and procurement

Gross disbursements by the IBRD to countries totaled $19,232 million, an increase of 37 percent over fiscal 1997's $ 13,998 million. IDA disbursements in fiscal 1998 reached $5,704 million (includes $74 million of development grants), of which $4,444 million was for investment projects; the overall level was only slightly below the record high of $5,979 million in fiscal 1997 *(see figure 4-1)*, reflecting sustained implementation efforts across all regions.

Disbursements by source of supply. Projects financed by the World Bank require procurement from foreign and local sources to achieve project goals. Disbursements are made primarily to cover specific costs for foreign procurement and some local expenditures.

Figure 4-2. IBRD and IDA Lending to the Poorest Countries, Fiscal Years 1989–98
(US$ millions)

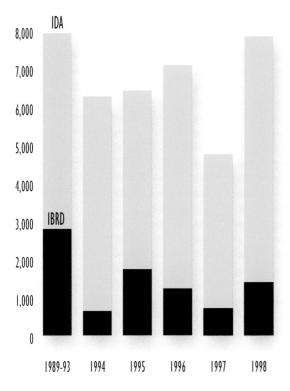

Note: The poorest countries are defined as those with a per capita income of $785 or less in 1997 U.S. dollars.

The procurement rules and procedures to be followed in the execution of each project depends on individual circumstances. Four considerations generally guide the Bank's requirements:
- economy and efficiency in the execution of a project;
- opportunity for all eligible bidders from borrowing and nonborrowing member countries to compete in providing goods and works financed by the Bank;
- development of local contractors and manufacturers in borrowing countries; and
- transparency in the procurement process.

In addition, in the face of growing concern about corruption in public procurement, a fraud and corruption provision is being added to all Bank standard bidding documents. The Bank prescribes conditions under which preferences may be given to domestic or regional manufacturers and, where appropriate, to domestic contractors.

Table 4-2 shows consolidated foreign and local disbursements for the IBRD and IDA through the end of fiscal 1993 and for period fiscal 1994 through fiscal 1998. Advance disbursements consist of payments made into special accounts of borrowers, from which funds are paid to specific suppliers as expenditures are incurred. Because balances in these accounts cannot be attributed to any specific supplying country until expenditures have been reported to the Bank, these are shown as a separate category.

Table 4-3 provides details on foreign disbursements by countries eligible to borrow from the World Bank and nonborrowing countries[4] for the IBRD and IDA separately.

Appendix 7 shows disbursements made in fiscal 1998 by the IBRD and IDA for local procurement by current borrowing countries and disbursements made for goods, works, and services procured from them by other Bank borrowers (foreign procurement) for projects funded by the Bank.

Appendix 8 shows the amounts disbursed from the IBRD and IDA separately for foreign procurement of goods, works, and services from

---

4. Appendix 6 list countries eligible for IBRD and IDA funds.

TABLE 4-2.   IBRD AND IDA DISBURSEMENTS FOR FOREIGN AND LOCAL EXPENDITURES

(amounts in millions of US dollars)

Period	IBRD and IDA						
	Foreign[a]		Local		Net advance disbursements[b]		Total amount
	Amount	%	Amount	%	Amount	%	
Cumulative to June 30, 1993	122,285	57	85,617	40	4,803	2	212,705
Fiscal 1994	9,010	56	7,442	47	-473	-3	15,979
Fiscal 1995	9,094	51	8,724	49	-97	—	17,720
Fiscal 1996	10,013[c]	52	8,787	46	456	2	19,256
Fiscal 1997	8,733	44	10,543	53	487	2	19,763
Fiscal 1998	14,218	57	10,112	41	449	2	24,779
Cumulative to June 30, 1998	173,352	56	131,224	42	5,625	2	310,201

NOTE: *Foreign expenditures are expenditures in the currency of any country other than that of the borrower or guarantor, for goods or services supplied from the territory of any country other than the territory of the borrower or guarantor. Local expenditures are expenditures in the currency of the borrower or guarantor or for goods or services supplied from the territory of the borrower or guarantor. Details may not add to totals because of rounding.*

a. *Amounts exclude debt-reduction disbursements of $3,038 million through FY93, $655 million in FY95, $213 million in FY97, and $82 million in FY98. Amounts include disbursements under simplified procedures for structural and sectoral adjustment loans of $556 million in FY96, $3,333 million in FY97, and $9,540 million in FY98.*

b. *Net advance disbursements are advances made to special accounts net of amounts recovered (amounts for which the Bank has applied evidence of expenditures to recovery of the outstanding advance).*

c. *Disbursements for FY96 include the refinanced/rescheduled overdue charges of $168 million for Bosnia and Herzegovina.*

selected member countries in fiscal 1998 and cumulatively through fiscal 1998.

Appendix 9 shows the proportion of foreign disbursements from the IBRD and IDA for specific categories of goods and services provided by selected member countries in fiscal 1998.

Appendix 10 provides a summary listing of the amounts paid to eligible World Bank borrowing country suppliers and nonborrowing country suppliers in each fiscal year from 1996 to 1998 under investment projects. Amounts disbursed are compared with respect to significant categories of goods procured from foreign suppliers. The extent to which eligible borrowing countries and nonborrowing countries participated in supplying these major categories of goods in each of the past three fiscal years is also compared.

Under simplified procedures for structural and sectoral adjustment loans approved by the executive directors in fiscal 1996, disburse-ments are no longer directly linked to procurement under adjustment loans. Thus, while appendixes 7 to 10 report on disbursements from the IBRD and IDA, they do not include disbursements under adjustment loans. The information in appendix 11 reflects adjustment loan disbursements to each borrower as pro-rata shares of that borrower's eligible imports from supplying countries using import data drawn from United Nations trade statistics.

In all these tables and appendixes, IBRD figures excludes disbursements for loans to the IFC and "B" loans. IDA figures include Special Facility for Sub-Saharan Africa and Interim Trust Fund credits. Disbursements for Project Preparation Facility advances are excluded for both the IBRD and IDA.

Strengthening partnerships

To help implement the Bank's commitment to strengthening partnerships with countries, development institutions, civil society, and the private sector, the Partnerships Group was established in 1997. It is helping transform the culture and practice of the Bank's work with partners, and will support a partnership knowledge database to help the development community at large.

The group's first task was to set up the Development Grant Facility (DGF) to bring together all of the Bank's grant-making activities under one umbrella *(see box 4-2)*. The group also coordinates partnership relations with foundations, the DAC, and the multilateral development banks. During the fiscal year, a partnerships strategy paper, laying out a strategy for enhancing development effectiveness through partnerships that place the country at the center of its development process, was reviewed by the executive directors. And partnership framework discussions were launched on a pilot basis with bilateral and multilateral development partners.

A roundtable on new approaches to commodity risk management in developing countries and meetings with the Council on Foundations and other new Bank partners were held in fiscal 1998.

Cofinancing and trust funds

Through its cofinancing and trust fund programs, the World Bank promotes financial partnerships to implement its strategic agenda and maximize the development impact of its operations. The cofinancing and trust funds program is a concrete financial manifestation of the Bank's broad partnership with other members of the international community.

Trends in cofinancing. In fiscal 1998 a significant turnaround in cofinancing activity reversed a four-year decline *(see table 4-4)*. The level of cofinancing mobilized through operations in the environment and the social sectors—in particular in education—continued to increase, accounting for 23 percent of the total, up from 13 percent in fiscal 1997. The number of cofinanced operations increased to 123 mobilizing $ 9,717 million in additional resources for the Bank's client countries, compared to 122 operations for $7,675 million in fiscal 1997.[5] Official

5. Cofinancing figures represent planned cofinancing at the time of Bank approval of each operation. The official cofinancing amounts shown, in most cases, are firm commitments at this stage; export credits and private cofinancing, however, are generally only estimates, to be firmed up during project implementation.

TABLE 4-3. IBRD AND IDA DISBURSEMENTS FOR FOREIGN EXPENDITURES, BY SOURCE OF SUPPLY

(amounts in millions of US dollars)

| | IBRD | | | | | IDA | | | | |
| | Countries not eligible to borrow | | Countries eligible to borrow | | Total | Countries not eligible to borrow | | Countries eligible to borrow | | Total |
Period	Amount	%	Amount	%	amount	Amount	%	Amount	%	amount
Cumulative to										
June 30, 1993	80,431	89	10,422	11	90,853	25,795	82	5,637	18	31,432
Fiscal 1994	4,260	78	1,197	22	5,457	2,435	69	1,118	31	3,553
Fiscal 1995	4,787	81	1,109	19	5,896	2,116	66	1,081	34	3,197
Fiscal 1996	5,264	77	1,541	23	6,806	1,762	66	891	34	2,652
Fiscal 1997	3,082	86	521	14	3,602	1,374	76	425	24	1,798
Fiscal 1998	2,734	85	468	15	3,202	1,103	75	374	25	1,477
Cumulative to										
June 30, 1998	100,557	87	15,257	13	115,815	34,584	78	9,526	22	44,110

NOTE: *Amounts exclude disbursements for debt reduction, net advance disbursements, and disbursements under simplified procedures for structural and sectoral adjustment loans. Countries eligible to borrow from IBRD and IDA are listed in Appendix 6. For consistency of comparison, the Republic of Korea is included as a country eligible to borrow for all periods covered by this table. Korea became eligible to borrow in December 1997. Details may not add to totals because of rounding.*

BOX 4-2   DEVELOPMENT GRANT FACILITY

The DGF became effective in October 1997. It aims to enhance the Bank's ability to make strategic choices in grantmaking based on institution-wide priorities and is a vital element of the Bank's work with partners. The DGF supports activities that are not suited to loans or credits and do not fit within the Bank's country-focused operational programs. DGF grants leverage Bank funds through partnerships that provide resources for innovations, cutting-edge approaches, and pilot projects.

At the end of fiscal 1998 the DGF was supporting some forty partnership initiatives in key sectors of Bank work. Examples include:
- in agriculture, with the Consultative Group on International Agricultural Research;
- in health, with riverblindness control programs;
- in capacity building, with the Institutional Development Fund and the Consultative Group to Assist the Poorest;
- in environment, with the Global Water Partnership; and
- in education, with the International Program for Improvement of Educational Outcomes.

The DGF's Annual Report will provide information on the status of grant programs and results achieved. Each year management recommends proposals for Bank participation in DGF-sponsored programs to the executive directors for the following fiscal year, including any plans for disengagement from ongoing programs.

DGF's budget of $122.1 million was approved for fiscal 1998.

---

sources of cofinancing continued to account for the largest share (78 percent), of which the Inter-American Development Bank (IDB) provided $537 million, the European Union (EU) institutions $914 million, and Japan $2,098 million, the largest amount. Specific investment loans remained the most attractive Bank lending instrument for cofinanciers (61 percent), particularly for infrastructure, water supply and sanitation, as well as social sector operations. Overall, the ratio of cofinancing to lending, excluding two large and quick-disbursing loans to the Republic of Korea, remained at 41 percent, about the same as in fiscal 1997.

Operations in South Asia attracted a significant level of cofinancing in fiscal 1998, raising 72 additional cents for each U.S. dollar lent. Cofinancing activities also increased significantly in the Middle East and North Africa, where a guarantee operation leveraged large amounts of private sector financing. However, the volume of cofinancing dropped in East Asia, due mainly to the financial crisis, and in Latin America and the Caribbean, due to changes in the composition of the Bank's lending program (*see figure 4-3 and table 4-5*).

TABLE 4-4   TOTAL IBRD AND IDA LENDING AND COFINANCING OPERATIONS, FISCAL YEARS 1995–1998

(amounts in millions of US dollars)

	1995	1996	1997	1998
	Amount	Amount	Amount	Amount
Lending[a]	22,522	21,352	19,142	23,594[c]
Cofinancing[b]	8,774	8,304	7,675	9,717
Cofinancing/Lending (ratio)	39.0	38.9	40.1	41.2

a. IDA commitments include $75 million in grants committed under the HIPC Debt initiative.

b. Based on cofinancing plans presented at the time of Board approval. Includes cofinancing with Bank loans, IDA credits and Bank guarantees and projects financed by Bank-managed trust funds.

c. This figure excludes $5,000 million in special loans to the Republic of Korea in the context of economic crisis.

Highlights for the year include:

• The Special Program of Assistance for Africa (SPA) remained one of the Bank's most important partnership programs. Now in its fourth phase (1997–99), donors and supporting institutions have pledged about $5,000 million—in addition to World Bank and IMF financing—in highly concessional, quick-disbursing cofinancing and coordinated assistance to support eligible countries' economic reform programs. In this phase, the SPA donors, in close coordination with recipient governments, will focus on improving aid effectiveness through greater harmonization and streamlining of implementation procedures. To this end, participating donors agreed to support pilot efforts to move toward common implementation arrangements for four sector programs.

• The reconstruction program in Bosnia and Herzegovina attracted $339 million in cofinancing support for six projects.

• Export credit cofinancing continued to recover, reaching $861 million from a ten-year low in the mid-1990s.

• Private cofinancing remained at about the same level as last year, amounting to $1,230 million, including one guarantee for $184 million, compared to $372 million in fiscal 1997.[6]

Trends in trust funds. The most significant trust fund developments in fiscal 1998 were a deceleration of the rate of external contributions to the trust-funds and a rapid and effective donor response to requests for assistance to deal with the financial crisis now affecting several

6. Private cofinancing includes parallel lending, NGO, and foundation grant support and guarantees.

FIGURE 4-3   Cofinancing by Region, Fiscal Years 1997–98
(US$ millions)

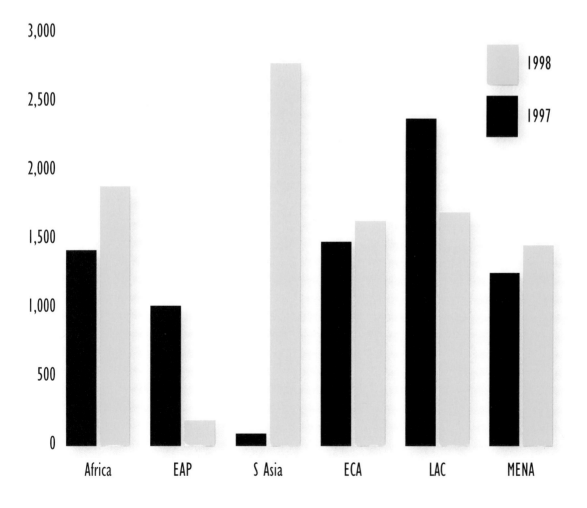

(amounts in millions of US dollars)

Region and year	Projects cofinanced No.	Amount	Official[a] No.	Amount	Export credit No.	Amount	Total private No.	Amount	(of which IBRD guarantees) No.	Amount	World Bank contribution IBRD	IDA	Total project costs
Africa													
1997	28	1,426	27	1,161	—	—	2	266	—	—	—	756	2,727
1998	34	1,899	34	1,747	1	60	3	92	—	—	57	1,667	7,972
East Asia and Pacific													
1997	16	1,022	13	297	3	320	2	405	—	—	2,306	174	8,552
1998	9	196	9	196	—	—	—	—	—	—	89	339	834
South Asia													
1997	5	93	5	93	—	—	—	—	—	—	—	285	544
1998	13	2,795	13	2,235	—	—	1	560	—	—	840	1,431	18,155
Europe and Central Asia													
1997	32	1,488	30	719	1	161	4	608	(2)	(320)	1,011	380	3,311
1998	33	1,647	33	1,647	—	—	2	—	—	—	1,606	259	4,001
Latin America and the Caribbean													
1997	26	2,384	26	2,384	—	—	—	—	—	—	2,797	12	9,866
1998	21	1,710	21	1,026	1	291	1	394	(1)	(56)	1,001	244	5,294
Middle East and North Africa													
1997	15	1,262	14	983	1	130	2	149	(1)	(52)	536	135	4,801
1998	13	1,469	13	775	1	510	2	184	(1)	(184)	285	155	2,854
Total													
1997	122	7,675	115	5,637	5	611	10	1,427	(3)	(372)	6,650	1,742	29,802
1998	123	9,717	123	7,626	3	861	9	1,230	(1)	(184)	3,878	4,095	39,109

— Zero.

NOTE: *The number of operations shown under different sources add up to a figure exceeding the total number of cofinanced projects because a number of projects were cofinanced from more than one source. Cofinancing data are reported by the fiscal year in which the project is presented to the Bank's Executive Board. Details may not add to totals because of rounding.*

a. These figures include cofinancing with untied loans from the Export-Import Bank of Japan

Bank member countries (*see box 4-3*). Despite a slowdown in external contributions, the demand for trust fund program resources continued to be strong. Trust fund disbursements grew to $1,100 million (*see figure 4-5 and table 4-6*). Trust fund resources enabled the Bank to finance a variety of activities consistent with the goals of its strategic agenda including debt relief, technical assistance, emergency reconstruction, and lending development.

The main impetus for growth in overall trust fund resources in fiscal 1998 came from the World Bank's own contributions to support mainly the HIPC Debt Initiative Trust Fund. External contributions to trust funds, measured in U.S. dollar equivalent, declined due mainly to severely constrained official development assistance programs and the realignment of major donor currencies vis-à-vis the U.S. dollar (*see figure 4-5*). The largest external contributors to the trust fund program were Japan ($209 million), the Netherlands ($143 million), Norway ($92 million), the United Kingdom ($76 million), and the United States ($64 million). The World Bank's contribution totaled $387 million.

Japan continued to make important contributions to the Bank's programs of assistance through the Policy and Human Resources Development (PHRD) Fund—even though contributions fell to $152 million from $175 million in fiscal 1997. This contraction resulted from the combined effect of a reduction in the level of

yen contributions and the depreciation of the yen. The PHRD Fund continued to support five important ongoing programs:
- technical assistance for project preparation;
- the Japanese Consultant Trust Fund;
- training and research at the Economic Development Institute;
- scholarships for graduate students from member countries; and
- post-conflict reconstruction.

In addition the PHRD Fund financed other important initiatives, such as a program of financial advisory services to help countries deal with the financial crisis in East Asia (*see box 4-3*); an action program to facilitate private sector participation in infrastructure activities; financial support to help alleviate debt of heavily indebted poor countries; and a program to advance capacity building in Africa.

The Consultant Trust Fund (CTF) program continued to finance activities consistent with the Bank's strategic agenda for issues of special interest to the development community, such as the environment, gender, governance, and participation. CTF disbursements grew in fiscal 1998 to $74.3 million. The CTF program helps to broaden the pool of expertise the Bank draws on to support its operational work, including economic and sector studies, policy-oriented studies, project appraisal, supervision and evaluation, and advisory services to client countries.

Implementation of the HIPC Debt Initiative gained momentum in fiscal 1998 (*see also table 2 in the Overview and box 5-1*). The HIPC Trust

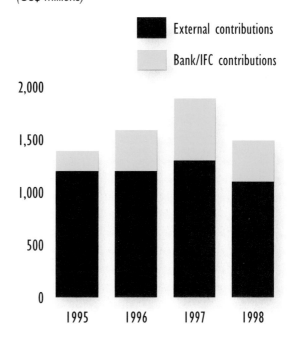

FIGURE 4-4
Trust Fund Contributions, Fiscal Years 1995–98
(US$ millions)

Fund received signed pledges from ten bilateral donors, totaling $134 million, and two multilateral contributors—the African Development Bank and the Nordic Development Fund (NDF)—totaling $14 million. Cash contributions amounted to $72 million from bilateral donors (of which $48 million was received in fiscal 1998) and $1 million from the NDF. In addition, the World Bank component of the HIPC Trust Fund—to be used to provide relief on IDA

BOX 4-3 RESPONDING TO THE EAST ASIAN FINANCIAL CRISIS

In fiscal 1998 the Bank and the donor community pooled resources to help meet the demand for advisory services to address the severe social and economic fallout of the financial crisis in Asia. Two major initiatives started during the year:

• The government of Japan provided $4.7 million (and committed another $6.9 million) through the PHRD Fund for initial funding to launch the Bank's Financial Sector Advisory Program (FSAP) in response to financial crises in Asian countries. The FSAP will provide technical assistance support to help

these countries address critical issues in financial sector management and banking reform.

• The Bank also agreed to administer the Asian European Meeting-European Union (ASEM-EU) Asia Financial Crises Response Fund. The United Kingdom, France, the European Commission (EC), and several other donors pledged over $35 million to this effort. Contributions from other European and Asian donors are anticipated. The fund will finance technical assistance in both the financial and social sectors, initially in seven countries in Asia.

TABLE 4-6. TRUST FUND DISBURSEMENTS, FISCAL YEARS 1997–1998[a]

(amounts in millions of US dollars)

	1997	1998
Multidonor special programs		
Highly Indebted Poor Countries (HIPC) Trust Fund	0.0	0.0
Global Environment Facility (excluding GEF cofinancing trust funds)	178.0	184.4
West Bank and Gaza	116.6	75.0
Montreal Protocol/Ozone Trust Fund	54.7	60.7
Consultative Group on International Agricultural Research (CGIAR)	51.5	44.2
Onchocerciasis Control (ONCHO)	10.5	33.4
Brazilian Rain Forest	14.9	16.1
Other trust fund programs		
Policy and Human Resources Development (PHRD) Fund[b]	165.5	147.9
Consultant Trust Fund Program (CTFP)[c]	68.1	74.3
Institutional Development Fund	18.4	20.2
Other trust funds[d]	626.4	479.3
Total	1,304.6	1,135.5

a. These figures do not take into account provision of debt service on IDA debt by HIPC trust funds. The amounts earmarked for these purposes thus far are $47 million for Bolivia and $52 million for Uganda, which would disburse over the next three to five years.

b. These figures exclude the portion of PHRD that is allocated to the Japanese Consultant Trust Fund (1997: $4.3 million, 1998: $0.2 million)

c. These figures include the Japanese Consultant Trust Fund disbursements.

d. This category includes smaller programs and single-purpose trust funds that finance debt reduction, cofinancing, technical assistance, and other advisory services.

debt—received $250 million from the IBRD in fiscal 1998, bringing total Bank contributions to $750 million.

Cofinancing and trust fund management. In fiscal 1998 the Bank established the Trust Fund and Cofinancing (TFC) Department, within the Vice Presidency for Resource Mobilization and Cofinancing (RMC), to reinvigorate cofinancing and trust fund activities. The TFC carries out a number of activities to strengthen cooperation with its cofinancing partners. In fiscal 1998 cofinancing framework agreements were finalized with Belgium and Sweden. The Bank also established a Netherlands-World Bank Global and Regional Partnership Trust Fund to serve as an umbrella fund for most Netherlands-World Bank partnership activities. TFC held nineteen consultations with donors, with an agenda covering a broad range of issues, including the Bank's response to the East Asian financial crisis, implementation of the Strategic Compact, the poverty agenda, as well as exploring new partnership opportunities. The TFC kept donors informed of the Bank's external resource needs through its biannual "Cofinancing Opportunities with the World Bank" and a new publication on financial partnership opportunities entitled "Mobilizing Resources for Development,"[7] which covers major Bank programs with ongoing external resource requirements.

The Bank continued to strengthen trust fund management oversight by mainstreaming trust fund activities in Bank planning and budgeting processes and improving financial controls and accountability. It also launched a program to monitor and evaluate trust fund activities. New partnership opportunities were pursued with bilateral and private sector groups, including foundations, nongovernmental organizations, and corporations.

7. "Cofinancing Opportunities with the World Bank" and "Mobilizing Resources for Development" can be obtained through the Resource Mobilization and Cofinancing (RMC) Vice Presidency.

Technical assistance

Because technical assistance loans (TALs) have historically shown comparatively poor performance, the Bank undertook a comprehensive study of the 190 TALs completed and evaluated since 1986 and 150 active TALs. A predictive model for the likelihood of success of a TAL was drawn up from the results. The outlook is encouraging: the study shows TALs' rate of success is likely to improve in the immediate future because countries with active TALs are those with improving economic policy environments and because the Bank has exercised more selectivity in its use of TALs in recent years.

The Bank has long used technical assistance loans as multipurpose lending instruments for a variety of development programs. Because they have often been relied on to meet difficult objectives—such as initial operations for new borrowers and for purposes that have not always received high-priority attention—they have also long been among the lending instruments most at risk for unsatisfactory outcomes. But contrary to the impression this gives—of an instrument that reduces portfolio quality—TALs are not very different from other Bank lending instruments. When they are examined in the context of the countries in which they operate, TALs perform similarly to other types of projects. The analysis found that TALs are not inherently more demanding, complex, or risky than any other type of project. There are some factors, within the control of the Bank or borrowers, or both, that can make a difference in performance, including selectivity based on borrower commitment and speed with which a TAL is put in place. These are being addressed.

TALs are, and will remain, an important tool. This prompted Bank management to assign more focused attention to technical assistance in fiscal 1998. To ensure consistent, specialized attention to the types of projects that TALs are supporting, and to improve the degree of knowledge sharing of good practice in technical assistance and technical cooperation, responsibility for these activities is being integrated into the Bank's public sector management operations.

Institutional Development Fund

Fiscal 1998 was the sixth year in which Institutional Development Fund (IDF) grants have been available for discrete, narrowly-targeted institution-building projects, primarily in poorer countries. IDF grants are usually provided for small projects (no more than $500,000) in countries where institution building is critical for success in governance and macroeconomic management, and where there is no imminent funding planned from the Bank or other donors to finance improvements in the area of need.

A review of IDF grants in May 1997 reported IDF grants have had a beneficial impact building up local capacity. Ninety percent of grants were judged satisfactory or better. IDF grants have also enabled the successful pioneering and testing of innovative approaches to institution building. In 1997 IDF grants included funding for the following projects:

• on-the-job training program for ten key staff of the Comoros government's privatization agency, which helped divest four state-operated utilities (air transport, gas, postal service, and telecommunications);

• a project in Ethiopia to help plan and implement gender-sensitive development inter-

FIGURE 4-5
Trust Fund Contributions and
Disbursements, Fiscal Years 1995–98
(US$ millions)

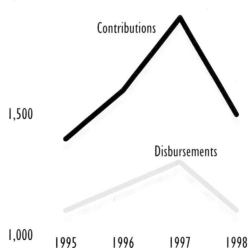

ventions to increase the economic participation of women and analyze constraints to the promotion of women's income-generating activities;

• a receiving station in Uganda for the African Virtual University, a project that is networking higher education institutions from East to West and North to South;

• a procurement improvement program (subscriptions to electronic mail and Internet access, for example) in Mali, where the system has been reformed through a new procurement code and procedural upgrading;

• development of competitive wholesale energy markets in China and Russia;

• a project to strengthen Indonesia's external development finance management and reverse a decline in the quality of economic analysis; and

• assistance to the Dominican Republic to set up an economic communications office to publicize the market-oriented policies recently adopted by the government.

Access to World Bank information

The new InfoShop, situated at the Bank's headquarters in Washington, D.C., was launched in November 1997 with the merger of the Public Information Center (PIC) and the World Bank Bookstore. The aim is to provide a one-stop shop to increase and facilitate greater public access to information about the Bank's work. The Bank also disseminates information to users worldwide from PICs in London, Paris, and Tokyo and from some of its resident missions. More than 5,000 World Bank documents are available to the public.

The expanded services of the InfoShop include a sales outlet for World Bank publications and operational documents; advice on how to search for Bank information; a comprehensive information and reference center; and facilities to demonstrate electronic media and video resources. The InfoShop carries material from other publishers of development-related subjects and partners such as the IMF and UN organizations.

In fiscal 1998 the InfoShop continued to improve and expand operations by increasing business hours to accommodate public demand and maintaining a telephone bank to respond to inquires on Bank publications, project-related information, and general information about the Bank. The InfoShop's Web site was revamped and reorganized to be more user friendly,[8] and electronic access to Bank information was increased through the Internet and CD-ROMs.

In fiscal 1998 the InfoShop responded to more than 15,500 requests for operational information, an increase of 17 percent over fiscal 1997. The increase is attributed to the merger of the PIC and the bookstore and to efforts to more widely make known the new information services. The business community remained the biggest users of PIC information (61 percent compared to 79 percent in fiscal 1997), followed by public agencies (12 percent compared to 7 percent in fiscal 1997), followed by academia at 6 percent and NGO's at 3 percent.

Administrative budget and corporate planning

The executive directors approved a total administrative budget of $1,423.9 million *(see appendix 5)* to carry out the Bank's fiscal 1998 work program and the Strategic Compact initiatives.[9] The budget reflected a decrease of 0.1 percent in real terms over fiscal 1997. The net administrative budget, which takes into account reimbursements and fee revenues that offset the costs of the programs not funded by the regular budget, amounted to $1,173 million, representing a reduction of 0.4 percent from the previous fiscal year. The decrease reflected the net impact of reduction in Bank contributions to the Staff Retirement Plan (SRP) and the charging of management fees for SRP and Retired Staff Benefits Plan to the respective assets instead of the administrative budget. (*Figure 4-6 shows* IBRD *and* IDA *income and expenditure at a glance.*)

The fiscal 1998 budget incorporated the vision outlined in the Strategic Compact of what the Bank wants to be in the year 2000: the most effective global development institution for fighting poverty. The budget supported programs to shift resources to front-line services (such as country services and the networks), develop new products for the Bank's clients, make knowledge an important element of develop-

8. http://www.worldbank.org/html/pic/PIC.html
9. This does not include $12.5 million, subsequently approved by the executive directors for the East Asian crisis.

◊§ Bangladesh

IDA (ITF)—$150 million. The first phase of the government's Primary Education Development Program, which will improve the quality and efficiency of the school system, particularly in underserved areas in the eastern region, will be supported. Total cost: $ 2,039.5 million.

‡§ Bhutan

IDA—$13.7 million. Basic education will be improved for some 8,000 students; an additional 5,000 student places will be available, particularly benefiting children from the poorest rural areas. Total cost: $21.18 million.

§ Bolivia

IDA—$75 million. Bolivia's education reform program will be complemented with activities to improve the quality of schooling and increase the number of years of schooling completed, particularly at the primary level. Girls in impoverished areas will especially benefit. Total cost: $116 million.

◊ Bosnia and Herzegovina

IDA (ITF)—$11 million. The provision of acceptable-quality education will be restored thereby improving school-age children's educational qualifications and productive potential. Total cost: $11 million.

◊ Brazil

IBRD—$155 million. The science and technology sector will be reformed and improved to promote scientific research and technological innovation. Total cost: $360 million.

§ Brazil

IBRD—$62.5 million. About 1.3 million primary school children, particularly those from the poorest regions, will benefit from more school places, adequate learning materials, certified and well-paid teachers, and committed parents. Total cost: $125 million.

Cameroon

IDA—$4.9 million. This learning and innovation loan will pilot a new model of public higher education that is more responsive to the needs of the economy. Total cost: $6.35 million.

◊§ Colombia

IBRD—$40 million. Basic education will be improved for poor and at-risk-of-violence communities in the department of Antioquia through better access to schools and better quality education. Total cost: $80 million.

◊‡§ Colombia

IBRD—$7.2 million. Some 95,000 children living in the municipality of Pasto (about 40 percent of whom live below the poverty line) will benefit from increased access to better-quality, basic education. Total cost: $12 million.

◊§ Côte d'Ivoire

IDA—$53.3 million. The government's National Education and Training Development Plan—one objective of which is to reach universal primary education by 2010—will be supported. Access to basic education will be increased in underserved areas. Total cost: $82.8 million.

◊§ El Salvador

IBRD—$58 million. The coverage of secondary schools will be expanded, including scholarship programs to low-income students, and their quality and efficiency improved. Total cost: $77.1 million.

◊‡§ El Salvador

IBRD—$88 million. This adaptable program loan will improve and expand the coverage, quality, and efficiency of education, especially in rural and marginal urban areas. Total cost: $119.1 million.

◊§ Ethiopia

IDA—$100 million. The first five-year phase of the Education Sector Development Program will be supported, which aims to achieve universal basic education by 2015 and improve overall educational attainment with greater social equity. Total cost: $1,799 million.

◊	Hungary	IBRD—$36.4 million. Youth unemployment will be reduced through improved vocational education. Total cost: $60.1 million.
	Hungary	IBRD—$150 million. The capacity of the higher education system will be increased and the quality and relevance of learning will be improved. Total cost: $250 million.
◊‡§	India	IDA—$152 million. Access and quality of primary education in the state of Bihar, particularly for disadvantaged groups, will be improved. Total cost: $199.7 million.
◊‡§	India	IDA—$59.4 million. Access and quality of primary education in Uttar Pradesh, particularly for disadvantaged groups, will be improved. Total cost: $75.7 million.
	Indonesia	IBRD—$103.5 million. The quality of basic education will be improved in West Java, and access to junior secondary education increased. Total cost: $130.2 million.
§	Lebanon	IBRD—$63 million. As part of Lebanon's reconstruction effort, the vocational and technical education system will be improved to make it more responsive to market needs and to give access to students from low-income families. Total cost: $68.87 million.
§	Macedonia, former Yugoslav Republic of	IDA—$5 million. More than fifty primary schools will be rehabilitated in predominately rural, high-poverty areas and the quality of education improved countrywide. Total cost: $12.6 million.
◊‡§	Madagascar	IDA—$65 million. More and better-trained students will graduate at all levels of education and at sustainable cost. And access to primary and secondary education in the poorest rural areas will be expanded. Total cost: $183 million.
◊	Malawi	IDA—$48.2 million. Secondary education will be expanded and improved. Total cost: $54.7 million.
◊‡§	Mexico	IBRD—$115 million. This adaptable program loan supports the government's compensatory education programs, working with poor, indigenous, and marginalized communities. Total cost: $150 million.
	Mexico	IBRD—$300 million. The generation, diffusion, and application of knowledge for innovation in support of economic and social development will be promoted. Total cost: $662.8 million.
◊§	Mexico	IBRD—$180.2 million. Access to higher education, particularly for financially needy students, will be improved and more effective and financially sustainable student loan institutions will be developed. Total cost: $287.9 million.
	Moldova	IDA—$5 million. This supplemental credit supports the General Education Project approved in fiscal 1997. Total cost: $20 million.
◊§	Pakistan	IDA—$22.8 million. More than a million children, particularly in poor areas, will benefit from improved school quality; overall elementary school enrollments in Northern Pakistan will expand by 28 percent; and the number of girls in school will double. Total cost: $36 million.
◊‡§	Pakistan	IDA—$250 million. Support for the Social Action Program will be continued to improve elementary education, primary health, population welfare, and rural water supply and sanitation services. Total cost: $1,270.2 million.

§   Romania   IBRD—$70 million. The quality and coverage of education in the poorest communities will be improved through rehabilitation of mainly rural schools and provision of adequate facilities. Total cost: $130 million.

§   Sri Lanka   IDA—$70.3 million. The quality, management, financing of, and access to, education programs will be improved. Deprived schools in slum areas will be targeted for improvement. Total cost: $83.4 million.

◊‡§ Tanzania   IDA—$20.9 million. School enrollments and the quality of learning will be raised in primary schools, and educational opportunities at the secondary level, particularly for poorer girls, will be improved. Total cost: $24 million.

◊   Tunisia   IBRD—$80 million. Access to quality higher education will be promoted and the public education sector will be improved. Total cost: $106.6 million.

◊§ Turkey   IBRD—$300 million. This adaptable program loan supports phase 1 of the government's basic education program aimed at achieving universal basic education coverage and improving its quality and relevance. Total cost: $2,512.2 million.

†   Uganda   IDA—$80 million. Budget support will be provided to implement the government's Universal Primary Education Policy, which supports universal primary education by offering all families free primary education for up to four children.

ELECTRIC POWER AND OTHER ENERGY

◊   Bangladesh   IDA—$235 million. Private participation in infrastructure development will increase thermal power generation capacity, enhance gas transmission infrastructure, and develop other infrastructure. Total cost: $886 million.

   Bosnia and   IDA—$25 million. Power generation, transmission, and distribution
   Herzegovina systems will be restored to reconnect consumers still without power after the war and reduce power outages and other quality of service defects. Total cost: $169.8 million.

◊§ Chad   IDA—$5.3 million. An economic and sustainable supply of energy will be provided for households, particularly those in poor areas, through a community-based participatory approach that includes environmental awareness. Total cost: $6.3 million.

   China   IBRD—$300 million. Power shortages in Hunan Province will be alleviated by providing an efficient, reliable, and environmentally sound power supply. Total cost: $747.2 million.

◊   China   IBRD—$250 million. Bottlenecks in power transmission infrastructure will be alleviated and the electricity trade commercialized in East China. Total cost: $888.6 million.

◊   Ethiopia   IDA—$200 million. Power sector efficiency and sustainability will be improved and electricity generation capacity increased. Total cost: $295.89 million.

	India	IBRD—$60 million. This adaptable program loan will support the first phase of the Haryana Power Sector Restructuring and Development Program by establishing a new legal, regulatory, and institutional framework and initiating privatization of power distribution. Total cost: $79.7 million.
	Kyrgyz Republic	IDA—$15 million. Supplemental financing will be provided to complete the rehabilitation of the Bishkek combined heat-and-power plant. Total cost: $116.2 million.
◊	Lao People's Democratic Republic	IDA—$34.7 million. Some 50,000 households in 520 rural villages without electric power will be connected to the electricity grid. Total cost: $39.3 million.
	Macedonia, former Yugoslav Republic of	IBRD—$35 million. Electricity generating reliability and efficiency will be improved and capacity expanded. Total cost: $39.6 million.
	Senegal	IDA—$100 million. Energy sector reforms to provide more efficient electricity service and lower energy prices will be supported, thereby improving competitiveness and growth prospects, increasing job opportunities, reducing deforestation, and raising rural incomes and employment.
	Turkey	IBRD—$270 million. Adequate transmission grid capacity will be developed in a timely and environmentally sustainable manner and power sector reform will be continued. Total cost: $502 million.
	Ukraine	IBRD—$200 million. The Kiev district heating system will be improved. Total cost: $308.9 million.
	Vietnam	IDA—$199 million. The transmission network will be strengthened, distribution systems rehabilitated and expanded, and the distribution network in areas affected by Typhoon Linda will be reconstructed. Total cost: $332 million.
◊	Zambia	IDA—$75 million. Reform and rehabilitation will put the power sector on a least-cost and financially sustainable path. Total cost: $203.59 million.

ENVIRONMENT

◊	Argentina	IBRD—$18 million. Pollution management will be improved. Total cost: $36 million.
	Azerbaijan	IDA—$20 million. Four of Azerbaijan's most urgent environmental problems will be addressed: declining sturgeon and caviar stocks, mercury contamination, industry pollution, and the lack of effective environmental institutions. Total cost: $24.5 million.
◊§	Brazil	IBRD—$51 million. Access to quality water supplies will be improved in poor, rural areas, and efficient and participatory management and use of water will be promoted, in the State of Bahia. Total cost: $85 million.
§	Brazil	IBRD—$198 million. Rational and sutainable use and participatory management of water resources will be promoted in Brazil, particularly in the Northeast. Access to water for domestic and productive purposes will improve the quality of life for some 1.3 million of Brazil's poorest people. Total cost: $330 million.

Bulgaria	IBRD—$16 million. This pilot project will reduce environmental hazards at a copper smelter and provide a model for addressing past environmental damages and liabilities in the process of privatization. Total cost: $25 million.	
◊ **China**	IBRD—$63 million. Sustained increases in energy efficiency will be achieved along with reductions in growth of carbon dioxide emissions and other pollutants. Total cost: $150.8 million.	
◊§ **China**	IBRD—$72 million; IDA—$20 million. The urban poor, women, and ethnic minorities will especially benefit from improvements in the environment of Nanning and Guilin. Total cost $175 million.	
China	IBRD—$95 million. Environmental conditions in Shandong Province will be improved and wastewater and water supply infrastructure will be overhauled, ensuring a water supply for over one million people. Total cost: $202 million.	
◊‡ **Dominican Republic**	IBRD—$3 million. Through a learning and participatory process, this learning and innovation loan will create the basis for a longer-term program to reverse environmental degradation. Total cost: $3.7 million.	
◊‡§ **Ecuador**	IBRD—$25 million. The incomes and quality of life of about 815,000 poor indigenous and Afro-Ecuadorian people will be improved through more secured access to land and financing for subprojects. Total cost: $50 million.	
◊ **Egypt**	IBRD—$20 million; IDA—$15 million. Industrial pollution, which causes adverse health effects and ecological degradation, will be reduced. Total cost: $48.7 million.	
◊‡ **Ghana**	IDA—$9.3 million. This adaptable program credit will implement the first phase of the Natural Resource Management Program to protect, rehabilitate, and sustainably manage national land, forest, and wildlife resources; the income of rural communities who own the resources will be increased. Total cost: $25.7 million.	
◊‡§ **Indonesia**	IBRD—$6.9 million. A framework for a national coral reef management system, including a community-based fisheries management program to assist poor fisherfolk, will be established. Total cost: $12.8 million.	
◊ **Latvia**	IBRD—$7.9 million. The country's largest waste disposal site will be remediated and improved. Total cost: $25.21 million.	
◊ **Peru**	IBRD—$150 million. The government's efforts to mitigate the potentially severe impact of the 1997-98 El Niño phenomenon will be supported. Total cost: $430 million.	
◊§ **Venezuela**	IBRD—$28 million. Environmental management will be strengthened, private environmental services fostered, and the national cartography system modernized. People's general health and living conditions, particularly those living in poor areas, will be improved. Total cost: $45 million.	
◊‡§ **Vietnam**	IDA—$21.5 million. Natural forests with high biodiversity will be protected and managed, and the living conditions of villagers in forty communes or towns, many of whom are living below the poverty level, will be improved. Total cost: $32.29 million.	

◊‡ Zimbabwe   IDA—$62.5 million. The government's ability to manage and protect wildlife and their habitats will be enhanced. Total cost: $75 million.

FINANCE

Bolivia   IDA—$20 million. Technical assistance will be provided to prepare laws and regulations for the financial, infrastructure, and business sectors; to implement a privatization and corporatization program; and to implement the government's reform program and support project management. Total cost: $32.34 million.

Bosnia and   IDA—$5 million. Private enterprise activities will be restarted and
Herzegovina   expanded in Republika Srpska resulting in increased economic activity, employment, and income. Total cost: $20 million.

Brazil   IBRD—$20 million. The Central Bank's modernization effort will be complemented by a program to professionalize banking supervision and mainstream international best practices. Total cost: $24.6 million.

Croatia   IBRD—$30 million. Fresh capital will be provided to expand or restructure private or newly privatized enterprises; commercial banks will be strengthened; and a market for medium- and long-term financing of investment projects will be fostered. Total cost: $52 million.

◊   Ecuador   IBRD—$21 million. The state's institutional framework for international trade management will be modernized and international trade market access will be increased. Total cost: $42.6 million.

Guyana   IDA—$1.5 million. Funds from IDA reflows will be made available to supplement the Private Sector Development Adjustment Credit approved in fiscal 1995.

Indonesia   IBRD—$20 million. The structure, resilience, soundness, and efficiency of the banking system will be improved. Total cost: $20.5 million.

†   Korea, Republic of   IBRD—$3,000 million. Balance of payments assistance will support the financial and real sector reform program; support government efforts to deal with the immediate liquidity crisis; and support the medium-term reform program, including assessing the adequacy and targeting of fiscal expenditure on social assistance programs.

†   Korea, Republic of   IBRD—$2,000 million. A part of the internationally coordinated support package, this loan will help Korea deal with its immediate foreign exchange crisis and implement major programs of structural reforms in the financial and real sectors, including strengthening social safety nets to cushion the impact of the crisis and of reforms, on poor and vulnerable people.

Macedonia, former   IBRD—$25 million. Private sector growth will be promoted and
Yugoslav Republic of   competition in the domestic credit markets stimulated to help integrate the country's banking sector into international financial markets.

Mexico   IBRD—$400 million. The second phase of the Contractual Savings Development Program will be supported, focusing on implementing the legal, regulatory, and institutional framework for reforming Mexico's old age security system.

Morocco	IBRD—$100 million. Contractual savings institutions, including insurance companies, savings banks, and the pension system, will be reformed to improve the allocation of savings to productive investment.
Poland	IBRD—$22 million. A credit market for municipal investment in the infrastructure sector will be promoted. Total cost: $40 million.
Thailand	IBRD—$350 million. Balance of payments assistance will support the restructuring of finance companies and restore confidence in the country's financial sector.
Thailand	IBRD—$15 million. The structure, resilience, and soundness of the financial sector will be improved. Total cost: $22 million.
Uruguay	IBRD—$100 million. Development of the capitalized system of individual pension accounts, established as part of Uruguay's 1996 pension reform, will be supported.
Vietnam	IDA—$35 million. Implementation of Vietnam's agreement with its London Club creditors to settle its commercial debt in arrears will be supported. Total cost: $54.03 million.
Yemen	IDA—$80 million. The performance of the banking system and its role in mobilizing savings and extending credit for productive activities will be improved.

HEALTH, NUTRITION AND POPULATION

§ Albania	IDA—$17 million. Health services will be restored thereby preventing outbreaks of communicable diseases, avoidable complications of common illnesses, and premature deaths. Total cost: $28 million.
◊ Armenia	IDA—$10 million. Armenia's health reform program will be supported. Total cost: $12.1 million.
◊‡§Bangladesh	IDA—$250 million. The quality of essential health and family planning services for vulnerable groups—particularly poor women and children—will be improved, public sector health and family planning services reformed, and the groundwork laid for broader health reform. Total cost: $2,895.9 million.
◊§ China	IDA—$85 million. About 45 million people in ten of China's poor provinces will benefit from improved basic health care. Total cost: $129.2 million.
§ Comoros	IDA—$8.4 million. Death from common diseases, particularly malaria, will be reduced; islands with the greatest numbers of poor people will particularly benefit. Total cost: $10 million.
◊§ Dominican Republic	IBRD: $30 million. Health care for the poorest people, particularly mothers and young children, will be expanded and improved. Total cost: $42 million.
◊‡§Ecuador	IBRD—$45 million. Health services will be expanded at the provincial and municipal levels to improve the health of poor and underserved people, particularly mothers and children under five years of age. Total cost: $65 million.

◊§	Egypt	IDA—$90 million. The first five-year phase of the government's comprehensive Health Sector Reform Program will be supported; poor people's access to basic health services will be especially targeted over the medium term. Total cost: $387 million.

◊§ **Egypt** — IDA—$90 million. The first five-year phase of the government's comprehensive Health Sector Reform Program will be supported; poor people's access to basic health services will be especially targeted over the medium term. Total cost: $387 million.

Eritrea — IDA—$18.3 million. The health of people living in rural and peri-urban areas will be improved, enhancing their quality of life and ability to participate in the country's socioeconomic development. Total cost: $21.1 million.

◊‡§ **Gambia** — IDA—$18 million. People living in rural and peri-urban areas will benefit from improved family health—including reproductive health, infant and child health, and good nutrition. Total cost: $19.9 million.

◊ **Ghana** — IDA—$35 million. Health sector reforms will be supported.

◊§ **Guinea-Bissau** — IDA—$11.7 million. The coverage and quality of health services will be increased and a minimum package of health care provided, principally benefiting women and children in poor areas. Total cost: $66.1 million.

◊‡§ **India** — IDA (ITF)—$76.4 million. An effective and sustainable health system will be established in Orissa. Poor people, women living in rural areas, and tribal people will especially benefit. Total cost: $90.7 million.

◊‡§ **India** — IDA (ITF)—$300 million. The nutrition and health of pre-school-aged children and women will be improved as the quality, impact, and cost-effectiveness of the Integrated Child Development Services program is improved in Kerala, Maharashtra, Rajasthan, Tamil Nadu, and Uttar Pradesh. Total cost: $422.3 million.

◊ **Indonesia** — IBRD—$42.5 million. The health of mothers and their newborn babies will be improved, unwanted pregnancies reduced, and adolescents prepared to lead a healthy reproductive life. Total cost: $61.9 million.

◊§ **Madagascar** — IDA—$27.6 million. The nutritional status of children and pregnant and lactating women will be improved through a community-based program. Total cost: $41.88 million.

◊§ **Mauritania** — IDA—$24 million. Health will be improved, especially for women, children, and underserved populations, through more accessible and affordable quality health services. Total cost: $191.6 million.

Mexico — IBRD—$700 million. The health system reform program will be supported.

◊ **Mexico** — IBRD—$25 million. Technical assistance will be provided to support the design and implementation of the health system reform program. Total cost: $30 million.

◊‡§ **Nicaragua** — IDA—$24 million. This adaptable program credit will finance the first phase of the Health Sector Modernization Program to improve the efficiency, effectiveness, and equity of the health system. The nutritional status of children under two years old and pregnant women living in poor areas will be improved. Total cost: $32 million.

◊§ **Philippines** — IBRD—$19 million. Services to ensure survival and promote the physical and mental development of children will be provided, particularly to those who are most vulnerable and disadvantaged. Total cost: $58.8 million.

◊§ Senegal	IDA—$50 million. Health will be improved, fertility lowered, and preventable infant and maternal death reduced, particularly among poor women and children under five living in peri-urban slums and rural areas.
Tunisia	IBRD—$50 million. The government's health sector reform program will be supported. Total cost: $101 million.
◊‡§Uganda	IDA—$34 million. Nutrition, health, and psycho-social and cognitive growth and development of children under six years of age will be improved. Total cost: $40 million.

INDUSTRY

Albania	IDA—$10.3 million. A political risks guarantee facility will help revive the private manufacturing sector. Total cost: $20.95 million.
◊‡§Bolivia	IDA—$62.8 million. People from 200 of the poorest rural municipalities will benefit from sustainable productive investments, based on local demand and generated through participatory planning. Total cost: $87.3 million.
West Bank and Gaza	Trust Fund for Gaza and West Bank—$10 million. About 50,000 people will benefit from jobs created as a result of private sector investment in the Gaza Industrial Estate and the creation of infrastructure for industry. Total cost: $84.5 million.

MINING AND OTHER EXTRACTIVE

◊ Argentina	IBRD—$39.5 million. Private investment in mining will be expanded. Total cost: $46.5 million.
◊ India	IBRD—$530 million; IDA—$2 million. Market-oriented coal sector reforms will be supported. Total cost: $1.697.6 million.
◊ Madagascar	IDA—$5 million. This learning and innovation credit will help lay the ground for private investment in mining and provide a training ground for long-term, developmentally sound, exploitation of the country's natural resources. Total cost: $7.75 million.
◊† Russia	IBRD—$800 million. The coal sector restructuring program will be supported to move the industry away from state support and increasingly toward privatization; the social safety net will be strengthened to meet the needs of those most affected by restructuring.

MULTISECTOR

Albania	IDA—$5 million. Government actions to facilitate private sector development, by improving the financial sector, macroeconomic management, and the legal framework, will be supported.
◊† Armenia	IDA—$60 million. Financial support to cover the short-term costs, including social safety nets, associated with continued economic reform will be provided.
◊ Armenia	IDA—$5 million. Technical assistance will be provided to enhance the government's capacity to implement the structural reform program supported by the Second Structural Adjustment Credit.

◊† **Azerbaijan**

IDA—$70 million. The government's efforts to accelerate structural reform, mainly in areas of trade liberalization, demonopolization and privatization, and banking, will be supported. Measures to mitigate the negative impact of utility price increases on poor households will be taken.

◊ **Cameroon**

IDA—$180 million. Cameroon's adjustment program will be supported to lay the groundwork for an increase in economic growth, to create jobs (especially for the young), and reduce poverty.

† **Cape Verde**

IDA—$30 million. The government's adjustment program—aimed at accelerating privatization, further liberalizing the economy, and maintaining a viable and stable macroeconomic framework necessary for growth, poverty reduction, and job creation—will be supported.

◊‡§ **Colombia**

IBRD—$5 million. This learning and innovation loan will support development of operational capacity of the *Consortium for the Program for Development and Peace of the Magdalena Medio Region* to reduce poverty and increase peaceful coexistence in the Region. Its success will contribute to the formulation of a national peace and development strategy and generate lessons for similar programs in other parts of the country. Total cost: $6.25 million.

Côte d'Ivoire

IDA—$50 million. The Commercial Debt Restructuring Program will be supported. Total cost: $237 million.

† **Georgia**

IDA—$60 million. Government reforms to strengthen public finance, develop the private sector, and reduce poverty will be supported.

Georgia

IDA—$5 million. Technical assistance to enhance the government's capacity to implement the Second Structural Adjustment Credit will be provided.

◊§ **Georgia**

IDA—$4.5 million. This learning and innovation credit will improve the management and promotion of Georgia's cultural heritage by testing approaches that could revive the tourism industry and engender social cohesion and national identity. Sites selected for rehabilitation and restoration house large numbers of very poor people. Total cost: $4.97 million.

◊ **Ghana**

IDA—$50 million. Support for completion of a phase in the Ghanaian economic reform program will be extended.

Ghana

IDA—$2.4 million. Funds from IDA reflows will be made available to help finance the Private Sector Adjustment Credit approved in fiscal 1995.

† **Guinea**

IDA—$70 million. Financial sustainability will be ensured, and public service effectiveness in sectors that benefit the poor—education, health, rural development, and road maintenance—will be improved.

Kenya

IDA—$17.5 million. Funds from IDA reflows will be made available to help finance the Structural Adjustment Credit approved in fiscal 1996.

Malawi

IDA—$2.4 million. Funds from IDA reflows will be made available to help finance the Fiscal Restructuring Deregulation Program Credit approved in fiscal 1996.

† **Malaysia**

IBRD—$300 million. The government's program of preemptive measures to stabilize the economy, resume medium-term growth, and protect the poor from the worst effects of the regional crisis will be supported.

◊† Moldova   IBRD—$55 million; IDA—$45 million. The government's economic reform program, including pension, compensation, and social benefits reform to protect vulnerable groups, will be supported.

Panama   IBRD—$12.7 million. Technical assistance will help improve the efficiency and quality, and expand the coverage, of infrastructure services. Total cost: $43.8 million.

Russia   IBRD—$800 million. The government's structural reform program will be supported.

† Tajikistan   IDA—$10 million. Funding for critical inputs and support for the social safety net to protect the most vulnerable people will be provided to help restore post-conflict production, employment, and consumption.

Tanzania   IDA—$2.6 million. Funds from IDA reflows will be made available to finance the Structural Adjustment Credit approved in fiscal 1997.

Thailand   IBRD—$15 million. The government's capacity to manage the economy in the aftermath of the currency and banking crisis will be improved. Total cost: $20 million.

OIL AND GAS

Bosnia and Herzegovina   IDA—$10 million. The gas transmission and distribution system will be reconstructed to restore a safe and reliable gas supply. Total cost: $44 million.

Brazil   IBRD—$130 million. A gas pipeline from Rio Grande in Bolivia to São Paulo in Brazil will help develop a gas market in South/Southeast Brazil and help create an export alternative for Bolivian gas. Total cost: $2,086 million.

PUBLIC SECTOR MANAGEMENT

Argentina   IBRD—$5 million. This learning and innovation loan will develop and implement a model court program in twelve Federal First Instance Courts. Total cost: $6.8 million.

Bolivia   IDA (ITF)—$15 million. The government's transition to a decentralized structure will be supported through modernization of the public sector's auditing and financial monitoring capabilities. Total cost: $17.3 million.

◊ Bolivia   IDA—$25 million. The disruption, loss of life, and deterioration of living standards resulting from El Niño will be minimized. Total cost: $28.3 million.

Bolivia   IDA—$2.9 million. Funds from IDA reflows will be made available to help finance the Capitalization Program Adjustment Credit approved in fiscal 1996.

Bosnia and Herzegovina   IDA—$63 million. Support for establishing public finance structures and implementing reform policies at the state and entity levels will be provided.

Brazil   IBRD—$250 million. The state of Rio de Janeiro's privatization and concession program will be supported, and urban transport and utility services will be delivered more efficiently. Total cost: $5,900 million.

Brazil	IBRD—$170 million. The state of Minas Gerais' privatization and concession program will be supported. Total cost: $1,360 million.
Brazil	IBRD—$5 million. This learning and innovation loan is providing technical assistance to help State Governments address, and move through the initial phases of, pension reform. Total cost: $10 million.
Bulgaria	IBRD—$100 million. The government's enterprise and banking sector reforms will be supported.
Cameroon	IDA—$18.1 million. Funds from IDA reflows will help finance the Second Structural Adjustment Credit approved in fiscal 1996.
Côte d'Ivoire	IDA—$12 million. Dependence on traditional exports will be reduced and the share of high value-added products in the export structure increased; foreign investment will be attracted and domestic investment promoted; and a more secure legal and judicial environment for new investors and existing businesses will be created. Total cost: $23.3 million.
Côte d'Ivoire	IDA—$36.6 million. Funds from IDA reflows will be made available to help finance the Private Sector Development Adjustment Credit approved in fiscal 1996.
◊ Ecuador	IBRD—$60 million. Emergency support for prevention and restoration of damaged infrastructure caused by El Niño will be provided. Total cost: $66 million.
Eritrea	IDA—$53 million. Development of Eritrea's human resources will help overcome bottlenecks to implementing the national development program and sustaining rapid economic growth. Total cost: $66 million.
Guatemala	IDA—$28.2 million. The creation of a Superintendency of Tax Administration to promote taxpayer compliance with tax laws, strengthen enforcement mechanisms, and enhance citizens' understanding of the rights and responsibilities within the new tax system will be supported. Total cost: $40.3 million.
Guatemala	IBRD—$15.7 million. Reforms initiated under the Integrated Financial Management Project will be expanded to increase the efficiency and transparency of public sector financial management and control. Total cost: $18 million.
◊§ Guinea	IDA—$5 million. This learning and innovation credit will test a performance-based capacity-building program methodology to transform microfinance agencies from donor-financed development projects into sustainable financial institutions. Total cost: $17 million.
Honduras	IDA—$14.2 million. Funds from IDA reflows will be made available to finance the Public Sector Modernization Structural Adjustment Credit approved in fiscal 1996.
† Hungary	IBRD—$150 million. Support for a comprehensive program of pension system reform will be provided, including introduction of a social assistance program for poor people who do not qualify for the minimum pension.
◊‡§ Indonesia	IBRD—$225 million. Rural incomes will be raised, *kecamatan* and village government and community institutions strengthened, and public infrastructure built through labor intensive methods. Total cost: $273 million.

Kazakhstan	IBRD—$230 million. More effective public resource mobilization and use will result from a wide ranging institutional and policy reform program.
Mauritania	IDA—$0.4 million. Funds from IDA reflows will be made available to finance the Public Resource Management Credit approved in fiscal 1996.
◊‡ Mongolia	IDA—$5 million. The government's financial management system will be improved and more effective revenue mobilized through introduction of a value-added tax on goods and services. Total cost: $5.5 million.
§ Morocco	IBRD—$70 million. About 4 million people's living standards will be improved as basic infrastructure services are provided to small- and medium-sized municipalities, which account for most of Morocco's underdeveloped areas. Total cost: $110.3 million.
◊ Nicaragua	IDA—$70 million. Support for undertaking major reforms in the state banking sector, and improving financial intermediation and the regulatory framework for private banking, will be provided.
Pakistan	IBRD—$250 million. Reforms to stabilize the economy and restructure the banking sector will be supported.
◊ Peru	IBRD—$22.5 million. The justice system will be improved, enabling an improved environment for private sector development and better access to better-quality justice for citizens. Total cost: $31.6 million.
Togo	IDA—$30 million. The state's role in productive and service activities will be reduced and private sector participation will be promoted. Total cost: $35.71 million.
Ukraine	IBRD—$16.4 million. The government's efforts to implement an automated treasury system for effective budget execution and cash management will be supported. Total cost: $16.4 million.
Uzbekistan	IBRD—$28 million. Enterprises will be restructured; revenue from sales and foreign direct investment will be increased through privatization; and public participation in capital markets will be wider. Total cost: $47.7 million.
Venezuela	IBRD—$8 million. Productive enterprises and transport infrastructure will be transferred to the private sector in four pilot states, and new competition and regulatory frameworks will be established for airports and ports. Total cost: $19.8 million.
◊ Venezuela	IBRD—$4.7 million. This learning and innovation loan will improve the Supreme Court's performance—transparency, efficiency of administration and case management, and timeliness of decisions—and through a demonstration effect, should facilitate further judicial reform. Total cost: $7.3 million.
Yemen	IDA—$1.5 million. A supplemental credit will complement the Institutional Development for Public Administration Project approved in fiscal 1989.

SOCIAL PROTECTION AND OTHER SOCIAL SECTOR

† Albania	IDA—$25 million. The economic recovery program, addressing key structural weaknesses that contributed to the recent crisis and reducing poverty and unemployment generated by the crisis, will be supported.

◊‡§ Angola — IDA—$5 million. This learning and innovation credit will test a program to reintegrate displaced people and revitalize community activities, and serve as a basis for a larger post-conflict social project. Total cost: $5.9 million.

◊§ Argentina — IBRD—$284 million. The third phase of a social safety net program will be supported. Through execution of small infrastructure facilities it will improve living standards and create employment for poor workers. Total cost: $1,077 million.

◊‡§ Benin — IDA—$16.7 million. A social fund will support essential basic assets and services to poor communities, especially women and unemployed youth. Total cost: $20.5 million.

◊§ Comoros — IDA—$11.5 million. About 250,000 of the country's poorest people will benefit from replenishment of a social fund to support community initiatives, create employment, and improve access to basic social services. Total cost: $13.7 million.

◊‡§ India — IBRD—$301.3 million; IDA—$241.9 million. Support will be provided for priority expenditure in Andhra Pradesh's nutrition, primary health and education, rural roads and irrigation sectors, and public enterprise reform. Total cost: $830 million.

◊§ Jordan — IBRD—$5 million. This pilot project, targeted at the unemployed poor, will introduce an efficient and effective linkage between public expenditures for short-term training and business needs. Total cost: $6 million.

† Kazakhstan — IBRD—$300 million. Support will be provided for the pension reform law that was inaugurated in January 1998.

◊‡§ Mali — IDA (ITF)—$21.5 million. Poverty will be reduced in the most vulnerable rural communities through the financing of high priority subprojects identified by communities. Total cost: $23 million.

◊§ Philippines — IDA—$10 million. Access to basic economic and social infrastructure, services, and employment opportunities will be increased for people living in the poor and most conflict-affected areas of the Special Zone for Peace and Development. Total cost: $15.33 million.

§ Romania — IBRD—$5 million. This learning and innovation loan will test and promote community-based child welfare approaches to child care and reintegrating Bucharest's street children more fully into society. Total cost: $29.5 million.

◊§ Russia — IBRD—$28.6 million. Technical assistance, training, and equipment provision will support implementation of reforms in pensions, social assistance, social protection, child allowance, and unemployment assistance. Total cost: $35.95 million.

◊ West Bank and Gaza — Trust Fund for Gaza and West Bank—$10 million. Services to poor and marginalized people will be strengthened and expanded using NGOs as the delivery mechanism. Total cost: $17 million.

◊‡§ Zimbabwe — IDA—$60 million. The capacity of poor communities to organize themselves and plan and implement self-help projects will be strengthened and poverty monitoring will be improved. Total cost: $73 million.

TELECOMMUNICATIONS AND INFORMATION TECHNOLOGY

Indonesia	IBRD—$34.5 million. Private sector participation in the provision of information technology (IT) will be enhanced and IT and communications services will be modernized. Total cost: $53.2 million.
Organization of Eastern Caribbean States	IBRD—$3.6 million; IDA—$2.4 million. Pro-competition reforms will be introduced in the telecommunications sector and the supply of informatics-related skills increased in Dominica, Grenada, St. Kitts and Nevis, St. Lucia, and St. Vincent and the Grenadine. Total cost: $10.2 million.
Romania	IBRD—$30 million. Telecommunications sector reform will be supported and existing public sector telecommunications facilities will be privatized. Total cost: $44 million.

TRANSPORTATION

Albania	IDA—$17 million. The efficiency and capacity of the port of Durres will be improved. Total cost: $23 million.
Argentina	IBRD—$450 million. Roads will be rebuilt and upgraded and private sector investment in transport will be promoted. Total cost: $929 million.
Bosnia and Herzegovina	IDA (ITF)—$39 million. Primary transport networks will be rehabilitated and key transport links with the rest of Europe reconstructed, and Republika Srpksa's fiscal and trade reforms will be supported. Total cost: $184 million.
Brazil	IBRD—$45 million. Urban transport will be integrated as two suburban rail networks in São Paulo are linked. Private sector participation in the operation and management of the rail system will be increased. Total cost: $95.1 million.
Brazil	IBRD—$186 million. The quality of Rio de Janeiro's urban transport services will be improved and operating subsidies will be reduced. Total cost: $372.5 million.
China	IBRD—$200 million. Accessibility to the city center of Guangzhou will be improved through a more efficient and environmentally sustainable urban transport system. Total cost: $586.1 million.
◊‡ China	IBRD—$123 million. More efficient and productive inland waterway transport will reduce transport costs in Guangdong and Jiangsu Provinces as well as other inland provinces. Total cost: $289.3 million.
China	IBRD—$250 million. This third of a series of projects for the Jingzhu expressway in Guangdong, Hunan, Hubei, Henan, and Hebei Provinces will build on its predecessors to support an integrated approach to expressway corridor development. Total cost: $679 million.
China	IBRD—$230 million. Transport efficiency and safety will be improved along high priority highways and access to poor counties improved in Inner Mongolia, Gansu, and Ningxia Provinces. Total cost: $658.7 million.
Côte d'Ivoire	IDA—$180 million. Transport sector reform will be supported and funding for physical investments, maintenance, and capacity building in road transport and port subsectors will be provided. Total cost: $944.1 million.

	Egypt	IDA—$2 million. This learning and innovation credit will support development of regulatory, institutional, and financial arrangements to enable private sector participation in, and privatization of, the country's ports. Total cost: $2.3 million.
	Eritrea	IDA—$30.3 million. The productivity and capacity of the ports of Massawa and Assab will be increased. They will be rehabilitated and upgraded and the level of services raised to international standards. Total cost: $57.6 million.
	Ethiopia	IDA—$309.2 million. IDA's share in supporting the multi-donor Rural Sector Development Program will support improvements in access to markets and better transport services for rural people. Total cost: $2,757 million.
‡	Guatemala	IBRD—$66.7 million. Rural roads will be better administered and maintained, and will be improved in the region most affected by internal conflict before the 1996 Peace Accords. Total cost: $136.5 million.
	Indonesia	IBRD—$234 million. Transportation will be more efficient and accessible within the four provinces of the Northern Sumatra region and adjacent regions. Total cost: $369.3 million.
	Nepal	IDA—$23.5 million. Transport costs of Nepal's imports and exports will be reduced and customs procedures streamlined. Total cost: $28.5 million.
	Nicaragua	IDA—$47.4 million. Nicaragua's ongoing road rehabilitation program will be supported. Total cost: $108.5 million.
§	Niger	IDA—$28 million. Road conditions and road maintenance will be improved, especially in rural areas where the poorest people will benefit. Total cost: $30.5 million.
◊	Poland	IBRD—$300 million. The road sector will be modernized and flood-damaged roads and bridges will be repaired. Total cost: $540 million.
	Rwanda	IDA—$45 million. Supplemental financing will be provided to the ongoing Transport Sector Project.
◊	Togo	IDA—$50 million. Road improvements will reduce overall transport costs. Total cost: $55 million.
	Tunisia	IBRD—$50 million. This adaptable program loan will implement the first phase of a program promoting better, cheaper, and less polluting transport services. This phase focuses on the port and railway subsectors and strengthening overall transport sector management. Total cost: $80.2 million.
	Uganda	IDA—$30 million. Road sector management capability will be strengthened. Total cost: $33 million.
	Uganda	IDA—$27.6 million. Emergency recovery assistance will restore and rehabilitate roads and bridges severely damaged by flooding associated with the El Niño weather pattern. Total cost: $30 million.
◊	Vietnam	IDA—$73 million. The capacity, efficiency, and safety of inland waterway transport in the Vietnamese Mekong Delta will be enhanced. Total cost: $84.9 million.

| Yemen | IDA—$5.8 million. This supplemental credit for the Multi-Mode Transport project will finance additional work on the Harad-Huth Road project, necessitated by difficult and unforeseen geological problems which arose during construction. Total cost: $52.3 million. |

◊ **Zambia** — IDA—$70 million. The road network will be improved. Interventions are specifically targeted to rural areas where feeder roads will be rehabilitated and maintained to help reduce transport costs, increase mobility, and increase small-scale farmers' incomes. Total cost: $460 million.

URBAN DEVELOPMENT

◊‡ **Albania** — IDA—$10 million. Essential infrastructure will be extended to unserviced or neglected areas of greater Tirana. Total cost: $15.86 million.

◊§ **Algeria** — IBRD—$150 million. Living and housing conditions will be improved for people living in some 50,000 urban-slum and low-income households. Total cost: $218.3 million.

◊ **Argentina** — IBRD—$100 million. The province of Tucuman will reform and restructure its government to ensure efficient and responsive delivery of public services, notably social services, within fiscally sound policies.

◊ **Argentina** — IBRD—$75 million. The province of Rio Negro will reform and restructure its government to ensure efficient and responsive delivery of public services, notably social services, within fiscally sound policies.

Argentina — IBRD—$50 million. The province of San Juan will reform and restructure its government to ensure efficient and responsive delivery of public services, notably social services, within fiscally sound policies.

Argentina — IBRD—$75 million. The province of Salta will reform and restructure its government to ensure efficient and responsive delivery of public services, notably social services, within fiscally sound policies.

Argentina — IBRD—$42 million. The government's efforts to protect human lives and infrastructure, and rehabilitate damage sustained from the impacts of the 1997-98 El Niño phenomenon, will be supported. Total cost: $60 million.

◊ **Bosnia and Herzegovina** — IDA—$17 million. Reconstruction of Republika Srpska's agriculture, housing, water and sanitation, and electric power sectors will be supported. Total cost: $65 million.

China — IDA—$28.4 million. About 25,000 people living in impoverished areas damaged by a January 1998 earthquake will benefit from restoration of homes, schools, and health centers. Total cost: $40.6 million.

Colombia — IBRD—$75 million. The credit market for providers of urban public services will be expanded and solidified as long-term financing for urban infrastructure investments is enhanced. Total cost: $125 million.

Côte d'Ivoire — IDA (ITF)—$10 million. The efficiency and equity of urban land and housing markets will be improved. Total cost: $12 million.

Croatia — IBRD—$40.6 million. War damage to water sector infrastructure will be repaired and rebuilt, including clearing land mines in Eastern Slavonia, Baranja, and Western Srijem. The negative environmental impacts likely to occur to the adjacent nature park by the restart of local agriculture will be mitigated. Total cost: $61.1 million.

◊‡§ Georgia   IDA—$20 million. Access to basic social and economic services, especially for the poorest people, will be improved by rehabilitating existing infrastructure. Total cost: $28.3 million.

§   Georgia   IDA—$20.9 million. The ongoing decentralization process to foster the development of strong local governments will be supported. Basic services for vulnerable groups will be improved, and employment for low- and unskilled labor will be generated. Total cost: $26 million.

◊   Jordan   IBRD—$32 million. Sustainable and environmentally sound tourism will be increased, urban infrastructure developed, and the environment protected. Total cost: $44 million.

◊§ Jordan   IBRD—$30 million. About 1.6 million poor people's living conditions will be improved through provision of small-scale infrastructure. Total cost: $140 million.

Moldova   IDA—$15.9 million. A national unified real estate registration program will be developed to establish clear and enforceable ownership rights, promote the privatization of land, and develop a real estate market. Total cost: $24.6 million.

◊   Mongolia   IDA—$16.7 million. The quality of life of people living in informal housing areas of the capital Ulaanbaatar, including the urban poor, will be improved by provision of urban services and water supplies. Total cost: $23.6 million.

◊   Poland   IBRD—$200 million. Basic infrastructure will be restored in communities that were affected by the devastating flood of July 1997; urgent repairs will be made to the flood management system; and institutional capacity for flood management and mitigation will be improved. Total cost: $498.2 million.

◊‡§ Senegal   IDA—$75 million. Responsibility and accountability for urban services and infrastructure will be shifted to municipalities, which will improve their quality, particularly in low-income urban neighborhoods.

◊   Tajikistan   IDA—$10 million. Support for reintegrating the Karategin-Tavildara Valley area into the national economy through reconstruction of physical and social infrastructure, and emergency support of agriculture development, will help implement the Peace Agreement. Total cost: $11 million.

Uzbekistan   IBRD—$24 million. Tashkent's municipal solid waste management system will be restored. Total cost: $56 million.

WATER SUPPLY AND SANITATION

Armenia   IDA—$30 million. Emergency improvements will be made to the drinking water supply, in particular to reach the poor. The groundwork will be laid for private sector involvement in water supply and wastewater services. Total cost: $35.5 million.

◊§ Brazil   IBRD—$150 million. Water supply and sewage collection and treatment services will be expanded and improved. About 65 percent of beneficiaries are the urban poor. Total cost: $300 million.

Cambodia   IDA—$31 million. Drinking water quality and access will be improved in

Cambodia's two biggest cities. Total cost: $41.64 million.

◊ Croatia
IBRD—$36.3 million. Municipal wastewater pollutant discharges into the Kastela and Trogir Bays will be reduced; the safety, reliability, and delivery of drinking water improved; and water and wastewater utility performance improved to attract private sector participation. Total cost: $261.5 million.

◊‡ Lesotho
IBRD—$45 million. The capacity to transform water, Lesotho's principal natural resource of abundance, into export revenues will be put in place, providing the lowest cost alternative for supplying water to the Gauteng region. Total cost: $1,132 million.

◊§ Madagascar
IDA—$17.3 million. Cost-effective water supply and sanitation coverage will be expanded, particularly in rural areas where some 300,000 people will benefit from access to safe water. Total cost: $22.3 million.

Mauritius
IBRD—$12.4 million. Health and sanitary conditions will be improved and environmental pollution from wastewater will be reversed. Total cost: $65.6 million.

◊‡§Morocco
IBRD—$10 million. About 1.3 million rural people living in the poorest provinces will have improved access to safe, potable water. Total cost: $120 million.

Mozambique
IDA—$36 million. Sustainable water supply and sanitation services will be increased in five cities. Total cost: $56.9 million.

◊§ Paraguay
IBRD—$40 million. Poverty will be reduced, and productivity and health improved, as 340,000 people in impoverished communities gain access to water supply services and 140,000 to sewage disposal systems. Total cost: $55.7 million.

◊‡ Philippines
IBRD—$56.8 million. Sewerage, sanitation, and drainage investments will be financed in four cities and technical assistance provided to pilot and field-test a privatized public performance audit system in the metropolitan waterworks and sewerage system. Total cost: $80.7 million.

Turkey
IBRD—$13.1 million. The quality and reliability of the water supply will be improved and sewerage network rehabilitated in the Cesme-Alacanti area. Total cost: $24 million.

◊§ Uzbekistan
IBRD—$75 million. Safe drinking water, improved hygiene education, and sanitation facilities will be provided to two of the poorest regions, reducing the incidence of water-borne diseases. Total cost: $117 million.

A project must meet at least one of two criteria to be included in the PTI: (a) the project includes a specific mechanism for identifying and reaching the poor; or (b) the proportion of the poor among project beneficiaries is significantly larger than their proportion in the overall population. An adjustment operation is considered to be poverty-focused when it meets at least one of the following criteria: (a) it reorients public expenditures in favor of the poor, including spending on basic social services and rural infrastructure; (b) it eliminates distortions and regulations that limit poor people's access to labor and credit markets, productive resources, and basic social services—as well as policy-induced distortions in input or output pricing—in order to help the poor to increase their income-generating opportunities; (c) or it supports safety nets that protect the most vulnerable.

Member	Governor	Alternate
Afghanistan	(vacant)	(vacant)
Albania	Arben Malaj	Fatos Ibrahimi
Algeria	Abdelkrim Harchaoui	Ali Hamdi
Angola	Emmanuel Moreira Carneiro	Sebastiao Bastos Lavrador
Antigua and Barbuda +	John E. St. Luce	Ludolph Brown
Argentina	Roque Benjamin Fernandez	Pedro Pou
Armenia	Armen R. Darbinian	Garnik Nanagulyan
Australia	Peter Costello	Kathy Sullivan
Austria	Wolfgang Ruttenstorfer	Hans-Dietmar Schweisgut
Azerbaijan	Elman Siradjogly Rustamov	Fuad Akhundov
Bahamas, The +	Hubert A. Ingraham	Ruth Millar
Bahrain +	Ibrahim Abdul Karim	Zakaria Ahmed Hejres
Bangladesh	Shah A.M.S. Kibria	Masihur Rahman
Barbados +	Owen S. Arthur	Erskine R. Griffith
Belarus +	Gennady V. Novitsky	Vladimir N. Shimov
Belgium	Jean-Jacques Viseur	Alfons Verplaetse
Belize	Manuel Esquivel	Yvonne S. Hyde
Benin	Albert Tevoedjre	Felix Adimi
Bhutan	Dorji Tshering	Yeshey Zimba
Bolivia	Edgar Millares Ardaya	Miguel Lopez Bakovic
Bosnia and Herzegovina	Mirsad Kurtovic	Drago Bilandzija
Botswana	Ponatshego H.K. Kedikilwe	O.K. Matambo
Brazil	Pedro Sampaio Malan	Gustavo Henrique de Barroso Franco
Brunei Darussalam +	Haji Hassanal Bolkiah	Haji Selamat Haji Munap
Bulgaria +	Muravei Radev	Martin Zaimov
Burkina Faso	Tertius Zongo	Patrice Nikiema
Burundi	Astere Girukwigomba	Minani Evariste
Cambodia	Keat Chhon	Sun Chan Thol
Cameroon	Justin Ndioro	Daniel Njankouo Lamere
Canada	Paul Martin	Huguette Labelle
Cape Verde	Antonio Gualberto do Rosario	Jose Ulisses Correia e Silva
Central African Republic	Christophe Bremaidou	Anicet-Georges Dologuele
Chad	Ahmat Hamid	Abderhamane Dadi
Chile	Eduardo Aninat	Joaquin Vial
China	Xiang Huaicheng	Jin Liqun
Colombia	Antonio J. Urdinola	Cecilia Lopez
Comoros	Nidhoim Attoumane	Abdallah M'Sa
Congo, Democratic Republic of	Fernand Tala-Ngai	Jean-Claude Masangu Mulongo
Congo, Republic of	Paul Kaya	Alexandre Mbaloula
Costa Rica	Leonel Baruch	Eduardo Lizano Fait

Member	Governor	Alternate
Côte d'Ivoire	Daniel Kablan Duncan	N'Goran Niamien
Croatia	Borislav Skegro	Josip Kulisic
Cyprus	Christodoulos Christodoulou	Antonis Malaos
Czech Republic	Ivan Pilip	Pavel Kysilka
Denmark	Poul Nielson	Ellen Margrethe Loj
Djibouti	Yacin Elmi Bouh	Hawa Ahmed Youssouf
Dominica	Julius C. Timothy	Cary A. Harris
Dominican Republic	Hector Manuel Valdez Albizu	Luis Manuel Piantini M.
Ecuador	Marco Flores	Galo Perez Granja
Egypt, Arab Republic of	Atef Mohamed Mohamed Ebeid	Yousef Boutros Ghali
El Salvador	Manuel Enrique Hinds	Gino Bettaglio
Equatorial Guinea	Antonio Nve Ngu	Miguel Abia Biteo
Eritrea	Gebreselassie Yosief	(vacant)
Estonia +	Mart Opmann	Agu Lellep
Ethiopia	Sufian Ahmed	Girma Birru
Fiji	James Ah Koy	Savenaca Narube
Finland	Sauli Niinisto	Pekka Haavisto
France	Dominique Strauss-Kahn	Jean Lemierre
Gabon	Jean Ping	Richard Onouviet
Gambia, The	Famara L. Jatta	Yusupha A. Kah
Georgia	Mikhail Chkuaseli	Vladimer Papava
Germany	Carl-Dieter Spranger	Juergen Stark
Ghana	Richard Kwame Peprah	Victor Selormey
Greece	Yannos Papantoniou	Christos Pachtas
Grenada	Keith Mitchell	Brian Francis
Guatemala	Jose Alejandro Arevalo Alburez	Edin Homero Velasquez Escobedo
Guinea	Elh. Th. Mamadou Cellou Diallo	Cellou Dalein Diallo
Guinea-Bissau	Issufo Sanha	Paulo Gomes
Guyana	Bharrat Jagdeo	Michael Shree Chand
Haiti	Fred Joseph	Fritz Jean
Honduras	Gabriela Nunez de Reyes	Emin Barjum Mahomar
Hungary	Peter Medgyessy	Zoltan Bodnar
Iceland	Halldor Asgrimsson	Fridrik Sophusson
India	Yashwant Sinha	Montek Singh Ahluwalia
Indonesia	Bambang Subianto	Miranda S. Goeltom
Iran, Islamic Republic of	Hossein Namazi	Aliakbar Arabmazar
Iraq	Issam Rashid Hwaish	Hashim Ali Obaid
Ireland	Charlie McCreevy	Paddy Mullarkey
Israel	Jacob A. Frenkel	Ben-Zion Zilberfarb
Italy	Antonio Fazio	Mario Draghi

Member	Governor	Alternate
Jamaica +	Omar Lloyd Davies	Wesley Hughes
Japan	Hikaru Matsunaga	Masaru Hayami
Jordan	Rima Khalaf Hunaidi	Nabil Suleiman Ammari
Kazakhstan	Sauat M. Mynbaev	Yerzhan A. Utembayev
Kenya	Simeon Nyachae	Margaret Chemengich
Kiribati	Beniamina Tinga	Taneti Maamau
Korea, Republic of	Kyu Sung Lee	Chol-Hwan Chon
Kuwait	Ali Salem Al-Ali Al-Sabah	Bader Meshari Al-Humaidhi
Kyrgyz Republic	Talaybek J. Koichumanov	Urkaly T. Isaev
Lao People's Democratic Republic	Xaysomphone Phomvihane	Phiane Philakone
Latvia	Roberts Zile	Laimonis Strujevics
Lebanon	Fuad A.B. Siniora	Nabil Al-Jisr
Lesotho	Leketekete Victor Ketso	Molelekeng E. Rapolaki
Liberia	Elias E. Saleeby	Sandra P. Howard
Libya	Mohamed A. Bait Elmal	Bashir Ali Khallat
Lithuania +	Algirdas G. Semeta	Jonas Niaura
Luxembourg	Luc Frieden	Jean Guill
Macedonia, Former Yugoslav Republic of	Taki Fiti	Zlatka Popovska
Madagascar	Pierrot J. Rajaonarivelo	Constant Horace
Malawi	Cassim Chilumpha	Ted A. Kalebe
Malaysia	Anwar bin Ibrahim	Aris Othman
Maldives	Fathulla Jameel	Adam Maniku
Mali	Ahmed El Madani Diallo	Soumaila Cisse
Malta +	Leo Brincat	Joseph P. Portelli
Marshall Islands	Ruben R. Zackhras	Michael Konelios
Mauritania	Sid'El Moctar Ould Nagi	Mohamed Lemine Ould Deidah
Mauritius	Rundheersing Bheenick	Dharam Dev Manraj
Mexico	Jose Angel Gurria Trevino	Martin M. Werner
Micronesia, Federated States of	John Ehsa	Sebastian L. Anefal
Moldova	Anatol Arapu	Dumitru Ursu
Mongolia	Bat-Erdene Batbayar	Jigjid Unenbat
Morocco	Fathallah Oualalou	Abdeltif Loudyi
Mozambique	Adriano Afonso Maleiane	Luisa Dias Diogo
Myanmar	Khin Maung Thein	Soe Lin
Namibia +	Saara Kuugongelwa	Usutuaije Maamberua
Nepal	Ram Sharan Mahat	Ram Binod Bhattarai
Netherlands	Gerrit Zalm	Johannes Pieter Pronk
New Zealand	Winston Peters	Alan Bollard
Nicaragua	Esteban Duque Estrada	Mario De Franco
Niger	Yacouba Nabassoua	Mohamed Hamil Maiga

Borrower or guarantor	IBRD loans		IDA credits		Total	
	Number	Amount	Number	Amount	Number	Amount
El Salvador	32	820.6	2	25.6	34	846.2
Equatorial Guinea	—	—	9	45.0	9	45.0
Eritrea	—	—	5	125.4	5	125.4
Estonia	7	125.7	—	—	7	125.7
Ethiopia	12	108.6	60	2,827.7	72	2,936.3
Fiji	13	152.9	—	—	13	152.9
Finland	18	316.8	—	—	18	316.8
France	1	250.0	—	—	1	250.0
Gabon	13	222.0	—	—	13	222.0
Gambia, The	—	—	24	178.2	24	178.2
Georgia	—	—	15	373.0	15	373.0
Ghana	9	207.0	89	3,221.0	98	3,428.0
Greece	17	490.8	—	—	17	490.8
Grenada	1	3.8	1	8.8	2	12.7
Guatemala	29	891.1	—	—	29	891.1
Guinea	3	75.2	49	1,073.8	52	1,149.0
Guinea-Bissau	—	—	21	234.9	21	234.9
Guyana	12	80.0	15	293.8	27	373.8
Haiti	1	2.6	36	626.5	37	629.1
Honduras	33	717.3	19	694.9	52	1,412.2
Hungary	39	4,302.0	—	—	39	4,302.0
Iceland	10	47.1	—	—	10	47.1
India	169	25,428.1	225	25,506.5	394	50,934.6
Indonesia	231	24,438.2	46	931.8	277	25,370.0
Iran, Islamic Republic of	39	2,058.1	—	—	39	2,058.1
Iraq	6	156.2	—	—	6	156.2
Ireland	8	152.5	—	—	8	152.5
Israel	11	284.5	—	—	11	284.5
Italy	8	399.6	—	—	8	399.6
Jamaica	62	1,326.0	—	—	62	1,326.0
Japan	31	862.9	—	—	31	862.9
Jordan	47	1,672.0	15	85.3	62	1,757.3
Kazakhstan	16	1,503.6	—	—	16	1,503.6
Kenya	46	1,200.0	72	2,830.8	118	4,030.8
Korea, Republic of	112	13,599.0	6	110.8	118	13,709.8
Kyrgyz Republic	—	—	15	438.5	15	438.5
Lao People's Democratic Republic	—	—	25	546.2	25	546.2
Latvia	10	256.3	—	—	10	256.3
Lebanon	15	783.5	—	—	15	783.5
Lesotho	2	155.0	25	271.0	27	426.0
Liberia	21	156.0	14	114.5	35	270.5
Lithuania	11	273.2	—	—	11	273.2
Luxembourg	1	12.0	—	—	1	12.0
Macedonia, FYR	7	173.5	5	203.8	12	377.3
Madagascar	5	32.9	72	1,612.0	77	1,644.9
Malawi	9	124.1	62	1,661.1	71	1,785.2
Malaysia	84	3,746.6	—	—	84	3,746.6
Maldives	—	—	6	47.3	6	47.3
Mali	—	1.9	58	1,201.5	58	1,203.4
Malta	1	7.5	—	—	1	7.5

(continued next page)

(amounts in millions of US dollars)

Borrower or guarantor	IBRD loans		IDA credits		Total	
	Number	Amount	Number	Amount	Number	Amount
Mauritania	3	146.0	39	481.9	42	627.9
Mauritius	30	413.1	4	20.2	34	433.3
Mexico	167	29,059.7	—	—	167	29,059.7
Moldova	9	302.8	3	79.9	12	382.7
Mongolia	—	—	10	163.7	10	163.7
Morocco	117	7,995.3	3	50.8	120	8,046.1
Mozambique	—	—	30	1,636.0	30	1,636.0
Myanmar	3	33.4	30	804.0	33	837.4
Nepal	—	—	68	1,540.0	68	1,540.0
Netherlands	8	244.0	—	—	8	244.0
New Zealand	6	126.8	—	—	6	126.8
Nicaragua	27	233.6	17	635.9	44	869.5
Niger	—	—	43	734.0	43	734.0
Nigeria	84	6,248.2	14	902.9	98	7,151.1
Norway	6	145.0	—	—	6	145.0
OECS Countries	1	3.6	—	2.4	1	6.0
Oman	11	157.1	—	—	11	157.1
Pakistan	83	6,264.2	106	5,378.1	189	11,642.3
Panama	39	1,029.5	—	—	39	1,029.5
Papua New Guinea	29	597.0	9	113.2	38	710.2
Paraguay	36	807.9	6	45.5	42	853.4
Peru	80	4,715.6	—	—	80	4,715.6
Philippines	145	9,943.1	5	294.2	150	10,237.3
Poland	27	4,642.5	—	—	27	4,642.5
Portugal	32	1,338.8	—	—	32	1,338.8
Romania	54	4,855.8	—	—	54	4,855.8
Russia	39	9,791.5	—	—	39	9,791.5
Rwanda	—	—	46	789.4	46	789.4
São Tomé and Principe	—	—	8	58.9	8	58.9
Senegal	19	164.9	69	1,585.0	88	1,749.9
Seychelles	2	10.7	—	—	2	10.7
Sierra Leone	4	18.7	21	403.7	25	422.4
Singapore	14	181.3	—	—	14	181.3
Slovak Republic	2	135.0	—	—	2	135.0
Slovenia	3	153.2	—	—	3	153.2
Solomon Islands	—	—	6	33.9	6	33.9
Somalia	—	—	39	492.1	39	492.1
South Africa	12	287.8	—	—	12	287.8
Spain	12	478.7	—	—	12	478.7
Sri Lanka	12	210.7	70	2,242.2	82	2,452.9
St. Kitts and Nevis	1	1.5	—	1.5	1	3.0
St. Lucia	3	8.5	—	11.2	3	19.7
St. Vincent and the Grenadines	1	1.4	1	6.4	2	7.8
Sudan	8	166.0	48	1,352.9	56	1,518.9
Swaziland	12	104.8	2	7.8	14	112.6
Syrian Arab Republic	17	613.2	3	47.3	20	660.5
Tajikistan	—	—	5	86.9	5	86.9
Tanzania	18	318.2	90	3,016.6	108	3,379.8
Thailand	114	6,279.1	6	125.1	120	6,404.2
Togo	1	20.0	40	728.5	41	748.5
Tonga	—	—	2	5.0	2	5.0

Borrower or guarantor	IBRD loans		IDA credits		Total	
	Number	Amount	Number	Amount	Number	Amount
Trinidad and Tobago	20	298.8	—	—	20	298.8
Tunisia	107	4,229.7	5	74.6	112	4,304.3
Turkey	122	13,242.5	10	178.5	132	13,421.0
Turkmenistan	3	89.5	—	—	3	89.5
Uganda	1	8.4	65	2,549.6	66	2,558.0
Ukraine	14	2,221.8	—	—	14	2,221.8
Uruguay	42	1,548.2	—	—	42	1,548.2
Uzbekistan	7	379.0	—	—	7	379.0
Vanuatu	—	—	4	15.4	4	15.4
Venezuela	36	3,212.4	—	—	36	3,212.4
Vietnam	—	—	20	2,046.3	20	2,046.3
Western Africa region	1	6.1	3	52.5	4	58.6
Western Samoa	—	—	8	46.6	8	46.6
Yemen, Republic of	—	—	109	1,449.4	109	1,449.4
Yugoslavia	90	6,114.7	—	—	90	6,114.7
Zambia	28	679.1	42	1,902.9	70	2,582.0
Zimbabwe	24	983.2	11	656.9	35	1,640.1
Other[a]	14	329.4	4	15.3	18	344.7
Total	4,201	316,021	2,911	109,056	7,112	425,076.4

— Zero

NOTE: *Joint IBRD/IDA operations are counted only once, as IBRD operations. When more than one loan is made for a single project, the operation is counted only once. Details may not add to totals because of rounding.*

a. *Represents IBRD loans and IDA credits made at a time when the authorities on Taiwan represented China in the World Bank (prior to May 15, 1980).*

(amounts in millions of US dollars)

Region and Country	IBRD loans		IDA credits		Total	
	Number	Amount	Number	Amount	Number	Amount
Africa						
Angola	—	—	1	5.0	1	5.0
Benin	—	—	2	20.7	2	20.7
Burkina Faso	—	—	1	41.3	1	41.3
Cameroon	—	—	2	203.0	2	203.0
Cape Verde	—	—	1	30.0	1	30.0
Chad	—	—	1	5.3	1	5.3
Comoros	—	—	2	19.9	2	19.9
Côte d'Ivoire	—	—	5	341.9	5	341.9
Eritrea	—	—	3	101.6	3	101.6
Ethiopia	—	—	4	669.2	4	669.2
Gambia	—	—	1	18.0	1	18.0
Ghana	—	—	3	96.7	3	96.7
Guinea	—	—	2	75.0	2	75.0
Guinea-Bissau	—	—	1	11.7	1	11.7
Kenya	—	—	—	17.5	—	17.5
Lesotho	1	45.0	1	6.8	2	51.8
Madagascar	—	—	4	114.9	4	114.9
Malawi	—	—	1	50.6	1	50.6
Mali	—	—	1	21.5	1	21.5
Mauritania	—	—	1	24.4	1	24.4
Mauritius	1	12.4	—	—	1	12.4
Mozambique	—	—	1	36.0	1	36.0
Niger	—	—	1	28.0	1	28.0
Rwanda	—	—	—	45.0	—	45.0
Senegal	—	—	4	233.0	4	233.0
Tanzania	—	—	2	45.3	2	45.3
Togo	—	—	3	106.2	3	106.2
Uganda	—	—	4	171.6	4	171.6
Zambia	—	—	2	145.0	2	145.0
Zimbabwe	—	—	3	131.3	3	131.3
Total	2	57.4	57	2,816.4	59	2,873.8
East Asia and Pacific						
Cambodia	—	—	1	31.0	1	31.0
China	14	2,323.0	2	293.4	16	2,616.4
Indonesia	9	703.2	—	—	9	703.2
Korea, Republic of	2	5,000.0	—	—	2	5,000.0
Lao, People's Democratic Republic	—	—	1	34.7	1	34.7
Malaysia	1	300.0	—	—	1	300.0
Mongolia	—	—	2	21.7	2	21.7
Papua New Guinea	1	5.0	—	—	1	5.0
Philippines	4	135.8	—	—	4	135.8
Thailand	3	380.0	—	—	3	380.0
Vietnam	—	—	5	395.4	5	395.4
Total	34	8,847.0	11	776.2	45	9,623.2
South Asia						
Bangladesh	—	—	4	646.4	4	646.4
Bhutan	—	—	1	13.7	1	13.7
India	5	1,068.0	6	1,073.6	11	2,141.6
Nepal	—	—	3	127.6	3	127.6
Pakistan	1	250.0	3	557.8	4	807.8
Sri Lanka	—	—	2	127.3	2	127.3
Total	6	1,318.0	19	2,546.4	25	3,864.4
Europe and Central Asia						
Albania	—	—	6	84.2	6	84.2
Armenia	—	—	6	134.5	6	134.5
Azerbaijan	—	—	2	90.0	2	90.0
Bosnia and Herzegovina	—	—	8	177.0	8	177.0

Region and Country	IBRD loans		IDA credits		Total	
	Number	Amount	Number	Amount	Number	Amount
Bulgaria	2	116.0	—	—	2	116.0
Croatia	3	106.9	—	—	3	106.9
Georgia	—	—	5	110.4	5	110.4
Hungary	3	336.4	—	—	3	336.4
Kazakhstan	3	545.0	—	—	3	545.0
Krygyz Republic	—	—	2	65.0	2	65.0
Latvia	1	7.9	—	—	1	7.9
Macedonia	3	67.5	1	10.0	4	77.5
Moldova	1	55.0	2	70.9	3	125.9
Poland	3	522.0	—	—	3	522.0
Romania	4	130.5	—	—	4	130.5
Russian Federation	3	1,628.6	—	—	3	1,628.6
Tajikistan	—	—	2	19.9	2	19.9
Turkey	4	603.1	—	—	4	603.1
Ukraine	2	216.4	—	—	2	216.4
Uzbekistan	3	127.0	—	—	3	127.0
Total	35	4,462.3	34	761.9	69	5,224.2
Latin America and the Caribbean						
Argentina	12	1,332.5	—	—	12	1,332.5
Bolivia	—	—	5	200.7	5	200.7
Brazil	15	1,617.5	—	—	15	1,617.5
Colombia	5	132.2	—	—	5	132.2
Dominican Republic	2	33.0	—	—	2	33.0
Ecuador	5	171.0	—	—	5	171.0
El Salvador	2	146.0	—	—	2	146.0
Guatemala	3	110.6	—	—	3	110.6
Guyana	—	—	—	1.5	—	1.5
Honduras	—	—	—	14.2	—	14.2
Mexico	7	1,767.2	—	—	7	1,767.2
Nicaragua	—	—	3	141.4	3	141.4
Organization of Eastern Caribbean States	1	3.6	—	2.4	1	6.0
Panama	1	12.7	—	—	1	12.7
Paraguay	1	40.0	—	—	1	40.0
Peru	2	172.5	—	—	2	172.5
Uruguay	1	100.0	—	—	1	100.0
Venezuela	3	40.7	—	—	3	40.7
Total	60	5,679.5	8	360.2	68	6,089.7
Middle East and North Africa						
Algeria	1	150.0	—	—	1	150.0
Egypt	1	20.0	3	122.0	4	142.0
Jordan	3	67.0	—	—	3	67.0
Lebanon	1	63.0	—	—	1	63.0
Morocco	4	200.0	—	—	4	200.0
Tunisia	4	222.0	—	—	4	222.0
Yemen, Republic of	—	—	3	124.5	3	124.5
Total	14	722.0	6	246.5	20	968.5
South Asia						
Bangladesh	—	—	4	646.4	4	646.4
Bhutan	—	—	1	13.7	1	13.7
India	5	1,068.0	6	1,073.6	11	2,141.6
Nepal	—	—	3	127.6	3	127.6
Pakistan	1	250.0	3	557.8	4	807.8
Sri Lanka	—	—	2	127.3	2	127.3
Total	6	1,318.0	19	2,546.4	25	3,864.4
Grand total	105	17,282.0	124	7,060.4	229	24,342.4

— Zero.

NOTE: *Supplements are included in the amount but are not counted as separate lending operations. Joint IBRD/IDA operations are counted only once, as IBRD operations.*

	IBRD	IDA	Total
Agriculture			
Argentina	75.0	—	75.0
Armenia	—	14.5	14.5
Bangladesh	—	11.4	11.4
Benin	—	4.0	4.0
Bosnia and Herzegovina	—	7.0	7.0
Brazil	55.0	—	55.0
Brazil	60.0	—	60.0
Brazil	80.0	—	80.0
Burkina Faso	—	41.3	41.3
China	100.0	—	100.0
China	150.0	—	150.0
China	90.0	60.0	150.0
China	100.0	100.0	200.0
China	300.0	—	300.0
Colombia	5.0	—	5.0
Ecuador	20.0	—	20.0
Egypt, Arab Republic of	—	15.0	15.0
Ethiopia	—	60.0	60.0
India	96.8	100.0	196.8
India	—	52.9	52.9
India	79.9	50.0	129.9
India	—	39.0	39.0
Indonesia	16.3	—	16.3
Indonesia	20.5	—	20.5
Kazakhstan	15.0	—	15.0
Kyrgyz Republic	—	15.0	15.0
Kyrgyz Republic	—	35.0	35.0
Lesotho	—	6.8	6.8
Macedonia, Former Yugoslav Republic of	7.5	5.0	12.5
Mexico	47.0	—	47.0
Moldova	—	5.0	5.0
Morocco	20.0	—	20.0
Nepal	—	79.8	79.8
Nepal	—	24.3	24.3
Pakistan	—	285.0	285.0
Papua New Guinea	5.0	—	5.0
Philippines	50.0	—	50.0
Romania	25.5	—	25.5
Senegal	—	8.0	8.0
Sri Lanka	—	57.0	57.0
Tanzania	—	21.8	21.8
Togo	—	26.2	26.2
Tunisia	42.0	—	42.0
Turkey	20.0	—	20.0
Vietnam	—	66.9	66.9
Yemen, Republic of	—	24.7	24.7
Yemen, Republic of	—	12.5	12.5
Zimbabwe	—	8.8	8.8
Total	1,480.50	1,236.90	2,717.40
Education			
Argentina	119.0	—	119.0
Armenia	—	15.0	15.0
Bangladesh	—	150.0	150.0
Bhutan	—	13.7	13.7

	IBRD	IDA	Total
Bolivia	—	75.0	75.0
Bosnia and Herzegovina	—	11.0	11.0
Brazil	155.0	—	155.0
Brazil	62.5	—	62.5
Cameroon	—	4.9	4.9
Colombia	40.0	—	40.0
Colombia	7.2	—	7.2
Côte d'Ivoire	—	53.3	53.3
El Salvador	58.0	—	58.0
El Salvador	88.0	—	88.0
Ethiopia	—	100.0	100.0
Hungary	36.4	—	36.4
Hungary	150.0	—	150.0
India	—	152.0	152.0
India	—	59.4	59.4
Indonesia	103.5	—	103.5
Lebanon	63.0	—	63.0
Macedonia, Former Yugoslav Republic of	—	5.0	5.0
Madagascar	—	65.0	65.0
Malawi	—	48.2	48.2
Mexico	115.0	—	115.0
Mexico	300.0	—	300.0
Mexico	180.2	—	180.2
Moldova	—	5.0	5.0
Pakistan	—	22.8	22.8
Pakistan	—	250.0	250.0
Romania	70.0	—	70.0
Sri Lanka	—	70.3	70.3
Tanzania	—	20.9	20.9
Tunisia	80.0	—	80.0
Turkey	300.0	—	300.0
Uganda	—	80.0	80.0
Total	1,927.80	1,201.50	3,129.30
Electric power and other energy			
Bangladesh	—	235.0	235.0
Bosnia and Herzegovina	—	25.0	25.0
Chad	—	5.3	5.3
China	300.0	—	300.0
China	250.0	—	250.0
Ethiopia	—	200.0	200.0
India	60.0	—	60.0
Kyrgyz Republic	—	15.0	15.0
Lao People's Democratic Republic	—	34.7	34.7
Macedonia, Former Yugoslav Republic of	35.0	—	35.0
Senegal	—	100.0	100.0
Turkey	270.0	—	270.0
Ukraine	200.0	—	200.0
Vietnam	—	199.0	199.0
Zambia	—	75.0	75.0
Total	1,115.00	889.00	2,004.00
Environment			
Argentina	18.0	—	18.0
Azerbaijan	—	20.0	20.0
Brazil	51.0	—	51.0
Brazil	198.0	—	198.0
Bulgaria	16.0	—	16.0
China	63.0	—	63.0
China	72.0	20.0	92.0

(continued next page)

(amounts in millions of US dollars)

	IBRD	IDA	Total
China	95.0	—	95.0
Dominican Republic	3.0	—	3.0
Ecuador	25.0	—	25.0
Egypt, Arab Republic of	20.0	15.0	35.0
Ghana	—	9.3	9.3
Indonesia	6.9	—	6.9
Latvia	7.9	—	7.9
Peru	150.0	—	150.0
Venezuela	28.0	—	28.0
Vietnam	—	21.5	21.5
Zimbabwe	—	62.5	62.5
Total	753.8	148.3	902.1
Finance			
Bolivia	—	20.0	20.0
Bosnia and Herzegovina	—	5.0	5.0
Brazil	20.0	—	20.0
Croatia	30.0	—	30.0
Ecuador	21.0	—	21.0
Guyana	—	1.5	1.5
Indonesia	20.0	—	20.0
Korea, Republic of	3000.0	—	3000.0
Korea, Republic of	2000.0	—	2000.0
Macedonia, Former Yugoslav Republic of	25.0	—	25.0
Mexico	400.0	—	400.0
Morocco	100.0	—	100.0
Poland	22.0	—	22.0
Thailand	350.0	—	350.0
Thailand	15.0	—	15.0
Uruguay	100.0	—	100.0
Vietnam	—	35.0	35.0
Yemen, Republic of	—	80.0	80.0
Total	6,103.0	141.5	6,244.5
Health, nutrition and population			
Albania	—	17.0	17.0
Armenia	—	10.0	10.0
Bangladesh	—	250.0	250.0
China	—	85.0	85.0
Comoros	—	8.4	8.4
Dominican Republic	30.0	—	30.0
Ecuador	45.0	—	45.0
Egypt, Arab Republic of	—	90.0	90.0
Eritrea	—	18.3	18.3
Gambia, The	—	18.0	18.0
Ghana	—	35.0	35.0
Guinea-Bissau	—	11.7	11.7
India	—	76.4	76.4
India	—	300.0	300.0
Indonesia	42.5	—	42.5
Madagascar	—	27.6	27.6
Mauritania	—	24.0	24.0
Mexico	700.0	—	700.0
Mexico	25.0	—	25.0
Nicaragua	—	24.0	24.0
Philippines	19.0	—	19.0
Senegal	—	50.0	50.0
Tunisia	50.0	—	50.0
Uganda	—	34.0	34.0
Total	911.5	1,079.4	1,990.9

	IBRD	IDA	Total
Industry			
Albania	—	10.3	10.3
Bolivia	—	62.8	62.8
Total	—	73.1	73.1
Mining			
Argentina	39.5	—	39.5
India	530.0	2.0	532.0
Madagascar	—	5.0	5.0
Russian Federation	800.0	—	800.0
Total	1,369.5	7.0	1,376.5
Multisector			
Albania	—	5.0	5.0
Armenia	—	60.0	60.0
Armenia	—	5.0	5.0
Azerbaijan	—	70.0	70.0
Cameroon	—	180.0	180.0
Cape Verde	—	30.0	30.0
Colombia	5.0	—	5.0
Côte d'Ivoire	—	50.0	50.0
Georgia	—	60.0	60.0
Georgia	—	5.0	5.0
Georgia	—	4.5	4.5
Ghana	—	50.0	50.0
Ghana	—	2.4	2.4
Guinea	—	70.0	70.0
Kenya	—	17.5	17.5
Malawi	—	2.4	2.4
Malaysia	300.0	—	300.0
Moldova	55.0	45.0	100.0
Panama	12.7	—	12.7
Russian Federation	800.0	—	800.0
Tajikistan	—	10.0	10.0
Tanzania	—	2.6	2.6
Thailand	15.0	—	15.0
Total	1,187.7	669.4	1,857.1
Oil and gas			
Bosnia and Herzegovina	—	10.0	10.0
Brazil	130.0	—	130.0
Total	130.0	10.0	140.0
Public sector management			
Argentina	5.0	—	5.0
Bolivia	—	15.0	15.0
Bolivia	—	25.0	25.0
Bolivia	—	2.9	2.9
Bosnia and Herzegovina	—	63.0	63.0
Brazil	250.0	—	250.0
Brazil	170.0	—	170.0
Brazil	5.0	—	5.0
Bulgaria	100.0	—	100.0
Cameroon	—	18.1	18.1
Côte d'Ivoire	—	12.0	12.0
Côte d'Ivoire	—	36.6	36.6
Ecuador	60.0	—	60.0
Eritrea	—	53.0	53.0

(continued next page)

	IBRD	IDA	Total
Guatemala	28.2	—	28.2
Guatemala	15.7	—	15.7
Guinea	—	5.0	5.0
Honduras	—	14.2	14.2
Hungary	150.0	—	150.0
Indonesia	225.0	—	225.0
Kazakhstan	230.0	—	230.0
Mauritania	—	0.4	0.4
Mongolia	—	5.0	5.0
Morocco	70.0	—	70.0
Nicaragua	—	70.0	70.0
Pakistan	250.0	—	250.0
Peru	22.5	—	22.5
Togo	—	30.0	30.0
Ukraine	16.4	—	16.4
Uzbekistan	28.0	—	28.0
Venezuela	8.0	—	8.0
Venezuela	4.7	—	4.7
Yemen, Republic of	—	1.5	1.5
Total	1,638.50	351.70	1,990.20
Social sector			
Albania	—	25.0	25.0
Angola	—	5.0	5.0
Argentina	284.0	—	284.0
Benin	—	16.7	16.7
Comoros	—	11.5	11.5
India	301.3	241.9	543.2
Jordan	5.0	—	5.0
Kazakhstan	300.0	—	300.0
Mali	—	21.5	21.5
Philippines	10.0	—	10.0
Romania	5.0	—	5.0
Russian Federation	28.6	—	28.6
Zimbabwe	—	60.0	60.0
Total	933.9	381.6	1,315.5
Telecommunications			
Indonesia	34.5	—	34.5
Organization of Eastern Caribbean States	3.6	2.4	6.0
Romania	30.0	—	30.0
Total	68.1	2.4	70.5
Transportation			
Albania	—	17.0	17.0
Argentina	450.0	—	450.0
Bosnia and Herzegovina	—	39.0	39.0
Brazil	45.0	—	45.0
Brazil	186.0	—	186.0
China	200.0	—	200.0
China	123.0	—	123.0
China	250.0	—	250.0
China	230.0	—	230.0
Côte d'Ivoire	—	180.0	180.0
Egypt, Arab Republic of	—	2.0	2.0
Eritrea	—	30.3	30.3
Ethiopia	—	309.2	309.2
Guatemala	66.7	—	66.7
Indonesia	234.0	—	234.0

	IBRD	IDA	Total
Nepal	—	23.5	23.5
Nicaragua	—	47.4	47.4
Niger	—	28.0	28.0
Poland	300.0	—	300.0
Rwanda	—	45.0	45.0
Togo	—	50.0	50.0
Tunisia	50.0	—	50.0
Uganda	—	30.0	30.0
Uganda	—	27.6	27.6
Vietnam	—	73.0	73.0
Yemen, Republic of	—	5.8	5.8
Zambia	—	70.0	70.0
Total	2,134.7	977.8	3,112.5

Urban development
	IBRD	IDA	Total
Albania	--	10.0	10.0
Algeria	150.0	—	150.0
Argentina	100.0	—	100.0
Argentina	75.0	—	75.0
Argentina	50.0	—	50.0
Argentina	75.0	—	75.0
Argentina	42.0	—	42.0
Bosnia and Herzegovina	—	17.0	17.0
China	—	28.4	28.4
Colombia	75.0	—	75.0
Côte d'Ivoire	—	10.0	10.0
Croatia	40.6	—	40.6
Georgia	—	20.0	20.0
Georgia	—	20.9	20.9
Jordan	32.0	—	32.0
Jordan	30.0	—	30.0
Moldova	—	15.9	15.9
Mongolia	—	16.7	16.7
Poland	200.0	—	200.0
Senegal	—	75.0	75.0
Tajikistan	—	10.0	10.0
Uzbekistan	24.0	—	24.0
Total	893.6	223.9	1,117.5

Water supply and sanitation
	IBRD	IDA	Total
Armenia	—	30.0	30.0
Brazil	150.0	—	150.0
Cambodia	—	31.0	31.0
Croatia	36.3	—	36.3
Lesotho	45.0	—	45.0
Madagascar	—	17.3	17.3
Mauritius	12.4	—	12.4
Morocco	10.0	—	10.0
Mozambique	—	36.0	36.0
Paraguay	40.0	—	40.0
Philippines	56.8	—	56.8
Turkey	13.1	—	13.1
Uzbekistan	75.0	—	75.0
Total	438.6	114.3	552.9
Grand total	21,086.20	7,434.70	28,520.90

NOTE: *Supplements are included in the amount but are not counted as separate lending operations.*
Joint IBRD/IDA operations are counted only once, as IBRD operations.
— *Zero.*

COMMUNIQUÉ

The 56th meeting of the Development Committee was held in Hong Kong, China, on September 22, 1997, under the chairmanship of Driss Jettou, Minister of Finance, Commerce, Industry and Handicrafts of Morocco. Zhu Rongji, Vice Premier of China, James D. Wolfensohn, President of the World Bank, Michel Camdessus, Managing Director of the International Monetary Fund, and Antonio Casas González, Governor of the Central Bank of Venezuela and Chairman of the Group of Twenty-Four, addressed the plenary session. Observers from a number of international and regional organizations also attended.

1. *Helping Countries Combat Corruption and Improve Governance.* Ministers agreed that corruption and weak governance undermine macroeconomic stability, private sector activity, and sustainable development objectives and may erode international support for development cooperation. They emphasized that corruption is a global problem that requires complementary actions by all countries. While stressing that member governments have the primary responsibility for combating corruption and strengthening governance, they welcomed the more active involvement of the Bank and the Fund, each within its respective mandate, in responding to member governments' requests to strengthen their institutions and performance in these areas, including the introduction of greater transparency in the public sector. They welcomed the relevant strategies and guidelines recently issued by the Bank and the Fund. The Committee stressed the importance of a consistent and evenhanded approach, as well as the need to take governance issues and corruption explicitly into account in lending and other decisionmaking when they significantly affect project or macroeconomic and country performance. The Committee asked that the Bank and Fund report to the Committee in a year's time on the implementation of their respective strategies and guidelines.

2. *Ministers invited other Multilateral Development Banks (MDBs) to develop similar strategies and guidelines.* The MDBs were encouraged, as a matter of urgency, to establish procurement procedures and oversight mechanisms of the highest standard and as uniform as possible, including anti-bribery provisions. Ministers noted the ultimate responsibility of borrowers for ensuring fair and effective procurement and stressed the importance of MDBs increasing their assistance to help build borrower capacity and accountability.

3. Ministers welcomed the efforts underway in other international and regional bodies to coordinate efforts to combat corruption. In particular, the Committee encouraged governments to criminalize international bribery in an effective and coordinated way.

4. *Multilateral Investment Guarantee Agency* (MIGA). Ministers reiterated their support for MIGA's continued growth in response to the expanding demand for its services. They welcomed the consensus on addressing MIGA's resource constraints by means of a three-part funding package comprising an IBRD grant of US$150 million, paid-in capital of US$150 million, plus US$700 million of callable capital. Ministers urged the IBRD management and Board of Executive Directors to move swiftly to implement the US$150 million grant. Ministers urged MIGA's Board to reach agreement on implementation of the remainder of the package. They also urged the MIGA Board to reach clear understandings on core policy issues as soon as possible. These measures would relieve MIGA's short term financial constraints and provide it with a sustainable capital structure for the medium to long term. Ministers urged the MIGA board and other relevant parties to come to closure on the capital increase by the time of the Committee's next meeting in April 1998.

5. *Private involvement in infrastructure.* Ministers welcomed the World Bank Group Action Program designed to strengthen the Group's ability to increase private participation in infrastructure in the context of its overall objectives to support poverty reduction and sustainable development. While ministers recognized that governments continue to play a significant role in infrastructure investment, they emphasized the important and increasing opportunities for more active private sector involvement. Ministers encouraged the Bank Group to strengthen its catalytic role through early and effective implementation of the action program's comprehensive range of assistance in the areas of finance, advisory services, risk mitigation, and knowledge and information. The Committee stressed the importance of coordination among the Bank Group, based on agreed country frameworks and strategies.

6. *Implementation of the Debt Initiative for Heavily Indebted Poor Countries* (HIPCs). The Committee welcomed the further progress that had been made in implementing the initiative to support governments that show strong commitment to reform. The Committee also encouraged eligible countries to undertake the policy actions necessary to put them on the path to securing debt relief. Decisions to provide assistance of about US$0.9 billion (in present value terms), which will generate debt service reduction of about US$1.5 billion, have been made for Bolivia, Burkina Faso, and Uganda; decisions on Côte d'Ivoire, Guyana, and Mozambique are expected in the near future. Ministers stressed the importance of adequate interim financing by all creditors. The Committee expressed appreciation for the continuing close collaboration among creditors in implementing the initiative, including understandings among them on the approach to burden-sharing. Ministers also appreciated that bilateral contributions of about US$100 million had already been made or pledged to the HIPC Trust Fund (administered by the World Bank) and urged other governments to contribute as well. They also encouraged international financial institutions that have not yet finalized mechanisms for participation in the initiative to do so as soon as possible. Ministers noted that additional resources will be needed to help finance the African Development Bank's full participation in the initiative. They also noted the need for additional resources to finance the Fund's contribution to the HIPC Initiative for countries beyond those noted above and, more generally, the need to complete the funding of ESAF.

7. *Strategic Compact.* The Committee welcomed the progress made in beginning to meet the compact's ambitious objectives to strengthen the Bank's effectiveness, as reflected in management's first semi-annual progress report to the Executive Directors.

8. *Bank/Fund Collaboration on Strengthening Financial Sectors.* Ministers noted the importance for macroeconomic stability and growth of strengthening the financial systems of developing countries, as recent events have shown. They welcomed an increased emphasis on this area in Bank and Fund operations. Ministers viewed enhanced cooperation between the Bank and the Fund as an urgent priority and welcomed the recent agreement guiding increased collaboration to help member countries strengthen their financial systems.

COMMUNIQUÉ

The 57th meeting of the Development Committee was held in Washington, D.C. on April 17, 1998, under the chairmanship of Dato' Seri Anwar Ibrahim, Deputy Prime Minister and Minister of Finance of Malaysia. James D. Wolfensohn, President of the World Bank, Michel Camdessus, Managing Director of the International Monetary Fund, and Abdelkrim Harchaoui, Minister of Finance of Algeria and Chairman of the Group of Twenty-Four, addressed the plenary session. Observers from a number of international and regional organizations also attended.

1. *Implications of the Asian Financial Crisis.* The Committee reviewed, in the context of a globalized economy, the implications of the Asian financial crisis for the World Bank Group. In a wide-ranging discussion, ministers recognized that the crisis risks damaging the region's remarkable development achievements, particularly its especially effective anti-poverty performance. Ministers expressed strong support for the active role played by the Bank Group and the International Monetary Fund, together with the Asian Development Bank, in the international effort to restore confidence and sustainable growth and to help ensure stability in the international financial system. They especially appreciated these organizations' rapid and substantial response to the crisis, including significant financial assistance to underpin stabilization measures, programs of structural reform, and technical assistance in key sectors in the most affected countries. Ministers also noted that although the region has vast potential for sustained high levels of economic growth through its own efforts, significant external support would still be required for a number of these countries over the foreseeable future.

2. Members welcomed the efforts of the World Bank and the IMF to help governments address the social consequences of crises, including shielding targeted public expenditures, improving labor standards, and strengthening social safety nets for the most vulnerable. They expressed strong support for the Bank's actions to help governments protect the poor, enhance the quality of social services, improve the design and financing of social funds, and promote sustainable environmental management. Ministers also welcomed the active support of the Bank and the Fund for the design and implementation of financial and corporate restructuring and governance and for enhanced country capacity

for better economic management and financial resiliency.

3. Ministers urged the Bank, in implementing the Strategic Compact and in maintaining support for all its members, to strengthen its ability to address situations of this kind rapidly and to help governments avoid such crises in the future. Thus, the Committee urged the Bank to assist countries in strengthening key institutions and structural policies and to augment its skills and capacities in related areas, including particularly the financial sector, corporate restructuring and governance, and poverty reduction and social sustainability.

4. Given the breadth and depth of the issues involved in helping member governments confront such difficult situations, Ministers urged the Bank and the Fund, building on their long tradition of working together, to review and reinforce their partnership based on their respective mandates. This partnership has become even more important in light of the growing significance of structural factors in assisting member governments and the increased demands on both institutions.

5. *Implementation of the Debt Initiative for Heavily Indebted Poor Countries* (HIPCs). The Committee was pleased by the increasing momentum in the implementation of the HIPC Initiative. Ministers congratulated Uganda on its continued strong economic reform effort and on becoming the first country to reach its completion point under the HIPC Initiative, resulting in savings in nominal debt service of about $650 million (about $350 million in NPV terms). The Committee welcomed decisions made since its last meeting by the Executive Boards of the IMF and IDA/IBRD to add Guyana, Côte d'Ivoire and Mozambique to the group of countries for which debt reduction packages have been agreed upon. In the case of Mozambique, this involved exceptional commitments by members of the Paris Club, and in particular Russia as Mozambique's largest creditor, as well as contributions from other countries and extraordinary assistance by IDA and the Fund to secure the large debt relief required. The six countries that have qualified for assistance under the Debt Initiative would be eligible to receive estimated debt relief amounting to about $5.7 billion (the equivalent of $3 billion in NPV terms).

6. Ministers noted that Mali and Guinea-Bissau are expected to join this group shortly and that the Boards' consideration of eligibility under the Debt Initiative for other countries will occur as soon as their track records and progress in negotiation of Bank/Fund-supported programs warrant action. Ministers encouraged potentially eligible countries to undertake such programs in a timely manner so that by the year 2000 as many as possible could be included in the Debt Initiative. Ministers welcomed the increasing number of countries that were contributing bilaterally to the HIPC Trust Fund. They also stressed the importance of additional contributions to the HIPC Initiative to assist all multilateral institutions to meet their share of the cost, including in particular the African Development Bank.

7. *Multilateral Investment Guarantee Agency* (MIGA). Ministers welcomed the successful conclusion of deliberations by the MIGA Board of Directors on MIGA's $850 million general capital increase (including a $150 million paid-in portion) as well as the agreement by IBRD governors to transfer $150 million as a grant to MIGA. These measures, reflecting agreements reached by the Committee at its last meeting, will relieve MIGA's short-term financial constraints and provide it with a sustainable capital structure for the medium to long term, thus enabling it to respond to continuing growth in demand for its services. The Committee also welcomed the progress achieved by the MIGA board on core policy issues and urged the board to continue its discussions and to reach clear understandings on the remaining issues as soon as possible.

8. *Report of the Multilateral Development Banks* (MDBs). Ministers expressed appreciation to the presidents of the four regional development banks and the World Bank for their comprehensive report on MDB follow-up to the recommendations of the Committee's MDB Task Force. The Committee welcomed the progress made by the MDBs in implementing programs designed to strengthen the effectiveness of each institution. Ministers also welcomed the efforts made by the MDB presidents to strengthen their collaboration on important areas—such as program evaluation and procurement rules—and their commitment to expand this cooperation, consistent with their respective mandates, in additional areas of high priority such as governance, corruption, and capacity building; financial sector fundamentals and reform; and infrastructure financing. Members also agreed on the importance of MDBs' addressing the considerable challenges that

remain in further strengthening this cooperation, and they suggested in particular that practical objectives be established for the next few years in areas such as evaluation. They urged the MDBs to continue to work closely with member governments to implement practical measures designed to ensure more effective in-country coordination, based on a shared strategic view, and enhanced development impact.

9. Members requested that the World Bank president inform the Committee at the spring 1999 meeting of progress achieved in strengthening World Bank cooperation with the regional development banks.

10. Ministers also noted that the Committee had made notable progress over the last two years on a number of important issues with broad systemic significance for all MDBs and the IMF, such as the HIPC Initiative and governance. This meeting's discussion of the implications of the Asian financial crisis is a further example, and ministers agreed that the Committee should continue to develop this practice, as recommended in the MDB Task Force Report, drawing on contributions where appropriate from other MDBs.

11. *World Bank Net Income Dynamics.* Ministers considered issues raised by a decline in IBRD net income at the same time that potential demands on this income were increasing. They urged the Bank's Board of Directors to review, on an urgent basis, all available options and to make appropriate recommendations and decisions in the next three months.

MANAGEMENT'S DISCUSSION AND ANALYSIS, JUNE 30, 1998

FINANCIAL STATEMENTS OF THE INTERNATIONAL BANK FOR RECONSTRUCTION AND DEVELOPMENT

Certain forward-looking statements contained herein are subject to risks and uncertainties. IBRD's actual results may differ materially from those set forth in such forward-looking statements.

Management's Discussion and Analysis

1. Financial Overview

The International Bank for Reconstruction and Development (IBRD) is an international organization established in 1945 and owned by its member countries. IBRD's main goals are promoting sustainable economic development and reducing poverty. It pursues these goals primarily by providing loans, guarantees and related technical assistance for projects and programs in its developing member countries. IBRD's ability to intermediate funds from international capital markets for lending to its developing member countries is an important element in achieving its development goals. IBRD's objective is not to maximize profit, but to earn adequate net income to ensure its financial strength and to sustain its development activities on an ongoing basis.

The table below presents selected financial data for the last five fiscal years:

	1998	1997	1996	1995	1994
For the Year U.S. $ millions					
Loan Income	6,881	7,235	7,922	8,187	7,822
Interest	6,775	7,122	7,804	8,069	7,707
Commitment Charges	106	113	118	118	115
Provision for Loan Losses	(251)	(63)	(42)	(12)	—
Investment Income	1,233	834	720	1,082	711
Borrowing Expenses	(6,144)	(5,952)	(6,570)	(6,944)	(6,646)
Net Noninterest Expense	(476)	(769)	(843)	(959)	(836)
Net Income	1,243	1,285	1,187	1,354	1,051
Performance Ratios %					
Net Return on Average Earning Assets:[a]	0.98	1.04	0.91	1.00	0.85
Gross Return on:					
Average Earning Assets[a]	6.38	6.51	6.62	6.94	6.82
Average Outstanding Loans[a]	6.54	6.75	6.92	7.12	7.45
Average Cash and Investments	5.62	5.00	4.43	5.69	3.53
Cost of Average Borrowings (after swaps)	6.10	6.14	6.44	6.62	5.49
Interest Coverage Ratio	1.20	1.22	1.18	1.19	1.16
Reserves-to-Loans Ratio [b]	14.06	14.49	14.36	14.49	14.35
Total at Year-end U.S. $ millions					
Total Assets	204,971	161,945	152,004	168,579	157,399
Cash and Liquid Investments [c]	24,648	18,107	15,898	18,274	19,095
Loans Outstanding	106,576	105,805	110,246	123,499	109,291
Accumulated Provision for Loan Losses	(3,240)	(3,210)	(3,340)	(3,740)	(3,324)
Borrowings Outstanding [d]	103,589	96,679	96,719	108,290	98,815
Total Equity	26,514	27,228	28,300	30,461	26,946

a. Includes commitment charges.

b. On July 30, 1998, the Executive Directors approved a change in the computation of the Reserves-to-Loans ratio. Prior year amounts have been restated for comparability.

c. Includes investments designated as held-to-maturity.

d. Outstanding borrowings, before swaps, net of premium/discount.

The financial strength of IBRD is based on the support it receives from its shareholders and on its array of financial policies and practices. Shareholder support for IBRD is reflected in the capital backing it has received from its members and in the record of its borrowing members in meeting their debt-service obligations to it. IBRD's financial policies and practices have led it to build reserves, to diversify its funding sources, to hold a large portfolio of liquid investments and to limit a variety of risks, including credit, market and liquidity risks.

IBRD's principal assets are its loans to member countries. The bulk of IBRD's outstanding loans are priced on a cost pass-through basis, in which the cost of funding the loans – and hence the benefits of IBRD's intermediation efficiency – are passed through to the borrower, plus a fixed spread of 50 basis points. During FY 1992 - FY 1998 IBRD provided waivers of a portion of commitment charges and interest to eligible borrowers.

From year to year IBRD's net income is affected by a number of factors, including the level of nonaccrual loans, changes in interest rates (which flow through with a lag to the pass-through lending rates) and the level of the lending rates (which determine the earnings on equity funding loans). IBRD holds its assets and liabilities primarily in U.S. dollars, Deutsche mark and Japanese yen. IBRD mitigates its exposure to currency exchange rate risks by matching the currencies of its assets, liabilities and reserves; however, reported income is affected by exchange rate movements. The increasing strength of the U.S. dollar, IBRD's reporting currency, has reduced assets, liabilities and reported net income during the last three fiscal years. This financial statement reporting effect does not impact IBRD's risk bearing and earning capacity.

IBRD's primary consideration in the allocation of net income is the adequacy of its reserves. In recent years IBRD has had sufficient net income to allow it to fund significant transfers to the International Development Association (IDA), the Heavily Indebted Poor Countries (HIPC) Debt Initiative Trust Fund and other development priorities of its shareholders.

During FY 1998 IBRD experienced unprecedented growth in its loan disbursements and commitments, prompted primarily by the financial crisis in East Asia and adjustment lending in Eastern Europe and Central Asia. This loan growth has reduced IBRD's reserves-to-loans ratio from 14.49% at June 30, 1997 to 14.06% at June 30, 1998. However, the implications of this reduction in the reserves-to-loans ratio for IBRD's risk-bearing capacity depend on changes in credit risks in the loan portfolio. On July 30, 1998, to ensure that the reserves-to-loans ratio continues to be adequate, IBRD's Executive Directors approved the allocation of $750 million of FY 1998 net income to reserves. The maturity of high interest, fixed rate loans from the early 1980s and, more broadly, the effects of lower lending rates on net income via the investment in loans of IBRD members' equity (free funds), contribute to an outlook of declining net income. IBRD continues to evaluate additional measures for enhancing its risk bearing capacity.

2. Development Activities

IBRD offers a range of instruments to its member countries to meet their development needs. These financial instruments fall into two primary categories, loans and guarantees.

Loans

From its establishment through June 30, 1998, IBRD had approved loans totaling $323,449 million to borrowers in 128 countries. The loans held by IBRD, including loans approved but not yet effective, at June 30, 1998 totaled $157,641 million, of which $106,576 million was disbursed and $51,065 million was undisbursed. Cumulative loan repayments at June 30, 1998, based on exchange rates at the time of disbursement, were $121,421 million.

IBRD's lending operations have conformed generally to five principles derived from its Articles of Agreement (the Articles). These principles, taken together, seek to ensure that IBRD loans are made to member countries for financially and economically sound purposes to which those countries have assigned high priority, and that funds lent are utilized as intended. The five principles are:

(i) IBRD makes loans to governments, governmental authorities or private enterprises in the territories of member countries. A loan that is not made directly to the member in whose territories the project is located must be guaranteed as to principal, interest and other charges by the member or its central bank or a comparable agency of the member acceptable to IBRD. A guarantee by the member itself has been obtained in all such cases to date.

(ii) IBRD's loans are designed to promote the use of resources for productive purposes in its member countries. Projects financed by IBRD loans are required to meet IBRD's standards for technical, economic, financial, institutional and environmental soundness.

(iii) In making loans, IBRD must act prudently and pay due regard to the prospects of repayment. Decisions to make loans are based upon, among other things, studies by IBRD of a country's economic structure, including assessments of its resources and ability to generate sufficient foreign exchange to meet debt-service obligations.

(iv) IBRD must be satisfied that in the prevailing market conditions (taking into account the member's overall external financing requirements), the borrower would be unable to obtain financing under conditions which, in the opinion of IBRD, are reasonable for the borrower. IBRD is intended to promote private investment, not to compete with it.

(v) The use of loan proceeds is supervised. IBRD makes arrangements to ensure that funds loaned are used only for authorized purposes and, where relevant, with due attention to considerations of cost-effectiveness. This policy is enforced primarily by requiring borrowers (a) to submit documentation establishing, to IBRD's satisfaction, that the expenditures financed with the proceeds of loans are made in conformity with the applicable lending agreements and (b) to procure goods and services through procedures, including international competitive bidding, which IBRD judges to be likely to lead to cost-efficient procurement.

Within the scope permitted by the Articles, these policies must necessarily be developed and adjusted in light of experience and changing conditions.

The process of identifying and appraising a project and approving and disbursing a loan often extends over several years. The appraisal of projects is carried out by IBRD's operational staff (engineers, financial analysts, economists and other sector and country specialists). With minor exceptions, all loans must be approved by the IBRD's Executive Directors. Loan disbursements are subject to the fulfillment of conditions set out in the loan agreement. IBRD is in the process of revising its financial project management and disbursement procedures with the intention of making them more efficient and effective, through the Loan Administration Change Initiative. During project implementation IBRD staff with experience in the sector or the country involved periodically visit project sites to review progress, monitor compliance with IBRD policies and assist in resolving any problems that may arise. Subsequent to completion the project is evaluated to determine the extent to which its major objectives were met. Similar appraisal, approval, supervision and evaluation procedures apply in the case of IBRD structural and sectoral adjustment and other non-project loans.

Lending Instruments

IBRD lending may take the form of any of the following instruments:

Investment Lending

IBRD has several products that support investment activities, either discrete projects or programs of investments. These loans broadly fall into the following categories:

- *Specific Investment Loans* fund the creation of new productive assets or economic, social, and institutional infrastructure or their rehabilitation to full capacity.

- *Sector Investment and Maintenance Loans* are designed to bring investments, policies, and performance in specific sectors or subsectors in line with agreed economic priorities.

- *Financial Intermediary Loans* support the development of financial institutions and provide funds to be channeled through intermediaries for general credit or for the development of sectors or subsectors. The primary objective of these loans is to improve the operational efficiency of financial institutions in a competitive environment.

- *Emergency Recovery Loans* are made to restore assets and productivity immediately after a major emergency (such as war, civil disturbance, or natural disaster) that seriously disrupts the country's economy.

- *Technical Assistance Loans* are designed to strengthen capacity in entities concerned with policies, strategies and institutional reforms in such areas as public enterprise reform and divestiture, civil service and judicial reform, government budgetary management, and the formulation of economic policy.

IBRD's management is also developing a range of new lending instruments. The first of these new products are the Adaptable Lending (AL) instruments, which include:

- *Learning and Innovation Loans* (LILs): These are designed to support small, time-sensitive programs to build capacity, pilot promising initiatives, or to experiment with and develop locally-based models prior to large scale interventions. LILs are modest in size with each loan not exceeding $5 million. Approvals of LILs are at the management level rather than at the Executive Director level.

♦ *Adaptable Program Loans* (APLs): These are designed to provide for funding of a long-term development program through a series of operations. Succeeding operations are committed on the basis of satisfactory performance on agreed milestones, indicators, periodic reviews, and the evaluation of implementation progress and emerging needs. Authority for approval is with the Executive Directors for the first loan of each program and the long-term program agreement. Authority for approval of subsequent APLs is with IBRD's management subject to oversight and review by the Executive Directors.

The introduction of LILs and APLs was approved by the Executive Directors on September 4, 1997.

A breakdown of IBRD's investment lending approved in FY 1998 and in each of the two preceding fiscal years is as follows:

In millions of U.S. dollars

Instruments	FY 1998		FY 1997		FY 1996	
	Amount	As a % of total loans	Amount	As a % of total loans	Amount	As a % of total loans
Adaptable Program Loans	$ 749	4	$ -	-	$ -	-
Emergency Recovery Loans	410	2	-	-	318	2
Financial Intermediary Loans	122	*	92	1	75	1
Learning and Innovation Loans	33	*	-	-	-	-
Sector Investment and Maintenance Loans	599	3	545	4	1,933	13
Specific Investment Loans	9,000	43	9,477	65	9,136	62
Technical Assistance Loans	238	1	273	2	364	3
Total	$11,151	53	$ 10,387	72	$ 11,826	81

* Indicates amounts less than 0.5%.

Adjustment Lending

Most IBRD loans are for specific projects. IBRD also makes adjustment loans designed to support the introduction of basic changes in economic, financial and other policies of key importance for the economic development of member countries. Disbursements on these loans are conditional on certain performance objectives. The Executive Directors have agreed that adjustment lending, excluding debt and debt-service reduction loans, will normally not exceed 25% of total IBRD lending. As a result of several adjustment and similar loans made by IBRD this fiscal year, 47% of IBRD's lending in FY 1998 consisted of such loans. The Executive Directors considered the matter and are fully aware that, in light of the specific and unusual financial circumstances in Asia at present, the guideline has been exceeded this fiscal year, and may possibly be exceeded again in subsequent years. Adjustment loans are broadly classified as follows:

♦ *Structural Adjustment Loans* support specific policy changes and institutional reforms. Agreement on a satisfactory macroeconomic framework and policy actions that can be monitored on a specific schedule are required.

♦ *Sector Adjustment Loans* support comprehensive policy changes and institutional reforms in major sectors. They also require agreement on a satisfactory macroeconomic framework and its implementation, and a specific action program that can be monitored.

♦ *Rehabilitation Loans* provide support for government policy reform programs to assist the private sector where foreign exchange is required for urgent rehabilitation of key infrastructure and productive facilities.

♦ *Debt and Debt-Service Reduction Loans* assist an eligible, highly-indebted country in financing an approved debt and debt-service reduction operation on its commercial debt that is designed to reduce the debt to a manageable level and contribute to a viable medium-term financing plan and the attainment of medium-term growth objectives.

A breakdown of IBRD's adjustment lending approved in FY 1998, and in each of the two preceding fiscal years is as follows:

In millions of U.S. dollars

Instruments	FY 1998		FY 1997		FY 1996	
	Amount	As a % of total loans	Amount	As a % of total loans	Amount	As a % of total loans
Structural adjustment loans[a]	$ 8,285	39	$ 1,295	9	$ 350	2
Sector adjustment loans	1,650	8	2,590	18	2,450	17
Rehabilitation loans	-	-	70	*	-	-
Total	$ 9,935	47	$ 3,955	27	$ 2,800	19
Debt and Debt-Service Reduction Loans	$ -	-	$ 183	1	$ 30	*

a. Includes a $3,000 million economic reconstruction loan to the Republic of Korea.

* Indicates amounts less than 0.5%.

Enclave Lending

On rare occasions an IBRD loan will be made for a large, foreign exchange generating project in an IDA-only country. In these circumstances appropriate risk mitigation measures are incorporated (including off-shore escrow accounts and debt-service reserves acceptable to IBRD) to ensure that the risks to IBRD are minimized. At June 30, 1998, IBRD had less than $150 million in outstanding loans for enclave projects.

Lending by Sector

A breakdown by sector of IBRD's outstanding loans and loans approved in each of the last three fiscal years is as follows:

| Sectors | Total loans outstanding at end FY 1998 | | Loans approved during | | | | | |
| | | | FY 1998 | | FY 1997 | | FY 1996 | |
	USD M	%	USD M	%	USD M	%	USD M	%
Agriculture	$ 11,564	11	$ 1,481	7	$ 2,811	19	$ 1,414	10
Education	4,749	5	1,928	9	762	5	921	6
Electric Power and Other Energy	13,625	13	1,115	5	1,613	11	2,459	17
Environment	1,310	1	754	4	23	*	535	4
Finance	14,822	14	6,103	29	994	7	1,199	8
Health, Population and Nutrition	2,309	2	911	4	246	2	1,495	10
Industry	5,924	5	-	-	145	1	217	2
Mining and Other Extractive	1,817	2	1,369	7	300	2	571	4
Multi-Sector	17,194	16	1,188	6	1,373	9	906	6
Oil and Gas	3,975	4	130	1	114	1	30	*
Public Sector Management	4,764	4	1,638	8	730	5	1,036	7
Social	1,857	2	934	4	1,304	9	440	3
Telecommunications and Informatics	1,254	1	68	*	-	-	35	*
Transportation	12,581	12	2,135	10	3,085	21	2,237	15
Urban Development	5,084	5	894	4	646	5	632	4
Water Supply and Sanitation	3,293	3	438	2	380	3	529	4
Total [a]**	$ 106,122	100	$21,086	100	$ 14,525	100	$ 14,656	100

a. Excludes loans to the IFC.

* Indicates amounts less than 0.5%.

** May differ from sum of individual figures shown due to rounding.

Financial Terms of Lending Instruments

Any of the previously described instruments can be offered with various financial terms. Presently IBRD offers new loans with three types of financial terms: multicurrency pool loans, LIBOR-based single currency loans, and fixed rate single currency loans. This product offering is intended to provide borrowers flexibility to select terms that are compatible with their debt management strategy and suited for their debt-servicing capability. All loans carry a three- to five-year grace period for principal and amortize over a period that in most cases ranges from 12 to 20 years.

In general IBRD charges a spread on its outstanding loans of 50 basis points over its average cost of borrowings, with the exception of the two loans described under "single currency loans" below. In addition, all loans carry a commitment charge of 75 basis points per annum on undisbursed amounts.

Waivers of a portion of interest owed by all eligible borrowers are in effect and have been for each of the previous seven fiscal years. Waivers of a portion of the commitment charge owed on undisbursed portion of loans made to or guaranteed by members are in effect and have been for each of the last nine fiscal years. Further details are provided in the Notes to Financial Statements–Note C.

Multicurrency Pool Loans

The currency composition of multicurrency pool loans is determined on the basis of a pool, which provides a currency composition that is the same for all loans in the pool. Pursuant to a policy established by the Executive Directors and subject to their periodic review, at least 90% of this pool is in fixed currency ratios of one U.S. dollar to 125 Japanese yen to two Deutsche mark equivalent.

The lending rate on these loans is variable, adjusted every six months to reflect the previous semester average cost of outstanding borrowings allocated to fund these loans, weighted by the average composition of the pool. IBRD adds its standard spread of 50 basis points to that average cost.

Loan Conversion Options

In FY 1997 in response to borrower demand for broader currency choice, the Executive Directors approved a policy to offer currency choice for all IBRD multicurrency pool loans for which the invitation to negotiate was issued by September 1, 1996. The purpose of this invitation was to provide borrowers the flexibility to amend the terms of their existing multicurrency pool loans to reflect the offered currency of their choice. Under this offer which extended from September 1, 1996 to June 1, 1998, borrowers had three options: (a) retain the terms of their existing multicurrency pool loans; (b) convert undisbursed loan amounts to single currency loan (SCL) terms; and (c) convert disbursed loan balances and undisbursed loan amounts (to the extent not converted to SCL terms) to one of four new single currency pools (SCPs).

Conversion to Single Currency Loan Terms

Aggregate conversions of undisbursed balances through July 1, 1998 to SCL terms were $21,115 million, with U.S. dollars comprising 79.7% of the total.

Conversion to Single Currency Pools

Single currency pool terms are not available for new commitments. Borrowers selecting conversion to single currency pool terms had the choice of four different pools (U.S. dollar, Japanese yen, Deutsche mark or Swiss franc). All variable rate multicurrency pool loans that were converted to single currency pools carry the applicable pool's variable lending rate, reset semi-annually to reflect the previous semester average cost of outstanding borrowings allocated to fund that pool weighted by the shares of currencies in the pool, plus the standard spread of 50 basis points.

Aggregating the conversions which took place on the conversion dates of July 1, 1997, January 1, 1998, and July 1, 1998, borrowers converted U.S. dollar equivalent $48,549 million (of which $615 million was undisbursed) from the multicurrency pool to single currency pools. Among the four currency choices, conversion to the U.S. dollar SCP loan pool accounted for 85.6% and conversion to the Deutsche mark pool accounted for 14.2 % of the total converted loan volume.

- ♦ *Implementation.* Given the cost pass-through nature of the loan products, special efforts were taken to ensure an equitable initial re-allocation of outstanding borrowings to fund the SCPs. This was achieved by allocating similar debt profiles to each of the currency pools on the basis of overall cost and maturity considerations. IBRD will reconfigure the currency composition of each pool to at least 90% of the pool's target currency by July 1, 1999, and maintain it at or above 90% thereafter, subject to available funding and swap access in the necessary currencies.

- ♦ *Lending Rates.* Lending rates for the U.S. dollar and Deutsche mark SCP loans for the January 1, 1998 to June 30, 1998 semester were 8.37% and 6.92%, respectively. The U.S. dollar rate of 8.37% is significantly higher than the 6.54% rate in effect for the July 1 to December 31, 1997 semester. This is because as the U.S. dollar SCP was converted from a multicurrency pool to a U.S. dollar pool, it involved swapping lower nominal cost non-U.S. dollar liabilities to U.S. dollar liabilities, thus reflecting the difference in market interest rates between these currencies and the U.S. dollar. This difference was greatest in the case of Japanese yen where market interest rates were substantially lower than for U.S. dollars.

Single Currency Loans

Borrowers may select LIBOR-based or fixed rate SCL terms for new loans. IBRD currently offers SCLs in U.S. dollars, Japanese yen, Deutsche mark, French francs, pounds sterling, Swiss francs, and Netherlands guilders and will consider borrower requests for such loans in other currencies.

LIBOR-based SCLs carry a lending rate that is reset semi-annually. The lending rate consists of a base rate, which is the prevailing six-month interbank offered rate (LIBOR, or PIBOR for French franc denominated SCLs) for the applicable currency on the loan's rate reset date, plus a spread. The spread consists of: (a) IBRD's average cost margin for funding allocated to these loans relative to the base rate, and (b) IBRD's standard spread of 50 basis points. These variable rate loans are designed to pass through to its borrowers IBRD's funding spread to LIBOR. This spread is set every six months, in January and July. At June 30, 1998, LIBOR-based SCLs make up 14.1% of the total outstanding loans. At the end of FY 1998, the proportion of outstanding LIBOR-based SCLs denominated in U.S. dollars was 97.3%, with the remaining portion denominated in Deutsche mark, French francs, Japanese yen and other currencies.

IBRD approved and disbursed two LIBOR-based single currency loans to the Republic of Korea in FY 1998 that have non-standard financial terms. The first, a $3,000 million economic reconstruction loan, carries a 6-month LIBOR interest rate plus a fixed spread of 100 basis points and has a loan origination charge. The second, a $2,000 million structural adjustment loan, carries a 6-month LIBOR interest rate plus a fixed spread of 75 basis points and has a loan origination charge. Neither loan is eligible for interest waivers.

Fixed rate SCLs carry lending rates that are set on specified semi-annual rate fixing dates for amounts disbursed during the preceding six months. The lending rate consists of a base rate, which reflects market interest rates for the applicable currency on the rate-fixing date for the equivalent loan maturity, plus a spread. The spread consists of: (a) IBRD's funding cost margin relative to the base rate for these loans, (b) a risk premium to compensate IBRD for market risks it incurs in funding these loans, and (c) IBRD's standard spread of 50 basis points.

SCLs continue to be IBRD's fastest growing loan product, with the outstanding balance more than doubling during FY 1998.

The following table presents a breakdown of IBRD's loan portfolio by product:

In millions of U.S. dollars

Loan Product	FY 1998 Principal Balance	As a % of Total Loans	FY 1997 Principal Balance	As a % of Total Loans	FY 1996 Principal Balance	As a % of Total Loans
Adjustable rate multicurrency pool loans						
Outstanding	$ 56,274	53	$ 91,842	87	$ 96,856	88
Undisbursed	8,765	17	27,422	53	44,786	82
LIBOR-based single currency loans						
Outstanding	15,018	14	4,493	4	957	1
Undisbursed	29,801	58	19,144	37	7,387	14
Fixed rate single currency loans						
Outstanding[1]	5,683	5	2,563	2	1,307	1
Undisbursed	12,356	24	5,007	10	2,335	4
Single currency pool loans						
Outstanding	25,658	24	–	–	–	–
Undisbursed	131	*	–	–	–	–
Other loans						
Outstanding	3,943	4	6,907	7	11,126	10
Undisbursed	12	*	3	*	12	*
Total loans **						
Outstanding	$ 106,576	100	$105,805	100	$110,246	100
Undisbursed	$ 51,065	100	$ 51,576	100	$ 54,520	100

[1] Includes $1,114 million of fixed rate single currency loans whose rate had not yet been fixed at June 30, 1998.

* Indicates amounts less than 0.5%.

** May differ from the sum of individual figures due to rounding.

For more information see the Notes to Financial Statements–Note C.

Guarantees

IBRD offers guarantees to its members and in exceptional cases will offer enclave guarantees in IDA-only countries subject to a limit of $300 million. IBRD guarantees are flexible instruments that provide the credit enhancement required to mobilize private capital. IBRD's objective in offering guarantees is to help mobilize private funding and to leverage IBRD's participation in these projects by providing required credit enhancements. IBRD guarantees can be customized to suit varying country and project circumstances. They can be targeted to mitigate specific risks – generally risks relating to political, regulatory and government performance – which the private sector is not normally in a position to absorb or manage. Two types of guarantees are offered:

♦ *Partial risk guarantees* cover debt-service defaults that may result from nonperformance of government obligations. These are defined in the contracts negotiated between the government or a government-sponsored entity and the private company responsible for implementing the project. The IBRD guarantee is limited to backing the government's obligations; the obligations of the private company contained in the project agreements are not covered and thus the private lenders assume the risk of nonperformance by the private company.

♦ *Partial credit guarantees* are used for private sector projects when there is a need to extend loan maturities, but not necessarily to cover sovereign contractual obligations. This approach may be most appropriate when the lenders are not willing to accept the sovereign risk of the host government for a term long enough to meet the needs of the project. By guaranteeing later maturities, such partial credit guarantees help induce the market to extend the term to the maximum risk it can bear. The presence of the guarantee may also induce a lower interest rate.

Each guarantee requires the counter-guarantee of the member government as does any loan not made to a member government. Guarantees are priced within a limited range to reflect the risks involved, and preparation fees may be charged where there are exceptional costs involved for IBRD.

IBRD applies the same country creditworthiness and project evaluation criteria for guarantees as it applies for loans. Projects in any country that is eligible for IBRD lending are eligible for IBRD guarantees. IBRD offers partial credit guarantees and partial risk guarantees to private investors where the government requests such support and the operation meets other IBRD determined criteria.

IBRD's exposure at June 30, 1998 on its guarantees (measured as their present value in terms of their first call date) was $1,501 million. The face value of such guarantees was $2,047 million, of which $371 million was subject to call. IBRD charges a fee of 25 basis points per annum on its exposure on guarantees. Additional information is provided in the Notes to Financial Statements–Note C.

IBRD may also provide partial risk guarantees for export-oriented projects in an IDA-only country (enclave guarantees) if the project is expected to generate foreign exchange outside the country, and IBRD determines that the country will have adequate foreign exchange to meet its obligations under the counter-guarantee if the guarantee is called. The government is expected to use revenue accruing to it from any such project for productive development purposes. A project covered by an enclave guarantee includes security arrangements with appropriate risk mitigation measures—such as offshore revenue escrow accounts and debt-service reserves acceptable to IBRD—to minimize IBRD's exposure and the risk of a call on the guarantee. The annual commitment of enclave guarantees is initially limited to an aggregate guaranteed amount of $300 million.

Lending Limit

Under IBRD's Articles, as applied, the total amount outstanding of callable guarantees, participation in loans and direct loans made by IBRD may not be increased to exceed the statutory lending limit (the sum of IBRD's subscribed capital, reserves and surplus.) At June 30, 1998, outstanding loans and callable guarantees totaled $106,947 million, or 52.9% of the statutory lending limit. The Executive Directors have issued guidelines pursuant to which all guarantees issued by IBRD are included in the calculation of this ratio from the time those guarantees first become callable.

In 1991 the Executive Directors decided that discussions on an additional capital increase would be initiated if IBRD's lending commitments during any fiscal year reach 80% of the sustainable level of lending (the level that in IBRD's judgment could be sustained without the need for additional capital). IBRD's lending commitments for FY 1998 were $21,086 million, or 77.7% of the sustainable level of lending. In May 1998 IBRD reviewed the lending program and concluded that the risk of breaching the statutory lending limit was low and that discussions on additional capital increases for the purpose of commitment authority were not currently warranted.

Other Activities

In addition to its financial operations, IBRD has furnished technical assistance to its member countries, both in connection with and independently of loan operations. Such assistance has taken a variety of forms, including the assignment of qualified professionals to survey development possibilities of member countries, to analyze their fiscal, economic and other development problems, to assist member countries in drawing up development programs, to appraise projects suitable for investment and to assist member countries in improving their asset and liability management techniques. To assist its developing member countries, IBRD also established an Economic Development Institute, which provides courses and other training activities dealing with economic policy, development and administration for selected groups of government officials, and has made contributions for research and other developmental activities. Furthermore, IBRD has on a number of occasions at the request of members concerned, facilitated efforts toward the settlement of international economic and financial disputes. Additionally, IBRD, alone or jointly with IDA, administers on behalf of donors, funds restricted for specific uses. These funds are held in trust and are not included in the assets of IBRD. See the Notes to Financial Statements–Note H.

3. Risk Management

IBRD assumes various kinds of risks in the process of providing development banking services. Its activities can give rise to three major types of risk: credit risk, market risk, and liquidity risk. IBRD is also exposed to operating risk. These risks are described below.

The objective of Asset-Liability Management (ALM) at IBRD is to ensure adequate funding for each product at the most attractive available cost, and to manage the currency composition, maturity profile and interest rate sensitivity characteristics of the portfolio of liabilities supporting each product in accordance with the particular requirements for that product and within prescribed risk parameters.

The major risk inherent to IBRD is (country) credit risk, or loan portfolio risk. IBRD is also subject to commercial credit, market (interest and exchange rate), operating and liquidity risk, which it actively manages. The risk management governance structure begins with the **Asset-Liability Management Committee (ALCO)** which makes decisions or recommendations to senior management in the areas of financial policy, the adequacy and allocation of risk capital, and oversight of financial reporting. There are three standing subcommittees reporting to ALCO:

The **Market Risk and Currency Management Subcommittee** develops and monitors the policies under which market and commercial credit risks faced by IBRD are measured, reported and managed. The subcommittee also monitors compliance with policies governing commercial credit exposure and currency management. Specific areas of activity include establishing guidelines for limiting balance sheet and market risks and the use of derivative instruments, and monitoring of matches between assets and their funding.

The role of the **Financial Policy and Information Technology Subcommittee** is to identify, discuss and resolve issues in financial policies and information technology initiatives under development in IBRD's financial complex.

The role of the **Strategic Credit Subcommittee** is to monitor global economic and political trends for their effect on individual country risks, portfolio concentration characteristics, trends in exposures to risk clusters, and aggregate changes in the magnitude, nature and composition of credit risk in the portfolio. Strategic issues such as the credit risk implications of new IBRD lending products, the allocation of capital, loan loss provisioning, arrears clearance and debt repayment workouts form a significant portion of this subcommittee's agenda.

For the day-to-day management of risk, IBRD's risk management structure extends into its business units. Risk management processes have been established to facilitate, control, and monitor risk-taking. These processes are built on a foundation of initial identification and measurement of risks by each of the business units.

The processes and procedures by which IBRD manages its risk profile continually evolve as its activities change in response to market, credit, product, and other developments. The Executive Directors periodically review trends in IBRD's risk profiles and performance as well as any significant developments in risk management policies and controls.

Credit Risk

Credit risk, the risk of loss from default by a borrower or counterparty, is inherent in IBRD's business. Under the direction of the ALCO, policies and procedures for measuring and managing such risks are formulated, approved and communicated throughout IBRD. Senior managers represented on ALCO are responsible for maintaining sound credit assessments, addressing transaction and product risk issues, providing an independent review function and monitoring the loans, investments and borrowings portfolios.

IBRD faces two main types of credit risk: country credit risk and commercial credit risk.

Country Credit Risk

Country credit risk is the primary risk faced by IBRD. It has three components. Expected losses from all three components are covered by the Accumulated Provision for Loan Losses, while unexpected losses are covered by IBRD's risk-bearing capital and income generating capacity. IBRD continuously reviews the creditworthiness of its member countries as borrowers and adjusts its overall country programs and lending operations to reflect the results of these reviews.

(i) The first component is idiosyncratic risk or the risk that individual countries will accumulate extended debt-service arrears (or move closer to accumulating extended payment arrears) for country specific reasons.

(ii) The second component is covariance risk. This is the risk that one or more borrowers will accumulate extended payment arrears (or move closer to accumulating extended payment arrears) as a result of a common shock. This shock could be, for example, a regional political crisis or an adverse change in the global environment (such as a fall in commodity prices or a rise in international interest rates).

(iii) The third component is portfolio concentration risk. This reflects the concentration in IBRD's portfolio that results from lending to a relatively small group of borrowers. This concentration exacerbates the idiosyncratic and covariance risk described above. This risk is managed using the portfolio concentration limit described below.

In 1997 the Executive Directors approved an approach to portfolio concentration under which IBRD's largest loan portfolio exposure to a single borrowing country is restricted to the lower of an equitable access limit or a concentration risk limit. The equitable access limit is equal to 10% of IBRD's subscribed capital, reserves and unallocated surplus. The concentration risk limit is based on the adequacy of IBRD's equity capital relative to its largest loan portfolio exposure to a single borrowing country. The concentration risk limit takes into account not only current exposure, but also projected exposure over the ensuing three- to five-year period. This limit is determined by the Executive Directors each year at the time they consider IBRD's reserves adequacy and the allocation of its net income for the preceding fiscal year. For FY 1998 the concentration risk limit was set at $13.5 billion. The equitable access limit was $20.2 billion. IBRD's largest loan portfolio exposure (including the present value of guarantees) to a single borrowing country was $11.4 billion at June 30, 1998.

Overdue and Non-performing Loans

It is IBRD's policy that if a payment of principal, interest or other charges with respect to an IBRD loan or IDA credit becomes 30 days overdue, no new loans to that member country, or to any other borrower in that country, will be presented to the Executive Directors for approval, nor will any previously approved loan be signed, until payment for all amounts 30 days overdue or longer has been received. In addition, if such payments become 60 days overdue, disbursements on all loans to or guaranteed by that member country are suspended until all overdue amounts have been paid. Where the member country is not the borrower, the time period for suspension of the approval and signing of new loans to or guaranteed by the member country is 45 days and the time period for suspension of disbursements is 60 days. It is the policy of IBRD to place all loans made to or guaranteed by a member of IBRD in nonaccrual status, if principal, interest or other charges on any such loan are overdue by more than six months, unless IBRD's management determines that the overdue amount will be collected in the immediate future. IBRD maintains an Accumulated Provision for Loan Losses to recognize the risk inherent in current and potential overdue payments. The methodology for determining the Accumulated Provision for Loan Losses is discussed in detail below. Additional information on IBRD's provisioning policy and status of nonaccrual loans can be found in the Summary of Significant Accounting and Related Policies and Note C of the Financial Statements.

In 1991 the Executive Directors adopted a policy to assist members with protracted arrears to IBRD to mobilize sufficient resources to clear their arrears and to support a sustainable growth-oriented adjustment program over the medium term. Under this policy IBRD will develop a lending strategy and will process loans, but not sign or disburse such loans, during a pre-clearance performance period with respect to members that: (a) agree to and implement a medium-term, growth-oriented structural adjustment program endorsed by IBRD; (b) undertake a stabilization program, if necessary, endorsed, or financially supported, by the IMF; (c) agree to a financing plan to clear all arrears to IBRD and other multilateral creditors in the context of a medium-term structural adjustment program; and (d) make debt-service payments as they fall due on IBRD loans during the performance period. The signing, effectiveness and disbursement of such loans will not take place until the member's arrears to IBRD have been fully cleared.

Accumulated Provision for Loan Losses

IBRD's Accumulated Provision for Loan Losses reflects the following:

♦ Management's assessment of the overall collectibility risk in the total accruing loan portfolio (which includes callable guarantees); and

♦ The present value losses on nonaccruing loans. Such losses are equal to the difference between the discounted present value of the debt-service payments on a loan at its contractual terms and the expected cash flows on that loan.

The adequacy of the Accumulated Provision for Loan Losses is determined by assessing the amount required to cover potential expected losses in the accrual portfolio and losses inherent in the nonaccrual portfolio. The amount required to cover potential expected losses in the accruing portfolio is related to mean of the distribution of losses facing the institution over the next three years. This is calculated using a risk-adjusted capital allocation framework that takes into account the concentration and covariance risk in the portfolio. The amount required to cover losses inherent in the nonaccrual portfolio is based on the calculation of the discounted present value of cash flows.

Estimating potential losses is inherently uncertain and depends on many factors, including general macroeconomic and political conditions, unexpected correlations within the portfolio, and other external factors. IBRD periodically reviews such factors and reassesses the adequacy of the Accumulated Provision for Loan Losses accordingly.

Commercial Credit Risk

IBRD's commercial credit risk is concentrated in instruments issued by sovereigns, agencies, banks and corporate entities. The majority of these investments are with AAA and AA institutions.

In the normal course of its business, IBRD utilizes various derivatives and foreign exchange financial instruments to meet the financial needs of its borrowers, to generate income through its trading activities, and to manage its exposure to fluctuations in interest and currency rates.

Derivative and foreign exchange transactions involve, to varying degrees, credit risk. The effective management of credit risk is vital to the success of IBRD's trading and ALM activities. Because of changing market environment, the monitoring and managing of these risks is a continual process.

IBRD seeks to control the credit risk arising from derivatives and foreign exchange transactions through its credit approval process, the use of collateral agreements and risk control limits, and monitoring procedures. The credit approval process involves evaluating each counterparty's creditworthiness, assigning credit limits to each counterparty, and determining if there are specific transaction characteristics that alter the risk profile. Credit limits are calculated and monitored on the basis of potential exposures taking into consideration current market values and estimates of potential future movements in those values. If there is a collateral agreement with the counterparty to reduce credit risk, then the amount and nature of the collateral obtained is based on the credit rating of the counterparty. Collateral held includes cash and government securities.

IBRD's management treats the credit risk exposure as the replacement cost of the derivative or foreign exchange product. This is also referred to as replacement risk or the mark-to-market exposure amount. While notional principal is the most commonly used volume measure in the derivative and foreign exchange markets, it is not a measure of credit or market risk.

Mark-to-market exposure is a measure, at a point in time, of the value of a derivative or foreign exchange contract in the open market. When the mark-to-market is positive, it indicates the counterparty owes IBRD and, therefore, creates a replacement risk for IBRD. When the mark-to-market is negative, IBRD owes the counterparty and does not have replacement risk.

When IBRD has more than one transaction outstanding with a counterparty, and there exists a legally-enforceable master agreement with the counterparty, the "net" mark-to-market exposure represents the netting of the positive and negative exposures with the same counterparty. If this net mark-to-market is negative, then IBRD's exposure to the counterparty is considered to be zero. Net mark-to-market is, in IBRD's view, the best measure of credit risk when there is a legally-enforceable master netting agreement between IBRD and the counterparty. For the notional amounts and related credit risk exposure amounts by product, see the Notes to Financial Statements–Note E.

The following table provides details of IBRD's estimated credit exposure—by counterparty rating category—on its investments and swaps, net of collateral held:

In millions of U.S. dollars

| | At June 30, 1998 | | | | | At June 30, 1997 | |
| | Investments | | Swap Exposure | | | | |
Counterparty Rating	Sovereigns	Agencies, Banks & Corporates		Total Exposure to Investments and Swaps	% of Total	Total Exposure to Investments and Swaps	% of Total
AAA	$ 6,026	$ 3,587	$ 127	$ 9,740	37	$ 4,074	21
AA	2,299	12,075	351	14,725	56	12,889	68
A	-	1,800	139	1,939	7	2,134	11
Total	$ 8,325	$ 17,462	$ 617	$ 26,404	100	$ 19,097	100

The increase in credit exposure during the year reflects the increase in the size of the investment portfolio. The credit exposure from swaps declined from FY 1997 to FY 1998 by $38 million to $617 million. The increase in the relative weight of credit exposures to AAA-rated entities was mainly due to the addition of asset swaps and asset-backed securities to the investment instruments used.

Interest Rate Risk

There are two potential sources of interest rate risk to IBRD. The first is the interest rate sensitivity associated with the net spread between the rate IBRD earns on its assets and the cost of borrowings which fund those assets. The second is the interest rate sensitivity of the income earned from funding a portion of IBRD assets with equity. The borrowing cost pass-through formulation incorporated in the lending rates charged on most of IBRD's loans has traditionally helped limit the interest rate sensitivity of the net spread earnings on its loan portfolio. Such cost pass-through loans currently account for more than 87% of the existing outstanding loan portfolio. However, cost pass-through loans do entail some residual interest rate risk, given the one-semester lag inherent in the lending rate formulation. If new borrowings are at interest rates above the average in the debt pool, the higher average debt costs would not be passed through to the lending rate charged to the borrowers and thus not affect the interest income generated on cost pass-through loans until the following semester. The reverse is true when market interest rates decline.

In addition, the cost pass-through currency pool products have traditionally been funded with a large share of medium- and long-term fixed rate borrowings, so as to provide the borrowers with a reasonably stable interest basis. Given the sustained interest rate declines seen over the last several years, the cost of these historical fixed rate borrowings in the multicurrency pool and the single currency pools is currently considerably higher than IBRD's new borrowing costs. In particular, approximately $327 million of this historical (and currently 'above-market') debt allocated to the multicurrency pool has contractual maturities longer than that of the longest outstanding loans. In the absence of new disbursements and additions to the multicurrency pool, IBRD would be subject to some risk associated with potentially having to redeploy these above-market borrowings, as and when the loans mature.

Interest rate risk on non cost pass-through products, which currently account for 13% of the existing portfolio, is controlled by using interest rate swaps to closely align the rate sensitivity characteristics of the loan portfolio with that of their underlying funding. The interest rate risk on IBRD's liquid portfolio is managed within specified duration-mismatch limits and is further limited by stop-loss limits. As a result of changes in policy, liquidity has been funded by floating rate debt since June 1996. This has enabled the match-funding of liquidity with associated debt sharing the same interest rate characteristics as the liquid portfolio to take place.

IBRD's level of net income is sensitive to the level of nominal interest rates, reflecting the fact that these rates determine the level of earnings on its equity base ($23,300 million at June 30, 1998) that funds a portion of the outstanding loans (net of provisions). In general, lower nominal interest rates result in lower lending rates which, in turn, reduce the nominal earnings on IBRD's equity.

Interest rate risk also arises from a variety of other factors, including differences in the timing between the contractual maturity or repricing of IBRD's assets, liabilities and derivative financial instruments. For example, IBRD's net interest income and financial condition are affected by changes in the level of market interest rates as the repricing characteristics of its loans and other assets do not necessarily match those of its borrowings. With regard to floating rate assets and liabilities, IBRD is exposed to timing mismatches between the reset dates on its floating rate receivables and payables.

As part of its ALM process IBRD employs interest rate swaps to manage and align the rate sensitivity characteristics of its assets and liabilities. IBRD uses derivative instruments to adjust the interest rate repricing characteristics of specific on-balance sheet assets and liabilities, or groups of assets and liabilities with similar repricing characteristics.

Exchange Rate Risk

In order to minimize exchange rate risk in a multicurrency environment, IBRD matches its borrowing obligations in any one currency (after swap activities) with assets in the same currency, as prescribed by the Articles, primarily by holding or lending the proceeds of its borrowings in the same currencies in which they were borrowed. In addition, IBRD's policy is to minimize the exchange rate sensitivity of its reserves-to-loans ratio. It carries out this policy by undertaking currency conversions periodically to align the currency composition of its reserves to that of its outstanding loans. This policy is designed to minimize the impact of market rate fluctuations on the reserves to loans ratio, thereby preserving IBRD's ability to absorb potential losses from arrears regardless of the market environment.

The following graph summarizes IBRD's currency position in major currencies for FY 1998:

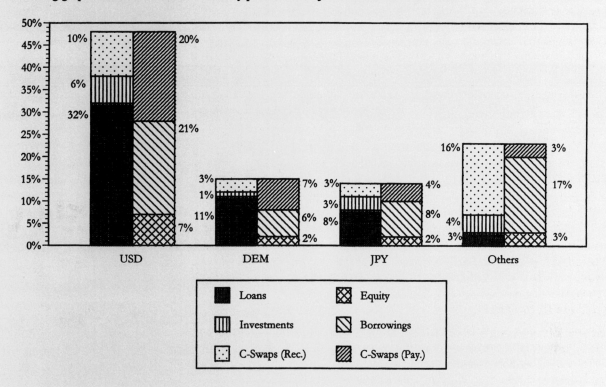

Operating Risk

Operating risk is the potential for loss arising from internal activities or external events caused by breakdowns in information, communication, physical safeguards, business continuity, supervision, transaction processing, settlement systems and procedures, and the execution of legal, fiduciary, and agency responsibilities. IBRD, like all financial institutions, is exposed to many types of operating risks, including the risk of fraud by staff or outsiders. IBRD attempts to mitigate operating risk by maintaining a comprehensive system of internal controls that is designed to keep operating risk at appropriate levels in view of the financial strength of IBRD and the characteristics of the activities and markets in which IBRD operates. In the past IBRD has suffered certain immaterial losses from operating risk and while it maintains an adequate system of internal controls, there can be no absolute assurance that IBRD will not suffer such losses in the future.

IBRD adopted the COSO[1] control framework and a self-assessment methodolgy to evaluate the effectiveness of its internal controls in FY 1996, and has an on-going program in place to cover all business units. Commencing in FY 1997, IBRD obtained an attestation from its external auditors on the effectiveness of internal controls over financial reporting.

Economic and Monetary Union in Europe (EMU)

The 1992 Maastricht Treaty on European Union set the framework for forming an Economic and Monetary Union (EMU), with a single currency, the euro, and a single monetary policy defined by a common independent authority, the European Central Bank. EMU creates various operating risks for IBRD because significant changes will have to be implemented including currency conversion, modification of payment and settlement systems, redenomination of currencies, and financial reporting changes. The main challenge posed by EMU is the extended transition period (three years) when payments can be made in each participating member state in euro and in the previous national currency which remains a sub-denomination of the euro during the transition. IBRD has created an internal euro task force which is working in conjunction with various

---

[1] The Committee of Sponsoring Organizations of the Treadway Commission (commonly referred to as COSO) was convened by the U.S Congress in response to the well publicized financial irregularities that occurred in the late 1980's.

business unit groups to identify and address the changes required by the introduction of the euro. Management expects that a plan will be adopted and changes will be implemented on a schedule which meets the EMU start date of January 1, 1999.

The Year 2000 Issue

The Year 2000 (Y2K) issue is the result of computer programs using two digits rather than four to define the applicable year. Some of IBRD's computer programs that have date-sensitive software may be unable to properly interpret dates beyond the year 1999. This could result in a system failure or miscalculations causing disruptions of operations, including, among other things, a temporary inability to process transactions. IBRD presently believes that timely modifications to existing software and or hardware will mitigate its Y2K risks.

Over the last five years, IBRD has revamped many of its systems, in the process making them Y2K compliant. Also, IBRD is currently replacing many of its individual systems with either an SAP or a Summit solution at a cost of approximately $45 million. Both these systems are Y2K compliant. This implementation is expected to be completed by June 30, 1999. The date on which IBRD plans to complete the Y2K modifications is based on management's best estimates, which were derived utilizing numerous assumptions of future events. However, there can be no guarantee that these estimates will be achieved and actual results could differ materially from those plans. Specific factors that might cause such material differences include, but are not limited to, the availability and cost of personnel trained in this area, the ability to locate and correct all relevant computer codes and similar uncertainties.

4. Liquidity Management

Liquidity risk arises in the general funding of IBRD's activities and in the management of positions. It includes the risk of being unable to fund its portfolio of assets at appropriate maturities and rates and the risk of being unable to liquidate a position in a timely manner at a reasonable price. The objective of liquidity management is to ensure the availability of sufficient cash flows to meet all of IBRD's financial commitments.

Under IBRD's liquidity management policy aggregate liquid asset holdings should be kept at or above a specified prudential minimum. That minimum is equal to the highest six months of debt-service plus one-half of net loan disbursements as projected for a fiscal year based on commitments at the beginning of that year. IBRD also holds liquid assets over the specified minimum to provide flexibility in timing its borrowing transactions and to meet working capital needs.

IBRD's liquid holdings are held principally in obligations of governments and other official entities, time deposits and other unconditional obligations of banks and financial institutions, asset-backed securities, and futures and options contracts pertaining to such obligations. The liquid asset holdings are separated into three sub-portfolios, each with different risk profiles, funding, and liquidity characteristics, but all contributing to the prudential purpose of liquidity. The three sub-portfolios are summarized below:

Stable Portfolio

The "stable" portfolio is the equivalent of the prudential minimum. In line with its purpose as a cash cushion in times of financial stress, the portfolio is held in an adequately liquid form to reasonably assure IBRD of the fund's availability to meet commitments over a six-month period. The portfolio size is relatively constant, allowing for consideration of a wide range of management strategies, including taking duration and credit risk.

The FY 1999 prudential minimum liquidity level has been set at $18,500 million, representing a $1,200 million increase over that for FY 1998.

Operational Portfolio

The "operational" portfolio is the equivalent of IBRD's operating cash account and meets IBRD's short-term cash requirements, i.e., working capital needs, by ensuring that funds are available as needed to meet payment obligations. Balances in this portfolio require a high degree of liquidity and only minimal credit or market risk is taken. The aggregate size of this portfolio is also influenced to an extent by this need, at times, to have balances in multiple currencies, especially those in which IBRD does not have a ready source of short-term funding.

Discretionary Portfolio

The "discretionary" portfolio is the locus of flexibility for IBRD's funding program and is governed by a comparison of the various costs and benefits of incremental borrowing and investment decisions. The size of the discretionary portfolio depends upon the perceived usefulness of borrowing in advance of immediate needs, on the relative attractiveness of market opportunities and on the usefulness of additional short-term borrowings for market presence purposes.

IBRD's cash and liquid investments amounted to $24,648 million (including $1,299 million classified as held-to-maturity investments) at June 30, 1998. This amount was equivalent to approximately 23.3% of IBRD's outstanding borrowings after swaps. The annualized financial return on average investments in IBRD's trading portfolio for FY 1998 was 5.45% compared to 4.73% in FY 1997. The return on its held-to-maturity portfolio for FY 1998 was 8.44% compared to 8.31% for FY 1997.

For further information, refer to the Notes to Financial Statements–Note B.

5. Funding Resources

Equity

Total shareholders' equity at June 30, 1998 was $26,514 million compared with $27,228 million at June 30, 1997. The slight decrease from FY 1997 primarily reflects the revaluation effects of exchange rate movements of $1,045 million which offset the increase in retained earnings of $539 million and the increase in paid-in capital of $240 million. At June 30, 1998, this equity comprised $11,288 million of paid-in capital and $16,733 million of retained earnings, reduced by $547 million of amounts to maintain value of currency holdings and payments on account of pending subscriptions, and $960 million of cumulative translation adjustment.

Capital

The authorized capital of IBRD at June 30, 1998 was $190,811 million, of which $186,436 million had been subscribed. Of the subscribed capital, $11,288 million had been paid in and $175,148 million was callable. Of the paid-in capital, $7,677 million was available for lending and $3,611 million was not available for lending. The terms of payment of IBRD's capital and the restrictions on its use that are derived from the Articles and from resolutions of IBRD's Board of Governors are:

(i) $2,370 million of IBRD's capital was initially paid in gold or U.S. dollars or was converted by the subscribing members into U.S. dollars. This amount may, under the Articles, be freely used by IBRD in its operations.

(ii) $8,918 million of IBRD's capital was paid in the currencies of the subscribing members. Under the Articles this amount is subject to maintenance-of-value obligations and may be loaned only with the consent of the member whose currency is involved. In accordance with such consents, $5,096 million of this amount had been used in IBRD's lending operations at June 30, 1998.

(iii) $149,149 million of IBRD's capital may, under the Articles, be called only when required to meet obligations of IBRD for funds borrowed or on loans guaranteed by it. This amount is thus not available for use by IBRD in making loans. Payment on any such call may be made, at the option of the particular member, either in gold, in U.S. dollars or in the currency required to discharge the obligations of IBRD for which the call is made.

(iv) $25,999 million of IBRD's capital is to be called only when required to meet obligations of IBRD for funds borrowed or on loans guaranteed by it, pursuant to resolution of the Board of Governors of IBRD (though such conditions are not required by the Articles). Of this amount, 10% would be payable in gold or U.S. dollars and 90% in the currencies of the subscribing members. While these resolutions are not legally binding on future Boards of Governors, they do record an understanding among members that this amount will not be called for use by IBRD in its lending activities or for administrative purposes.

No call has ever been made on IBRD's callable capital. Any calls on unpaid subscriptions are required to be uniform, but the obligations of the members of IBRD to make payment on such calls are independent of each other. If the amount received on a call is insufficient to meet the obligations of IBRD for which the call is made, IBRD has the right and is bound to make further calls until the amounts received are sufficient to meet such obligations. However, no member may be required on any such call or calls to pay more than the unpaid balance of its capital subscription.

At June 30, 1998, of the uncalled capital, $102,563 million (58.6%) was callable from the member countries of IBRD that are also members of the Development Assistance Committee of the Organization for Economic Cooperation and Development. This amount was equal to 97.1% of IBRD's outstanding borrowings after swaps at June 30, 1998. The capital subscriptions of those countries and the callable amounts are set out below:

In millions of U.S. dollars

Member Country [a]	Total Capital Subscription	Uncalled Portion of Subscription
United States	$ 31,965	$ 29,966
Japan	15,321	14,377
Germany	8,734	8,191
France	8,372	7,851
United Kingdom	8,372	7,832
Italy	5,404	5,069
Canada	5,404	5,069
Netherlands	4,283	4,018
Belgium	3,496	3,281
Switzerland	3,210	3,012
Australia	2,951	2,770
Spain	2,857	2,682
Sweden	1,806	1,696
Austria	1,335	1,254
Denmark	1,237	1,162
Norway	1,204	1,132
Finland	1,033	971
New Zealand	873	821
Portugal	659	620
Ireland	636	599
Luxembourg	199	190
Total	**$ 109,351**	**$ 102,563**

a. Details regarding the capital subscriptions of all members of IBRD at June 30, 1998 are provided in the Statement of Subscriptions to Capital Stock and Voting Power in the Financial Statements.

For a further discussion of capital stock, restricted currencies, maintenance of value and membership refer to the Summary of Significant Accounting and related policies and the Notes to Financial Statements–Note A.

Borrowings

IBRD diversifies its sources of funding by offering its securities to private and official investors globally on terms acceptable to IBRD. Official investors are governments, central banks and other governmental institutions. Under the Articles, IBRD may borrow only with the approval of the member in whose markets the funds are raised and the member in whose currency the borrowing is denominated, and only if each such member agrees that the proceeds may be exchanged for the currency of any other member without restriction.

In FY 1998 medium- and long-term debt raised from the market by IBRD amounted to $28,020 million. This excludes proceeds from continuous short-term issuance programs, i.e., Central Bank Facility and Discount Notes, and transactions with a maturity of less than one year. The increase in medium- and long-term borrowings in FY 1998 primarily reflected increased loan disbursements in response to the financial crisis in East Asia and adjustment lending in Eastern Europe and Central Asia.

Funding Operations

In millions of U.S. dollars	FY 1998	FY 1997
Total Medium- and Long-term Borrowings *	$ 28,020	$ 17,694
Average Maturity (years)	5.8	5.2
Number of Transactions	195	139
Number of Currencies	21	18

* Net proceeds on a trade date basis.

Most new funding was swapped initially into floating rates. Fixed rates were established subsequently for some of this funding in accordance with the requirements of different loan products and policy guidelines.

The after-swap currency composition of new funding was mostly in U.S. dollars and reflected the need to fund loan assets and liquidity. Borrowings were carried out in those currencies that provided the best market opportunities, resulting in 195 transactions during FY 1998.

IBRD buys its debt back strategically to reduce the cost of borrowings and to reduce exposure to refunding requirements in a particular year. During FY 1998 IBRD repurchased a total of $540 million of its outstanding borrowings and prepaid $561 million of its outstanding borrowings.

A more detailed analysis of borrowings is provided in the Notes to Financial Statements–Note D.

6. Results Of Operations

IBRD's net income can be seen as broadly comprising a spread on earning assets, plus the contribution of equity, less provisions for loan losses and administrative expenses. The significant factors affecting the spread on earning assets are described below:

♦ **Loans** are funded by a combination of debt and equity, with debt funding approximately 77% of loans.

Most loans are subject to a cost pass-through formulation with the loans carrying a variable lending rate linked to the particular borrowings allocated to them. Such cost pass-through loans currently account for approximately 87% of the outstanding loan portfolio. Other loans which are not cost pass-through products, comprise 13% of the existing loan portfolio.

Income generated from loans funded by equity is directly sensitive to the level of nominal interest rates with any changes in these rates directly impacting net income. Loans funded by equity comprise 23% of the loan portfolio.

♦ **Investments** are primarily funded by variable rate debt sharing the same interest rate characteristics as the investment portfolio. As a result the interest rate sensitivity of the spread of investment returns over its cost of funding has been substantially eliminated with net investment income being largely unaffected by interest rate fluctuations. Further, the impact on net income from the margin on the investment portfolio is not significant.

The following table is a comparison of the FY 1998 and FY 1997 results.

		FY 1998	FY 1997
Net Income U.S. $ millions			
Loan Income		6,881	7,235
Interest		6,775	7,122
Commitment Charges		106	113
Provision for Loan Losses		(251)	(63)
Investment Income		1,233	834
Borrowing Expenses		(6,144)	(5,952)
Net Interest Income		1,719	2,054
Net Noninterest Expense		(476)	(769)
Net Income		1,243	1,285
Performance Ratios %			
Return on Average Earning Assets[a]		6.38	6.51
Less: Average Cost of Borrowings Outstanding		6.10	6.14
Net Interest Margin on Average Earning Assets[a]		0.28	0.37
Less: Provision for Loan Losses		0.20	0.05
Net Non-Interest Expense		0.37	0.62
Contribution of Members' Equity		1.27	1.34
Net Income as a percentage of Average Earning Assets[a]		0.98	1.04
Average Assets and Liabilities U.S. $ millions			
Total Earning Assets		127,138	123,879
Cash and Investments		21,895	16,627
Disbursed and Outstanding Loans		105,243	107,251
Borrowings Outstanding [b]		100,718	96,929

a. Includes commitment charges

b. Borrowings outstanding, after swaps.

Net income as a percentage of average earning assets declined 6 basis points from 1.04% for FY 1997 to 0.98% for FY 1998. The following main factors contributed to the decline: increased loan loss provisioning, the negative effect of the conversions of multicurrency pool loans to single currency pool terms and lower nominal rates for loans funded by equity. These negative effects on net income were partially offset by gains attributed to IBRD's pension and other postretirement benefit accounts.

The negative effect of the conversions of the multicurrency pool loans to single currency pool (SCP) terms was the primary factor lowering the net interest income margin on average earning assets. The SCP conversions reduced the loan spread through the interaction of the change in currency composition, resulting in a higher nominal rate, with the lag in the pass-through lending rate. Effectively, this raised debt costs before raising the lending rate on the affected loans.

Net Interest Income

In millions of U.S. dollars	FY 1998 Amount	FY 1998 Average Return %	FY 1997 Amount	FY 1997 Average Return %	FY 1996 Amount	FY 1996 Average Return %
Loans						
Gross Interest Income	$ 7,090	6.74	$ 7,514	7.01	$ 8,271	7.22
Non-performing Loan Interest	(84)	(0.08)	(146)	(0.14)	(188)	(0.16)
Interest Waiver	(241)	(0.23)	(259)	(0.24)	(286)	(0.25)
Provision for Loan Losses	(251)	(0.24)	(63)	(0.06)	(42)	(0.04)
Commitment Charges	106	0.10	113	0.11	118	0.10
Prepayment Premiums	10	0.01	13	0.01	7	0.01
Loan Income	6,630	6.30	7,172	6.69	7,880	6.88
Investment Income	1,233	5.62	834	5.00	720	4.43
Total Interest Income	7,863	6.18	8,006	6.47	8,600	6.58
Cost of Borrowings	(6,144)	6.10	(5,952)	6.14	(6,570)	6.44
Net Interest Income	$ 1,719	1.35	$ 2,054	1.66	$ 2,030	1.56

The decrease in loan income of $542 million (7.6%) was primarily due to a falling interest rate environment in the major financial markets and the continuing maturity of high-interest, fixed rate loans. Of the decrease in loan interest income, $290 million was due to a decrease in the average interest rate of the loan portfolio, and $136 million was associated with the decrease in the balance of average loans outstanding in terms of U.S. dollars. The other major factor contributing to the change in loan income was the increase in the provision for loan losses. During FY 1998 the expected losses due to the changes in the credit quality of the portfolio combined with growth in net disbursements resulted in an increase in the provision for loan losses of $188 million from FY 1997 to FY 1998.

The following table provides a breakdown of the gross loan interest income by loan product.

In millions of U.S. dollars	FY 1998 Average Volume	FY 1998 Interest Income Amount	FY 1998 Interest Income Return %	FY 1997 Average Volume	FY 1997 Interest Income Amount	FY 1997 Interest Income Return %	FY 1996 Average Volume	FY 1996 Interest Income Amount	FY 1996 Interest Income Return %
Loans	$ 105,243	$ 7,090	6.74	$107,251	$ 7,514	7.01	$ 114,534	$ 8,271	7.22
Fixed Rate (excluding SCLs)	5,233	460	8.78	8,838	771	8.72	13,835	1,189	8.59
Multicurrency Pool (adjustable)	68,857	4,502	6.54	93,874	6,456	6.88	99,391	6,997	7.04
Single Currency Loans									
Fixed	3,273	225	6.89	1,962	136	6.94	747	51	6.88
Adjustable	10,052	615	6.12	2,577	151	5.86	561	34	6.06
Single Currency Pools (SCPs)									
Adjustable	17,828	1,288	7.23	—	—	—	—	—	—

During FY 1998 investment income increased by $399 million (47.7%). Of this increase, $103 million resulted from higher returns (up from 5.0% to 5.6%) mainly due to a shift from Japanese yen and Deutsche mark investments into higher-yield U.S. dollar investments. Higher average outstanding investment balances, reflecting the modified liquidity policy, accounted for the remaining increase of $296 million.

The cost of borrowings increased by $192 million (3.2%). The replacement of longer maturity fixed rate debt with variable rate debt, coupled with a falling interest rate environment, lowered the average cost of borrowings from 6.14% to 6.10%. This decrease was offset by a higher average borrowings balance, resulting in an increase of $231 million in borrowing costs.

FY 1997 versus FY 1996

Net interest income totaled $2,054 million in FY 1997, compared to $2,030 million in FY 1996. The reduction in total interest income of $594 million in FY 1997 as compared to FY 1996 was offset by a slightly larger decrease in the cost of borrowings of $618 million, resulting in a $24 million increase in net interest income.

The reduction in loan interest income arose from lower average loan interest rates driven by a decline in the average cost of borrowings, resulting from a declining interest rate environment in the financial markets. A 21 basis point decline in the average loan interest rate resulted in a reduction of $240 million, while a decrease of $7,283 million in the average outstanding loans balance accounted for a $517 million reduction in gross interest income. The negative effect of non-performing loan interest in FY 1997 was lower by $42 million primarily due to the clearance of arrears of loan interest and charges by Bosnia and Herzegovina in June 1996, and its subsequent debt-service payments during FY 1997.

Investment income increased by $114 million mainly due to a shift from Japanese yen and Deutsche mark investments into higher-yield U.S. dollar investments.

Net Noninterest Expense

The following table presents the main components of noninterest expense:

In millions of U.S. dollars	FY 1998	FY 1997	FY 1996
Gross Administrative Expenses			
Staff Salaries	263	255	255
Other Staff Costs	203	217	254
Consultant Fees	91	71	72
Operational Travel	94	81	79
Other Expense	293	277	250
Total Gross Administrative Expenses	944	901	910
Less:			
Pension & Postretirement Benefit Income	399	63	-
Reimbursements	69	67	64
Contribution to Special Programs	112	120	113
Total Net Administrative Expenses	364	651	733
Contribution to Special Programs	112	120	113
Net Other Income	-	(2)	(3)
Total Net Noninterest Expense	476	769	843

Net noninterest expenses declined by $293 million. This decrease is attributable to the recognition of additional income from pension and other postretirement benefit plans.

1997 versus 1996

Net noninterest expenses declined by $74 million in FY 1997. In FY 1997 income resulting from a change in assumptions associated with the Staff Retirement Plan of $112 million reduced total net noninterest expense.

INTERNATIONAL BANK FOR RECONSTRUCTION AND DEVELOPMENT

FINANCIAL STATEMENTS
JUNE 30, 1998

Balance Sheet

June 30, 1998 and June 30, 1997

Expressed in millions of U.S. dollars

	1998	1997
Assets		
DUE FROM BANKS		
Unrestricted currencies	$ 55	$ 26
Currencies subject to restrictions—Note A	712	615
	767	641
INVESTMENTS		
Trading—Notes B and E	23,284	17,229
Held-to-maturity—Notes B and E	2,673	1,279
Assets designated for other postretirement benefits—Notes B and J	1,456	—
	27,413	18,508
SECURITIES PURCHASED UNDER RESALE AGREEMENTS—Trading—Note B	466	97
NONNEGOTIABLE, NONINTEREST-BEARING DEMAND OBLIGATIONS ON ACCOUNT OF SUBSCRIBED CAPITAL	1,890	1,902
AMOUNTS RECEIVABLE FROM CURRENCY SWAPS		
Investments—Trading—Notes B and E	10,510	4,571
Borrowings—Notes D and E	55,767	29,031
	66,277	33,602
AMOUNTS RECEIVABLE TO MAINTAIN VALUE OF CURRENCY HOLDINGS	392	574
OTHER RECEIVABLES		
Amounts receivable from investment securities traded	262	29
Accrued income on loans	1,963	1,932
Accrued interest on investments	189	143
	2,414	2,104
LOANS OUTSTANDING (see Summary Statement of Loans, Notes C and E)		
Total loans	157,641	157,381
Less undisbursed balance	51,065	51,576
Loans outstanding	106,576	105,805
Less accumulated provision for loan losses	3,240	3,210
Loans outstanding net of accumulated provision	103,336	102,595
OTHER ASSETS		
Unamortized issuance costs of borrowings	652	492
Miscellaneous—Note I	1,364	1,430
	2,016	1,922
Total assets	$204,971	$161,945

Balance Sheet

June 30, 1998 and June 30, 1997

Expressed in millions of U.S. dollars

	1998	*1997*
Liabilities		
BORROWINGS—Notes D and E		
Short-term	$ 6,729	$ 7,648
Medium- and long-term	96,860	89,031
	103,589	96,679
SECURITIES SOLD UNDER REPURCHASE AGREEMENTS AND PAYABLE FOR CASH COLLATERAL RECEIVED—Note B		
Trading	860	294
Held-to-maturity	1,374	—
	2,234	294
AMOUNTS PAYABLE FOR CURRENCY SWAPS		
Investments—Trading—Notes B and E	10,113	4,694
Borrowings—Notes D and E	57,755	29,687
	67,868	34,381
AMOUNTS PAYABLE TO MAINTAIN VALUE OF CURRENCY HOLDINGS	2	4
OTHER LIABILITIES		
Amounts payable for investment securities purchased	255	135
Accrued charges on borrowings	2,519	2,167
Payable for Board of Governors-approved transfers—Note F	122	201
Accounts payable and miscellaneous liabilities	1,151	856
Liabilities under other postretirement benefits—Note J	717	—
	4,764	3,359
Total liabilities	178,457	134,717
Equity		
CAPITAL STOCK (see Statement of Subscriptions to Capital Stock and Voting Power, Note A)		
Authorized capital (1,581,724 shares—June 30, 1998; 1,558,478 shares—June 30, 1997)		
Subscribed capital (1,545,457 shares—June 30, 1998; 1,512,211 shares—June 30, 1997)	186,436	182,426
Less uncalled portion of subscriptions	175,148	171,378
	11,288	11,048
AMOUNTS TO MAINTAIN VALUE OF CURRENCY HOLDINGS—Note A	(554)	(106)
PAYMENTS ON ACCOUNT OF PENDING SUBSCRIPTIONS—Note A	7	7
RETAINED EARNINGS (see Statement of Changes in Retained Earnings, Note F)	16,733	16,194
CUMULATIVE TRANSLATION ADJUSTMENT (see Statement of Changes in Cumulative Translation Adjustment)	(960)	85
Total equity	26,514	27,228
Total liabilities and equity	$204,971	$161,945

The Notes to Financial Statements are an integral part of these Statements.

Statement of Income

For the fiscal years ended June 30, 1998, June 30, 1997 and June 30, 1996

Expressed in millions of U.S. dollars

	1998	1997	1996
INCOME			
Income from loans—Note C			
Interest	$6,775	$7,122	$7,804
Commitment charges	106	113	118
Income from investments—Note B			
Trading			
Interest	1,107	718	673
Net gains/(losses)			
Realized	(10)	47	31
Unrealized	1	(43)	(83)
Held-to-maturity			
Interest	176	103	100
Income from securities purchased under resale agreements—Note B	59	53	66
Income from investments designated for other postretirement benefits—Notes B and J	107	—	—
Income (expense) from Staff Retirement Plan—Note I	182	63	(60)
Other income	10	12	11
Total income	8,513	8,188	8,660
EXPENSES			
Borrowing expenses—Note D			
Interest	6,000	5,827	6,455
Prepayment (gains)/losses	(7)	16	9
Amortization of issuance and other borrowing costs	151	109	106
Interest on securities sold under repurchase agreements and payable for cash collateral received—Note B	100	44	67
Administrative expenses—Notes G and H	763	714	673
Other postretirement benefits expense—Note J	50	—	—
Provision for loan losses—Note C	251	63	42
Other expenses	10	10	8
Total expenses	7,318	6,783	7,360
OPERATING INCOME	1,195	1,405	1,300
Effect of accounting change—Note J	160	—	—
Contributions to special programs—Note G	(112)	(120)	(113)
NET INCOME	$1,243	$1,285	$1,187

The Notes to Financial Statements are an integral part of these Statements.

Statement of Changes in Retained Earnings

For the fiscal years ended June 30, 1998, June 30, 1997 and June 30, 1996

Expressed in millions of U.S. dollars

	1998	1997	1996
Retained earnings at beginning of the fiscal year	$16,194	$16,099	$15,502
Board of Governors-approved transfers to—Note F			
International Development Association	(304)	(600)	(250)
Debt Reduction Facility for IDA-Only Countries	—	—	(100)
Trust Fund for Gaza and West Bank	—	(90)	(90)
Trust Fund for Bosnia and Herzegovina	—	—	(150)
Heavily Indebted Poor Countries Debt Initiative Trust Fund	(250)	(500)	—
Multilateral Investment Guarantee Agency	(150)	—	—
Net income for the fiscal year	1,243	1,285	1,187
Retained earnings at end of the fiscal year	$16,733	$16,194	$16,099

Statement of Changes in Cumulative Translation Adjustment

For the fiscal years ended June 30, 1998, June 30, 1997 and June 30, 1996

Expressed in millions of U.S. dollars

	1998	1997	1996
Cumulative translation adjustment at beginning of the fiscal year	$ 85	$ 1,056	$ 3,308
Translation adjustment for the fiscal year	(1,045)	(971)	(2,252)
Cumulative translation adjustment at end of the fiscal year	$ (960)	$ 85	$ 1,056

The Notes to Financial Statements are an integral part of these Statements.

Statement of Cash Flows

For the fiscal years ended June 30, 1998, June 30, 1997 and June 30, 1996

Expressed in millions of U.S. dollars

	1998	1997	1996
Cash flows from lending and investing activities			
Loans			
Disbursements	$(19,283)	$(14,009)	$(13,321)
Principal repayments	10,146	10,710	11,494
Principal prepayments	1,372	1,311	812
Investments: Held-to-maturity			
Purchases of securities and repayments of securities sold under repurchase agreements	(33,202)	(8,911)	(5,417)
Maturities of securities and proceeds from securities sold under repurchase agreements	33,184	8,895	5,422
Net cash used in lending and investing activities	(7,783)	(2,004)	(1,010)
Cash flows from Board of Governors-approved transfers to			
International Development Association	(298)	(599)	(250)
Debt Reduction Facility for IDA-Only Countries	(18)	(1)	(86)
Trust Fund for Gaza and West Bank, Trust Fund for Bosnia and Herzegovina, and Emergency Assistance for Rwanda	(60)	(91)	(179)
Heavily Indebted Poor Countries Debt Initiative Trust Fund	(250)	(500)	—
Multilateral Investment Guarantee Agency	(150)	—	—
Net cash used in Board of Governors-approved transfers	(776)	(1,191)	(515)
Cash flows from financing activities			
Medium- and long-term borrowings			
New issues	27,748	14,928	9,851
Retirements	(13,569)	(14,137)	(10,330)
Net short-term borrowings	(1,009)	3,277	340
Net currency swaps	(300)	(266)	(649)
Net capital stock transactions	217	71	111
Net cash provided by (used in) financing activities	13,087	3,873	(677)
Cash flows from operating activities			
Net income	1,243	1,285	1,187
Adjustments to reconcile net income to net cash provided by operating activities			
Depreciation and amortization	855	541	399
Provision for loan losses	251	63	42
Changes in other assets and liabilities			
(Increase) decrease in accrued income on loans and investments	(204)	18	176
Decrease (increase) in miscellaneous assets	8	(153)	(80)
Increase in net assets associated with other postretirement benefits	(739)	—	—
Increase (decrease) in accrued charges on borrowings	448	(49)	(214)
Increase (decrease) in accounts payable and miscellaneous liabilities	335	35	(18)
Net cash provided by operating activities	2,197	1,740	1,492
Effect of exchange rate changes on unrestricted cash and liquid investments	(205)	(319)	(1,632)
Net increase (decrease) in unrestricted cash and liquid investments	6,520	2,099	(2,342)
Unrestricted cash and liquid investments at beginning of the fiscal year	16,829	14,730	17,072
Unrestricted cash and liquid investments at end of the fiscal year	$ 23,349	$ 16,829	$ 14,730

Statement of Cash Flows

For the fiscal years ended June 30, 1998, June 30, 1997 and June 30, 1996

Expressed in millions of U.S. dollars

	1998	*1997*	*1996*
Composition of unrestricted cash and liquid investments:			
Investments held in trading portfolio	$23,284	$ 17,229	$ 15,001
Unrestricted currencies	55	26	27
Net receivable (payable) for investment securities traded/purchased	7	(106)	857
Net receivable (payable) from currency swaps—Investments	397	(123)	2
Net payable for securities purchased/sold under resale/repurchase agreements and payable for cash collateral received	(394)	(197)	(1,157)
	$23,349	$ 16,829	$ 14,730
Supplemental disclosure			
Increase (decrease) in ending balances resulting from exchange rate fluctuations			
Loans outstanding	$ (6,994)	$ (6,429)	$(14,436)
Investments: Held-to-maturity	2	94	(29)
Borrowings	(7,239)	(4,701)	(11,731)
Currency swaps—Borrowings	1,632	(495)	(1,184)

The Notes to Financial Statements are an integral part of these Statements.